SUMMER CAMPS IN CANADA

SUMMER CAMPS IN CANADA

A COMPLETE GUIDE TO THE BEST SUMMER CAMPS FOR KIDS AND TEENS

Ann West

SUMMER CAMPS IN CANADA

Published by:
Polestar Press Ltd.
1011 Commercial Drive, Second Floor
Vancouver, British Columbia
Canada
V5L 3X1

Cover design: Jim Brennan
Editorial Assistant: Corene Dance
Printed in Canada by Best Book Manufacturers

Cover photographs courtesy of B.C. Pioneer Camps.
Interior photographs: page 13, 121 and 314 — Pioneer Chehalis; page 51 and 255 — Educo Adventure School; page 100, 143 and 150 — Pioneer Pacific; page 164 — Camp Kawartha; page 264 — Camp Edphy International. Thank you to all the camps that provided us with photographs.

Special thanks to the kind and helpful voices at the other end of the anonymous telephone void. Specific thanks to Earl Kagna, Nancy Hannum and Vivian Darroch-Lozowski.

Canadian Cataloguing in Publication Data
Main entry under title:
Summer camps in Canada
Includes index.
ISBN 1-896095-05-4
1. Camps—Canada—Directories. I. West, Ann, J., 1950-
GV195.C3S95 1995 796.54'2'02571 C95-910047-4

CONTENTS

Accreditation and Affiliation

Associations listed under "Accreditation"

ACA	Alberta Camping Association
ACA	American Camping Association
ACQ	Quebec Camping Association
BCCA	BC Camping Association
CCA	Canadian Camping Association
CCI	Christian Camping International
MCA	Manitoba Camping Association
NBCA	New Brunswick Camping Association
NLCA	Newfoundland & Labrador Camping Association
CANS	Camping Association of Nova Scotia
OCA	Ontario Camping Association
PEICA	PEI Camping Association
SCA	Saskatchewan Camping Association

Organizations and Agencies listed under "Affiliation"

Alberta Forest Service
Anglican Church
Assoc for Experimental Education
Assoc Garagona Inc.
Assoc of Neighbourhood Houses
Baptist Church
BC Forestry Assoc
BC Lions Society
Boys' & Girls' Club
Cdn Diabetes Assoc
Cdn Girls in Training
Cdn International Student Services
Cdn Parents for French
Cdn Sunday School Mission
Canyon Church Camp Assoc
Catholic Church
Christian (nondenominational)
Creative Centre for Learning & Dev't
Easter Seals Society
Evangelical
Fellowship of Christian Assemblies
Handicapped Freedom Tours Society
Inter Varsity Christian Fellowship
Jewish
Kiwanis Club
Les Frères Maristes
Lutheran Church
Mennonite Brethren
Mennonite Camping Assoc
Metro Toronto Assoc/Comm Living
Muslim
Native American Lore Camp
Ont Cancer Society
Ont Min/Community/Social Services
Ont Min/Culture, Tourism, Recreation
Ont Sailing Assoc
Presbyterian Church
Red Cross
Salvation Army
Scouts Canada
Seventh Day Adventists
Society of St. Vincent de Paul
Ukrainian Orthodox Church
United Church
YM-YWCA

PREFACE

Each summer, children across Canada troop home singing strange songs, brimming over with stories about new friends and first-time experiences, hand-crafted treasures spilling from suitcases of dirty laundry. They have taken part in a peculiarly North American rite of passage called "Summer Camp." This rite can occur in the mountains of British Columbia, by a spruce bog in Newfoundland, on a ranch in Alberta or in the heart of a town in Nova Scotia. It can take place over a period of a few days or several weeks. The rituals involve campfires, singing, and the study of various arts whether archery or canoeing, hockey or dinosaur digs. Whatever the rituals particular to their camp, the successful campers will emerge with a greater sense of confidence and independence, new friends, a wider knowledge of worlds outside their own and an eagerness to apply their new skills to other areas of their lives. As for those camp songs, well, they seem to last forever too.

To ensure that your child comes home singing, it is important to match her needs and expectations with what the camp has to offer. If what she really wants is to spend five days immersed in space technology, two weeks at a wilderness camp may not make for happy memories. Now is the time to discuss expectations and possibilities with your child and come up with an outline of your ideal camp.

In **Summer Camps in Canada**, you will find information on over 300 summer camps from Newfoundland to Vancouver Island. The book is divided into three sections. The first is a short introduction which suggests how to select a camp, how to prepare for camp, and some creative alternatives to residential summer camps.

The second section is the main body of the book. Divided by province, it lists basic information on each camp. The third section includes an index of camps both by name and by specialty.

Reading the introduction will help to clarify what you are looking for in a camp. The specialty index will help you locate the programs which interest you, and the individual listings will provide you with more specific information on each camp.

Whatever your criteria, **Summer Camps in Canada** will help you find just the right camp to make your child's summer experience memorable and ensure a winter-long supply of anecdotes and unforgettable songs.

INTRODUCTION

Selecting a camp

To begin the search for your child's ideal camp, ask yourself and your child the following questions: What activities does he most enjoy—canoeing, nature studies, star-gazing, horseback riding? What skills does she want to develop—to become a better goalie, earn a swimming badge, make new friends? Does he do better in a highly structured environment, or in one with more free time? Is she happier in a large group with plenty of activity or in a smaller, quieter group? Does he prefer to remain close to home or is he ready to test his independence further afield? Does your child have any special needs physically, emotionally, or developmentally? With the answers to these questions in mind, you will have a much clearer picture of what you are looking for.

Once you have located some camps which interest you—either by scanning the descriptions or by checking the specialty index—contact the camp directors. In addition to the latest brochure, you may want to request references from the parents of former campers. You may also want to make a list of questions to ask the director such as: Are there any additional costs? What kind of health care is available at the camp? What are the goals of the camp? What is the staff's response to disciplinary or behavioural problems? What are the meals like? With all of your questions answered, your application sent and your child accepted, it will almost be time to start packing.

Preparing for camp

If this is your child's first time at camp it will be important to clarify both your expectations and those of your child. Let him know that he will be expected to abide by the camp rules. Be sure to find out what the camp policy is on phone calls and visits from parents. Many camps discourage visits as they can work against the best interests of the child, but mail is always welcome.

What to bring

Most camps supply a "bring" list. In addition to the essentials, you may want to include some stamped and addressed envelopes—fold the notepaper inside so it doesn't get mislaid. Pack a few paperbacks and a walkman too if the camp allows them. Remember to include an inexpensive instant camera with which to record those extraordinary camp events. And to help battle any pangs of homesickness, pack a journal and pen, a favourite stuffed toy, or perhaps a small family photo album. Finally, be sure to label all clothing and items and don't send anything irreplaceable!

Medical concerns

Some camps require a physical examination and medical history before the camp application is considered complete. Whether the camp requires this formality or not, a pre-camp check-up seems prudent. In the unlikely event that your child should experience a medical problem while away, having current information on file with your family doctor will aid in treatment.

Most camps require an immunization history and will ask about allergies and any regular medication requirements. Fill in the forms thoroughly and honestly, and do tell the camp of any significant fears your child might have or if there are occasional problems such as bedwetting or severe nightmares.

Travel plans

If your child has a friend going to the same camp, consider letting them travel together, especially if they are travelling without parents by bus, train or plane. If you are driving to the camp, perhaps you can take another child along. Most young people find it reassuring to go through arrival, check-in, and orientation with another camper. If the camp is organizing part of the transportation, give yourself plenty of time to reach the drop-off and pick-up locations.

Expenses

The cost of sending a child to camp is usually more than the actual camp fee. Besides travel, there are other things to consider, such as new equipment (e.g. a sleeping bag), and a few long distance phone calls. In addition, there may be extra charges for laundry, movies, tuck shop, or special activities. Camp fees vary tremendously and many camp organizations offer some form of financial aid. If the fee for the camp you have chosen is beyond your budget, ask the camp if they have any subsidies, or contact your local school board for suggestions. Occasionally, non-profit societies have discretionary funds for children with special needs.

Training programs

Many camps have a teen program. Counsellor-in-Training programs may result in a summer job the following year and can be good references on future job applications. A few camps offer First Aid or Lifeguard training. Enquire about certificates, licenses, and school credit programs available within the camp activity structure. Volunteer opportunities exist with some camps, especially those designed for people with special needs.

Creative alternatives

Sometimes the ideal camp is a day camp, even a day camp in another city! If you or your child is set on a special ballet program or theatre school or the best-ever soccer round-up, phone the co-ordinator and enquire about billeting possibilities. Or perhaps you will be able to arrange to billet your child with a friend or relative in the area. Sending a child to a day program in another city requires a great deal of organization and a very realistic assessment of your child's ability to cope without either a parent or standard 24-hour camp supervision.

Do you travel on business? If you know your travel plans sufficiently in advance, why not take your son or daughter along? A business trip to Toronto can be combined with a children's day program at the Royal Ontario Museum; or a week away can be planned to coincide with a 5-day camp program nearby. You will have the pleasure of travelling to and from your home with your child, and it will be an adventure for her. If you are from a remote area of the country, a day or residential camp connected with a metropolitan university, art gallery or museum can be a marvelous and unusual opportunity for your child.

If she simply isn't ready to spend that much time away from home, there are still a wide variety of day camps to choose from. For example, most sport camps are day camps. Often week-long programs are offered by the Physical Education Department of the local university, and community centre playing fields are frequently the location for specially run soccer or baseball day programs. If hockey is your child's passion, check out the *Hockey News*. It's available at most newsstands and publishes a "Summer Program Supplement" early in the new year. For other sports camps, contact the relevant organizaton.

Universities and community colleges rarely run residential camps but they will sometimes offer special day programs; contact the appropriate department, whether it's for music, visual arts, or computer sciences, for information. Other places to enquire are music conservatories, dance studios, art galleries, community centres, the YM-YWCA, local school boards or libraries.

If you have a child with special needs, contact the school board, a

Kiwanis chapter, your provincial Social Service Ministry or the specific care agency (such as the Canadian Cancer Society, the Diabetes Foundation, or the Lung Association) for suggestions.

Eventually your teenager may feel he has outgrown camp. Many travel agencies, especially those affiliated with universities, offer supervised group travel experiences for teenagers in the summer. Call around and be aware that there may be age restrictions.

Whatever the particular needs of your child, you will be able to find a camp to suit them. You can discover the diverse opportunities available in **Summer Camps in Canada**. While every effort has been made to make the listings as complete as possible, oversights are bound to occur and changes may be made to programs or fees. Remember, this information is meant to be used as a starting point; it is no substitute for visiting a camp, speaking directly with a camp director, or conferring with parents of former campers. If you don't find your favourite camp listed here, please write and tell us. We will be happy to receive suggestions or additional information to include in the next edition.

So pack that favourite T-shirt, tune up those singing voices, and get ready to plan the best summer ever!

A special note about Quebec camps: Most of the material received from the camps in Quebec was bilingual. All camps, even those which indicated that the camp was conducted entirely in French, have been listed. You may want to enquire carefully as to the language or languages of operation for the Quebec camps, especially if your child is not comfortable in both languages.

A Guide to Camp Listings

The listings for each camp are fairly straightforward. Further notes, when they seem necessary, are below.

Summer Address/Winter Address:

Most camps have a summer address, which is generally the actual camp location, and a winter address, a person or office through which most of the off-season camp administration is handled. Both of these contact addresses are listed.

Contact Person:

The contact person is generally the Camp Director, but is often an employee or associate of the organization with which the camp is affiliated. Often the Winter listing is a home address and phone number — it's always best to try and make contact during regular working hours.

Accreditation:

Most camps in Canada are members of a provincial association, which in turn is a member of the Canadian Camping Association. Each provincial association has its own standards of accreditation or membership—please contact the individual associations for an outline.

Affiliation:

Camps are often organized and operated by larger groups with wider interests, such as a church diocese or a social service agency. The degree to which the concerns of these organizations are an integral part of camp life vary from camp to camp.

Specialty:

An "Index of Camps by Specialty" is on page 336.

Special Needs:

Camps that exist to satisfy the requirements of children with special needs are listed as such in the "Index of Camp by Specialty." However, many camps are able to accommodate special needs requirements. In all cases, the camp should be contacted to determine if their facilities are suitable for your child.

ALBERTA

ALBERTA 4-H CENTRE

SUMMER ADDRESS	Alberta 4-H Centre RR #1 Westerose T0C 2V0	**SUMMER PHONE**	ALTA 403-682-2153
WINTER ADDRESS	c/o 4-H Foundation of Alberta Box 550 Edmonton T5J 2K8	**WINTER PHONE**	ALTA 403-427-2541

CONTACT PERSON Vicki Berger
ACCREDITATION ACA
AFFILIATION 4-H Foundation of Alberta
YEARS IN OPERATION 25
DATES OPEN July through August
FEES $85 per 5-day session.
SCHOLARSHIPS Local 4-H clubs may sponsor participants.
ACCOMODATION Large dormitory, main dining hall, recreation rooms.
SPECIALTY Traditional
OBJECTIVES To enhance campers' environmental awareness, agricultural education & personal development.

ACTIVITIES Environmental studies on developed nature trails, hiking, canoeing, swimming, campfires, baseball, tetherball, archery, crafts.

EVALUATIONS No
MEDICAL FACILITIES First aid room; ambulance service 16 km away.
VISITORS Please enquire.
SPECIAL NEEDS FACILITIES Unspecified.
DESCRIPTION 6 km of hiking trails and a beachfront on 143 acres of land.

NEAREST CITY/TOWN Edmonton
AGE SPREAD 10 to 14 years
CAMPERS PER SESSION 80
STAFF PER SESSION 8
COUNSELLOR:CAMPER RATIO 1 to 6
BOYS OR GIRLS ☐ Boys only ☐ Girls only ☒ Co-ed
NOTES Subsidized by program sponsors & Alberta Agriculture. Family camping is an option; please enquire.

BAR HARBOUR CAMP

SUMMER ADDRESS	4715 55th Street		
	Stettler		ALTA
	T0C 2L2	**SUMMER PHONE**	403-742-5255
WINTER ADDRESS	Box 1568		
	Stettler		ALTA
	T0C 2L0	**WINTER PHONE**	403-742-4702

CONTACT PERSON Leroy Overacker
ACCREDITATION ACA
AFFILIATION United Church
YEARS IN OPERATION 60+
DATES OPEN July through August
FEES Please enquire.
SCHOLARSHIPS No
ACCOMODATION Cabins, dining hall, rec hall, flush toilets, showers, tents.
SPECIALTY Christian Development
OBJECTIVES To provide a Christian camping experience for young people.

ACTIVITIES Swimming, hiking, canoeing, crafts, nature walks, sports, games, orienteering.

EVALUATIONS No
MEDICAL FACILITIES First aid cabin; hospital 19 km away.
VISITORS Allowed
SPECIAL NEEDS FACILITIES Yes
DESCRIPTION Located on Buffalo Lake.

NEAREST CITY/TOWN Stettler
AGE SPREAD 6 years & up
CAMPERS PER SESSION 100
STAFF PER SESSION 15
COUNSELLOR:CAMPER RATIO 1 to 20
BOYS OR GIRLS ☐ Boys only ☐ Girls only ☒ Co-ed
NOTES Special needs refers to wheelchair accessibility. Family camping is an option; please enquire.

BIRCH BAY RANCH

SUMMER ADDRESS 51505 Range Road 215

Sherwood Park ALTA
T8E 1H1 **SUMMER PHONE** 403-922-2883

WINTER ADDRESS As above

WINTER PHONE

CONTACT PERSON Sharon Fraess
ACCREDITATION ACA, CCI
AFFILIATION Christian (nondenominational)
YEARS IN OPERATION 23
DATES OPEN July through August
FEES $250-$295 per session.
SCHOLARSHIPS No
ACCOMODATION Cabins, showers, main dining lodge.
SPECIALTY Christian Development & Horseback Riding
OBJECTIVES To provide a well-balanced program on a physical, mental & spiritual level in a Christian atmosphere. Campers are challenged to seek the meaning of a relationship with God.
ACTIVITIES Horsemanship, vaulting (gymnastics on horseback), canoeing, archery, gym, air riflery, rodeos, ropes course, crafts, field sports, devotions, campfires.

EVALUATIONS Horsemanship certificates are issued.
MEDICAL FACILITIES Nurse's cabin with staff trained in first aid.
VISITORS Allowed
SPECIAL NEEDS FACILITIES Yes
DESCRIPTION Situated on 130 acres of heavily wooded, lakefront property located on South Cooking Lake. Facilities include a barn, tack room, rodeo arena & 2 riding arenas.
NEAREST CITY/TOWN Edmonton
AGE SPREAD 5 to 18 years
CAMPERS PER SESSION Approximately 100
STAFF PER SESSION 35-40
COUNSELLOR:CAMPER RATIO Included in above figure.
BOYS OR GIRLS ☐ Boys only ☐ Girls only ☒ Co-ed
NOTES Special needs facilities refers to one week during summer with interpreters for the hearing impaired.

BRIGHTWOOD YOUTH RANCH CAMP

SUMMER ADDRESS Box 277

Evansburg ALTA
T0E 0T0 **SUMMER PHONE** 403-727-3840

WINTER ADDRESS As above

WINTER PHONE

CONTACT PERSON Irvin L. Reich
ACCREDITATION ACA, CCA, CCI
AFFILIATION Fellowship of Christian Assemblies (nondenominational)
YEARS IN OPERATION 10
DATES OPEN July through August
FEES $180 per 6-day session.
SCHOLARSHIPS No
ACCOMODATION Carpeted dorms, showers, flush toilets, main dining hall.
SPECIALTY Christian Development & Horseback Riding
OBJECTIVES To challenge campers in areas that develop respect & love for God's creatures, & to encourage friendship & goodwill among camp peers.
ACTIVITIES Swimming, canoeing, hiking, horsemanship, trail riding, archery, crafts, Bible studies, campfires.

EVALUATIONS Achievement cards are awarded.
MEDICAL FACILITIES First aid room.
VISITORS Allowed
SPECIAL NEEDS FACILITIES Unspecified
DESCRIPTION Located on a west-facing hillside, the ranch is surrounded by rolling property, fields, wooded areas & a stream.

NEAREST CITY/TOWN Edmonton
AGE SPREAD 8 to 16 years
CAMPERS PER SESSION Approximately 50
STAFF PER SESSION 18-20
COUNSELLOR:CAMPER RATIO 1 to 6
BOYS OR GIRLS ☐ Boys only ☐ Girls only ☒ Co-ed
NOTES Family camping is an option; please enquire.

BURN CAMP

SUMMER ADDRESS	Physiotherapy Dept., U of Alberta Hospital 8440 - 112th Street Edmonton ALTA T6G 2B7 **SUMMER PHONE** 403-492-6002
WINTER ADDRESS	As above
	WINTER PHONE
CONTACT PERSON	Sharon Doberstein
ACCREDITATION	ACA
AFFILIATION	Alberta Burn Society
YEARS IN OPERATION	7
DATES OPEN	Last week in August
FEES	No fee to camper
SCHOLARSHIPS	
ACCOMODATION	Cabins, tipis, full washrooms, dining hall.
SPECIALTY	Special Needs: Burn Victims
OBJECTIVES	To provide children with opportunities to make new friends, learn new skills and gain confidence in their abilities.
ACTIVITIES	Horseback riding, canoeing, kayaking, hiking, swimming, rock climbing, sports, outtrips, environmental education, archery, arts & crafts, rope courses.
EVALUATIONS	Yes
MEDICAL FACILITIES	Health centre with nurses, paramedic, & physical therapist.
VISITORS	Allowed
SPECIAL NEEDS FACILITIES	Yes
DESCRIPTION	The camp is held at Camp Chief Hector in the Rocky Mountains surrounded by forests & lakes.
NEAREST CITY/TOWN	Calgary
AGE SPREAD	6 to 18 years
CAMPERS PER SESSION	Maximum 80
STAFF PER SESSION	Maximum 50
COUNSELLOR:CAMPER RATIO	1 to 3
BOYS OR GIRLS	☐ Boys only ☐ Girls only ☒ Co-ed
NOTES	Children from anywhere in Canada are eligible to apply to this camp.

CAMP ADVENTURE

SUMMER ADDRESS	Boys' and Girls' Clubs of Calgary 1318 Regal Crescent NE Calgary ALTA T2E 6Y6 **SUMMER PHONE** 403-276-9981
WINTER ADDRESS	As above
	WINTER PHONE
CONTACT PERSON	Claude Gallant
ACCREDITATION	ACA
AFFILIATION	Boys' and Girls' Clubs of Calgary
YEARS IN OPERATION	33
DATES OPEN	July through August
FEES	$70-$90 Boys'/Girls' club members; $110-150 non-members.
SCHOLARSHIPS	Camperships are available.
ACCOMODATION	Tipi, sleeping cabins, main dining lodge, wash-house.
SPECIALTY	Disadvantaged Youth
OBJECTIVES	To provide fun & friendships in a wilderness environment, & a learning experience for children from difficult socio-economic backgrounds.
ACTIVITIES	Hiking, canoeing, backpacking, archery, swimming, sports, arts & crafts, nature study, environmental awareness, day trips, campfires.
EVALUATIONS	No, but certificates, medals, and T-shirts may be awarded.
MEDICAL FACILITIES	Nurse's cabin.
VISITORS	Allowed
SPECIAL NEEDS FACILITIES	Unspecified
DESCRIPTION	Located on Sibbald Lake in the Bow Crow Provincial Forest.
NEAREST CITY/TOWN	Calgary
AGE SPREAD	6 to 17 years
CAMPERS PER SESSION	50-72
STAFF PER SESSION	20
COUNSELLOR:CAMPER RATIO	1 to 5
BOYS OR GIRLS	☐ Boys only ☐ Girls only ☒ Co-ed
NOTES	

CAMP ALEXO

SUMMER ADDRESS	c/o Youth & Volunteer Centre 4633 49th Street Red Deer ALTA T4N 1T4 **SUMMER PHONE** 403-721-2189
WINTER ADDRESS	As above **WINTER PHONE** 403-342-6500
CONTACT PERSON	John Johnston
ACCREDITATION	ACA
AFFILIATION	None
YEARS IN OPERATION	10
DATES OPEN	July through August
FEES	Sliding fee structure.
SCHOLARSHIPS	Some campers can be subsidized.
ACCOMODATION	Cabins, tipis, main dining lodge, separate washrooms.
SPECIALTY	Disadvantaged Youth
OBJECTIVES	To provide a diversified camping experience emphasizing the development of self-esteem for the clientele of non-profit social service agencies.
ACTIVITIES	Backpacking, canoeing, archery, crafts, games, orienteering, environmental & outdoor educational programs.
EVALUATIONS	No
MEDICAL FACILITIES	Infirmary
VISITORS	Allowed
SPECIAL NEEDS FACILITIES	Unspecified
DESCRIPTION	Located in the Brazeau mountains near the David Thompson Highway.
NEAREST CITY/TOWN	Red Deer
AGE SPREAD	7 to 17 years
CAMPERS PER SESSION	60
STAFF PER SESSION	10
COUNSELLOR:CAMPER RATIO	1 to 5
BOYS OR GIRLS	☐ Boys only ☐ Girls only ☒ Co-ed
NOTES	Provide service to the clientele of non-profit social service agencies. No youth will be denied the opportunity to attend camp due to lack of funds.

CAMP CADICASU

SUMMER ADDRESS Box 59

Bragg Creek ALTA
T0L 0K0 **SUMMER PHONE** 403-949-3944

WINTER ADDRESS As above

WINTER PHONE

CONTACT PERSON Michael Nelson
ACCREDITATION ACA
AFFILIATION Catholic Church
YEARS IN OPERATION 63
DATES OPEN July through August
FEES $190 per one-week session.
SCHOLARSHIPS Subsidies are available.
ACCOMODATION Tents, cabins, main dining hall, swimming pool.
SPECIALTY Christian Development
OBJECTIVES To promote personal growth within a Christian environment by providing programs which are educational, social, spiritual & recreational.
ACTIVITIES Hiking, backpacking, swimming, archery, acclimatization, arts & crafts, horseback riding.

EVALUATIONS No
MEDICAL FACILITIES Nurse on staff.
VISITORS Not allowed.
SPECIAL NEEDS FACILITIES Unspecified
DESCRIPTION Please enquire.

NEAREST CITY/TOWN Calgary
AGE SPREAD 8 to 13 years
CAMPERS PER SESSION 120
STAFF PER SESSION 38
COUNSELLOR:CAMPER RATIO 1 to 8
BOYS OR GIRLS ☐ Boys only ☐ Girls only ☒ Co-ed
NOTES

CAMP CAROLINE

SUMMER ADDRESS Box 250

Caroline ALTA
T0M 0M0 **SUMMER PHONE** 403-722-3939

WINTER ADDRESS As above

WINTER PHONE

CONTACT PERSON Jim Crozier
ACCREDITATION ACA, CCI
AFFILIATION Baptist Church
YEARS IN OPERATION 21
DATES OPEN July through August
FEES $127 - $275 per session (depending on program chosen).
SCHOLARSHIPS Financial assistance may be available.
ACCOMODATION Two main sleeping lodges, main dining lodge, indoor pool.
SPECIALTY Christian Development
OBJECTIVES To promote a personal understanding of the teachings of Christ. Also to provide a quality program enhancing spiritual, emotional, mental & physical development.
ACTIVITIES Swimming, sports, drama, music, crafts, archery, riflery, whitewater canoeing & rafting, waterskiing, mountain biking, horsemanship, horsepacking, devotions, campfires.

EVALUATIONS No
MEDICAL FACILITIES First aid station; clinic 6 km away; hospital 20 minutes away.
VISITORS Not allowed.
SPECIAL NEEDS FACILITIES Unspecified
DESCRIPTION Situated on 320 acres of wilderness land.

NEAREST CITY/TOWN Calgary
AGE SPREAD All ages
CAMPERS PER SESSION 140
STAFF PER SESSION 60
COUNSELLOR:CAMPER RATIO 1 to 7
BOYS OR GIRLS ☐ Boys only ☐ Girls only ☒ Co-ed
NOTES Family camping is also an option; please enquire.

CAMP CHIEF HECTOR

SUMMER ADDRESS			
	Seebe		ALTA
	T0L 1X0	**SUMMER PHONE**	403-673-3858
WINTER ADDRESS	Rocky Mountain YM-YWCA 101 - 3 Street SW		
	Calgary		ALTA
	T2P 4G6	**WINTER PHONE**	403-269-6156

CONTACT PERSON Mike Walters
ACCREDITATION ACA
AFFILIATION YM-YWCA
YEARS IN OPERATION 63
DATES OPEN July through August
FEES $345/week; $685-$710/2 weeks; $1000-1370/4 weeks.
SCHOLARSHIPS Camperships are available.
ACCOMODATION Cabins, tipis, full washrooms, dining halls.
SPECIALTY Traditional
OBJECTIVES To promote individual growth & development in spirit, mind & body based on respect for oneself, others, the natural world & a sense of belonging to the global community.
ACTIVITIES Backpacking, horseback riding, canoeing, hiking, swimming, kayaking, arts & crafts, singing, environmental programs, archery, hayrides, sports, games, campfires.

EVALUATIONS Available upon request.
MEDICAL FACILITIES 2 health centres with 3 nurses & 1 paramedic.
VISITORS Not encouraged
SPECIAL NEEDS FACILITIES Yes
DESCRIPTION Located in the shadow of the Rocky Mountains on a 1000-acre site with forests & lakes.

NEAREST CITY/TOWN Calgary
AGE SPREAD 7 to 17 years
CAMPERS PER SESSION 320
STAFF PER SESSION 155
COUNSELLOR:CAMPER RATIO 1 to 4
BOYS OR GIRLS ☐ Boys only ☐ Girls only ☒ Co-ed
NOTES Special needs refers to special one week camps for Cystic Fibrosis & deaf/hearing-impaired campers. Equal access facility.

CAMP ENCOUNTER

SUMMER ADDRESS	RR #1		
	Gunn		ALTA
	T0E 1A0	**SUMMER PHONE**	403-967-2548
WINTER ADDRESS	As above		
		WINTER PHONE	

CONTACT PERSON David Kieser
ACCREDITATION ACA, CCA
AFFILIATION Catholic Church
YEARS IN OPERATION 8
DATES OPEN July through August
FEES $130 per one-week session.
SCHOLARSHIPS Assistance may be available.
ACCOMODATION Dormitories, modern washroom facilities, dining & rec hall.
SPECIALTY Christian Development
OBJECTIVES To provide youth ministry in the recreational, environmental, & religious education fields, in an outdoor Christian camp community.
ACTIVITIES Canoeing, swimming, hiking, co-operative games, crafts, outtripping, campfires.

EVALUATIONS No
MEDICAL FACILITIES Unspecified; please enquire.
VISITORS Allowed
SPECIAL NEEDS FACILITIES Yes
DESCRIPTION Located on Lac la Nonne.

NEAREST CITY/TOWN Edmonton
AGE SPREAD 8 to 18 years
CAMPERS PER SESSION 40-50
STAFF PER SESSION 15
COUNSELLOR:CAMPER RATIO 1 to 5
BOYS OR GIRLS ☐ Boys only ☐ Girls only ☒ Co-ed
NOTES Special needs refers to wheelchair accessibility. Family camping is an option; please enquire.

CAMP FREEDOM

SUMMER ADDRESS	435 Cannington Close SW		
	Calgary T2W 3E9	**SUMMER PHONE**	ALTA 403-224-9925
WINTER ADDRESS	As above		
		WINTER PHONE	403-281-3267

CONTACT PERSON Andy Stone
ACCREDITATION
AFFILIATION Handicapped Freedom Tours Society
YEARS IN OPERATION 5
DATES OPEN June through September
FEES Approximately $150-$175 per 4-day session.
SCHOLARSHIPS No
ACCOMODATION Cabins, dining lodge, washrooms, rec centre with hot tub.
SPECIALTY Special Needs
OBJECTIVES To allow outdoor learning & recreation for the disabled.

ACTIVITIES Trail riding, hot-air ballooning, fishing, canoeing, ATV, photography, campfires.

EVALUATIONS No
MEDICAL FACILITIES Small ICU & large infirmary.
VISITORS Allowed
SPECIAL NEEDS FACILITIES Yes
DESCRIPTION Please enquire for details.

NEAREST CITY/TOWN Calgary
AGE SPREAD 3 to 93 years
CAMPERS PER SESSION 36
STAFF PER SESSION 9
COUNSELLOR:CAMPER RATIO Included in above figure.
BOYS OR GIRLS ☐ Boys only ☐ Girls only ☒ Co-ed
NOTES Special needs refers to all disabilities. Hot-air ballooning is an all-day event; launch at 7am & return at 7pm.

CAMP GARDNER

SUMMER ADDRESS	Box 5, Site 1 RR #1 Calgary ALTA T2P 2G4
SUMMER PHONE	403-242-9267
WINTER ADDRESS	As above
WINTER PHONE	
CONTACT PERSON	Don Thome
ACCREDITATION	ACA
AFFILIATION	Scouts Canada
YEARS IN OPERATION	35
DATES OPEN	July through August
FEES	$175 per one-week session.
SCHOLARSHIPS	No
ACCOMODATION	Lodges, bunk-houses, tents, showers, main dining hall.
SPECIALTY	Traditional
OBJECTIVES	To provide a quality camping experience based on Scouting themes; sharing & learning in a group situation in harmony with nature.
ACTIVITIES	Swimming, hiking, crafts, environmental & nature studies, games, archery, sports, drama, campfires.
EVALUATIONS	No, but campers can work on earning badges.
MEDICAL FACILITIES	All staff have first aid & CPR training.
VISITORS	Allowed
SPECIAL NEEDS FACILITIES	Unspecified
DESCRIPTION	Located on the Elbow River.
NEAREST CITY/TOWN	Calgary
AGE SPREAD	All ages
CAMPERS PER SESSION	40
STAFF PER SESSION	13
COUNSELLOR:CAMPER RATIO	1 to 6
BOYS OR GIRLS	☐ Boys only ☐ Girls only ☒ Co-ed
NOTES	Camp is operated by Scouts Canada, Calgary Region.

CAMP HORIZON

SUMMER ADDRESS Box 540

Bragg Creek ALTA
T0L 0K0 **SUMMER PHONE** 403-949-3818

WINTER ADDRESS As above

WINTER PHONE

CONTACT PERSON Bob Williamson
ACCREDITATION ACA
AFFILIATION None
YEARS IN OPERATION 28
DATES OPEN July through August
FEES Please enquire.
SCHOLARSHIPS About 50% of actual cost is subsidized.
ACCOMODATION Heated dorms & cabins with showers, dining hall, pool.
SPECIALTY Special Needs: Physical & Mental Disabilities
OBJECTIVES To provide camping opportunities to children with physical & mental disabilities.

ACTIVITIES Rafting, climbing, tenting, nature programs, arts & crafts, sports, games, swimming, hay rides, campfires.

EVALUATIONS No
MEDICAL FACILITIES First aid room & trained staff.
VISITORS Not encouraged
SPECIAL NEEDS FACILITIES Yes
DESCRIPTION Situated on 44 acres of well-forested land with 3 km of wheelchair accessible trails.

NEAREST CITY/TOWN Calgary
AGE SPREAD 5 years & up
CAMPERS PER SESSION 36-100
STAFF PER SESSION 10-35
COUNSELLOR:CAMPER RATIO 1 to 4
BOYS OR GIRLS ☐ Boys only ☐ Girls only ☒ Co-ed
NOTES Special needs refers to disabled & mentally handicapped campers, as well as children with medical concerns (such as cancer, diabetes, severe asthma). Wheelchair accessible; site is barrier free. Family camping is an option; please enquire.

CAMP KASOTA EAST

SUMMER ADDRESS	General Delivery		
	Sylvan Lake		ALTA
	T0M 1Z0	**SUMMER PHONE**	403-887-5757
WINTER ADDRESS	24 Broughton Crescent		
	Red Deer		ALTA
	T4R 1L8	**WINTER PHONE**	403-343-6136

CONTACT PERSON Wayne Rumont
ACCREDITATION ACA
AFFILIATION United Church, Canyon Church Camp Association
YEARS IN OPERATION 60+
DATES OPEN June through August
FEES $50-$140 per session
SCHOLARSHIPS Sponsors may be available in special cases.
ACCOMODATION Cabins, wash-houses with showers, dining hall, craft lodge.
SPECIALTY Christian Development
OBJECTIVES To provide a Christian environment for education in a wilderness setting.

ACTIVITIES Crafts, canoeing, sailing, field sports, performing arts, photography, Bible study, square dancing, swimming, campfires.

EVALUATIONS No
MEDICAL FACILITIES Trained staff; hospital 6 km away.
VISITORS Not encouraged
SPECIAL NEEDS FACILITIES Yes
DESCRIPTION Please enquire for details.

NEAREST CITY/TOWN Red Deer
AGE SPREAD 6 years & up
CAMPERS PER SESSION Approximately 60
STAFF PER SESSION 10
COUNSELLOR:CAMPER RATIO 1 to 4
BOYS OR GIRLS ☐ Boys only ☐ Girls only ☒ Co-ed
NOTES Special needs refers to handicapped camps offered; please enquire.

CAMP KINNAIRD

SUMMER ADDRESS	Box 519		
	Sylvan Lake		ALTA
	T0M 1Z0	**SUMMER PHONE**	403-746-5668
WINTER ADDRESS	YM-YWCA		
	320 - 5th Avenue SE		
	Calgary		ALTA
	T2G 0E5	**WINTER PHONE**	403-263-1550

CONTACT PERSON Mark Irwin
ACCREDITATION ACA
AFFILIATION YM-YWCA
YEARS IN OPERATION 40
DATES OPEN July through August
FEES $225/6 days; $450/12 days; $650 for leadership program.
SCHOLARSHIPS Camperships are available.
ACCOMODATION Cabins, lodge, dining hall, showers, indoor toilets, tipis.
SPECIALTY Traditional
OBJECTIVES Personal growth & development of the individual through involvement in a variety of small group activities, outdoor challenges, & respect for the natural environment.
ACTIVITIES Sailing, windsurfing, canoeing, outtrips, kayaking, archery, arts & crafts, campfires, environmental activities.

EVALUATIONS No
MEDICAL FACILITIES Infirmary
VISITORS Allowed on Visitors Day.
SPECIAL NEEDS FACILITIES Unspecified
DESCRIPTION Located at Sylvan Lake on 28 acres of lakefront property.

NEAREST CITY/TOWN Red Deer
AGE SPREAD 6 to 17 years
CAMPERS PER SESSION 80-96
STAFF PER SESSION 15
COUNSELLOR:CAMPER RATIO 1 to 6
BOYS OR GIRLS ☐ Boys only ☐ Girls only ☒ Co-ed
NOTES

CAMP KURIAKOS

SUMMER ADDRESS	Box 372		
	Bentley T0C 0J0	**SUMMER PHONE**	ALTA 403-746-2702
WINTER ADDRESS	As above		
		WINTER PHONE	ALTA 403-748-3927

CONTACT PERSON David E. Larson
ACCREDITATION ACA
AFFILIATION Lutheran Church
YEARS IN OPERATION 63
DATES OPEN July through August
FEES $149-$159 per 5-day session.
SCHOLARSHIPS No
ACCOMODATION Cabins, dorms, tents, dining hall, washrooms with showers.
SPECIALTY Christian Development
OBJECTIVES Camp is meant to be a place set apart for renewal, refreshment & recreation. Kuriakos is a New Testament Greek word meaning "belonging to the Lord".
ACTIVITIES Crafts, backpacking, swimming, sailing, canoeing, archery, team sports, worship, orienteering, games, campfires.

EVALUATIONS No
MEDICAL FACILITIES Nurse on staff; hospital 10 km away.
VISITORS Allowed
SPECIAL NEEDS FACILITIES Yes
DESCRIPTION Please enquire for details.

NEAREST CITY/TOWN Red Deer
AGE SPREAD 8 to 18 years
CAMPERS PER SESSION 50-150 (depending on age group).
STAFF PER SESSION 3-25 (as above).
COUNSELLOR:CAMPER RATIO 1 to 6
BOYS OR GIRLS ☐ Boys only ☐ Girls only ☒ Co-ed
NOTES Family camping is an option; please enquire.

CAMP MANNAWANIS

SUMMER ADDRESS Box 2519

St. Paul ALTA
T0A 3A0 **SUMMER PHONE** 403-645-4490

WINTER ADDRESS As above

WINTER PHONE 403-645-4630

CONTACT PERSON Bob Harrison
ACCREDITATION ACA
AFFILIATION None
YEARS IN OPERATION 8
DATES OPEN July through August
FEES $125 per one-week session.
SCHOLARSHIPS No
ACCOMODATION A-frame cabins, dining hall, showers, indoor toilets.
SPECIALTY Cree Culture
OBJECTIVES To provide cultural & cross-cultural experiences for native & non-native children through exposure to the local Cree culture.

ACTIVITIES Swimming, canoeing, sailing, archery, crafts, storytelling, Pow Wows (singing, dancing, drumming), ceremonies.

EVALUATIONS No
MEDICAL FACILITIES All staff trained in advanced first aid; hospital 5 km away.
VISITORS Allowed
SPECIAL NEEDS FACILITIES Yes
DESCRIPTION Situated on the shores of lower Thieron Lake.

NEAREST CITY/TOWN St. Paul
AGE SPREAD 7 to 17 years
CAMPERS PER SESSION Maximum 50
STAFF PER SESSION 12
COUNSELLOR:CAMPER RATIO 1 to 5
BOYS OR GIRLS ☐ Boys only ☐ Girls only ☒ Co-ed
NOTES Special needs refers to many campers affected by Fetal Alcohol Syndrome. There are minimal facilities for physically handicapped children; please enquire.

CAMP OKOTOKS

SUMMER ADDRESS	General Delivery		
	Okotoks		ALTA
	T0L 1T0	**SUMMER PHONE**	
WINTER ADDRESS	3333 Richardson Way SW		
	Calgary		
	T3E 7B6	**WINTER PHONE**	403-249-8605

CONTACT PERSON Stephen Marston
ACCREDITATION ACA, CCA, CCI
AFFILIATION Christian Brethren
YEARS IN OPERATION 32
DATES OPEN July through August
FEES $96 - $155 per session.
SCHOLARSHIPS May be available upon request.
ACCOMODATION Cabins, central washrooms, main lodge, dining hall.
SPECIALTY Christian Development
OBJECTIVES To provide the best possible camping experience, along with the opportunity to give serious thoughts to the claims of Jesus Christ.
ACTIVITIES Chapel, Bible studies, tennis, riflery, archery, canoeing, swimming, crafts, games, team sports, table tennis, campfires.

EVALUATIONS No
MEDICAL FACILITIES Health centre with nurse or doctor.
VISITORS Not allowed
SPECIAL NEEDS FACILITIES Unspecified
DESCRIPTION Located on the Sheep River.

NEAREST CITY/TOWN Okotoks
AGE SPREAD 5 years & up
CAMPERS PER SESSION 100
STAFF PER SESSION 40
COUNSELLOR:CAMPER RATIO 1-2 per cabin
BOYS OR GIRLS ☐ Boys only ☐ Girls only ☒ Co-ed
NOTES Family camping is an option; please enquire.

CAMP SILVERSIDES

SUMMER ADDRESS Box 519

Bentley ALTA
T0C 0J0 **SUMMER PHONE** 403-748-2689

WINTER ADDRESS As above

WINTER PHONE

CONTACT PERSON Mark Archibald
ACCREDITATION ACA
AFFILIATION Canadian Sunday School Mission
YEARS IN OPERATION 64
DATES OPEN July through August
FEES $35 - $169 per session; please enquire.
SCHOLARSHIPS No
ACCOMODATION Cabins, main dining lodge, central washrooms, showers.
SPECIALTY Christian Development
OBJECTIVES To provide a fun-filled, wholesome & safe setting in which campers can find a personal relationship with God through faith in Jesus Christ.
ACTIVITIES Canoeing, windsurfing, trampolines, drama, archery, riflery, games, crafts, Bible study, & chapel.

EVALUATIONS No
MEDICAL FACILITIES Camp nurse & infirmary; hospital 5 km away.
VISITORS Allowed
SPECIAL NEEDS FACILITIES Yes
DESCRIPTION Located on Gull Lake.

NEAREST CITY/TOWN Red Deer
AGE SPREAD 8 years & up
CAMPERS PER SESSION 110
STAFF PER SESSION 40
COUNSELLOR:CAMPER RATIO 1 to 6
BOYS OR GIRLS ☐ Boys only ☐ Girls only ☒ Co-ed
NOTES Special needs refers to wheelchair-accessible buildings.

CAMP VALAQUA

SUMMER ADDRESS	PO Box 72 Water Valley ALTA T0M 2E0
SUMMER PHONE	403-637-2510
WINTER ADDRESS	As above
WINTER PHONE	
CONTACT PERSON	Tim or Donita Wiebe-Neufeld
ACCREDITATION	ACA, Mennonite Camping Association
AFFILIATION	Mennonite Brethren
YEARS IN OPERATION	34
DATES OPEN	July through August
FEES	$110 - $120 per one-week session.
SCHOLARSHIPS	Camperships are available.
ACCOMODATION	Cabins, main lodge, washrooms, showers.
SPECIALTY	Christian Development
OBJECTIVES	To provide a setting in which campers can experience God through worship, nature, recreation, & interaction with fellow campers & staff.
ACTIVITIES	Bible study, sports, crafts, archery, canoeing, trampoline, fishing, hiking, nature awareness, swimming, singing, campfires.
EVALUATIONS	No
MEDICAL FACILITIES	First aid room & nurse.
VISITORS	No
SPECIAL NEEDS FACILITIES	Unspecified
DESCRIPTION	Located on the Little Red Deer River near Water Valley.
NEAREST CITY/TOWN	Cochrane
AGE SPREAD	6 to 17 years
CAMPERS PER SESSION	72
STAFF PER SESSION	18 (plus 16 volunteers).
COUNSELLOR:CAMPER RATIO	1 to 5
BOYS OR GIRLS	☐ Boys only ☐ Girls only ☒ Co-ed
NOTES	

CAMP WARWA

SUMMER ADDRESS	Box 29		
	Darwell T0E 0L0	**SUMMER PHONE**	ALTA 403-892-3648
WINTER ADDRESS	As above		
		WINTER PHONE	

CONTACT PERSON Ian Hosler
ACCREDITATION ACA
AFFILIATION None
YEARS IN OPERATION 6
DATES OPEN July through August
FEES $33 per day or $165 per 5-day session.
SCHOLARSHIPS Camperships are available.
ACCOMODATION Cabins, wash-houses with showers & flush toilets, dining hall.
SPECIALTY Traditional
OBJECTIVES To encourage the enhancement of individual self-awareness & personal growth through outdoor-focussed programs.

ACTIVITIES Environmental education, canoeing, orienteering, kayaking, climbing, ropes course, swimming, crafts, field sports, camp-wide games, archery, campfires.

EVALUATIONS No
MEDICAL FACILITIES Infirmary with first aid attendant.
VISITORS Allowed
SPECIAL NEEDS FACILITIES Yes
DESCRIPTION Located on 23 acres at Lac Ste-Anne with access to Crown lands and islands.

NEAREST CITY/TOWN Edmonton
AGE SPREAD 6 to 18 years
CAMPERS PER SESSION 51
STAFF PER SESSION 19
COUNSELLOR:CAMPER RATIO 1 to 5
BOYS OR GIRLS ☐ Boys only ☐ Girls only ☒ Co-ed
NOTES Special needs means the camp can accommodate mildly physically or mentally challenged children. Cases are evaluated individually; please enquire.

CAMPUS AMICUS

SUMMER ADDRESS c/o Learning Disabilities Assoc. of Alberta
745B 37 Street NW
Calgary ALTA
T2N 4T1 **SUMMER PHONE** 403-283-6606

WINTER ADDRESS As above

WINTER PHONE

CONTACT PERSON Linda Miller
ACCREDITATION ACA
AFFILIATION Learning Disabilities Association of Alberta
YEARS IN OPERATION 10
DATES OPEN July through August
FEES Vary according to length of stay; please enquire.
SCHOLARSHIPS Funding is available.
ACCOMODATION Cabins, showers, main dining hall.
SPECIALTY Special Needs: Learning Disabilities
OBJECTIVES To provide campers with an experience which will enable them to raise their self-esteem while having fun developing appropriate social & problem-solving skills.
ACTIVITIES Horseback riding, archery, drama, ropes course, rodeo, outtrips, camp-wide games, campfires.

EVALUATIONS Yes
MEDICAL FACILITIES None
VISITORS Allowed
SPECIAL NEEDS FACILITIES Yes
DESCRIPTION Please enquire for details.

NEAREST CITY/TOWN Calgary
AGE SPREAD 8 to 15 years
CAMPERS PER SESSION Approximately 80
STAFF PER SESSION Approximately 1 staff per 2-3 campers.
COUNSELLOR:CAMPER RATIO Included in above figures.
BOYS OR GIRLS ☐ Boys only ☐ Girls only ☒ Co-ed
NOTES Special needs refers to learning-disabled children.

CANYON CAMP

SUMMER ADDRESS Red Rock Canyon Road
Waterton Lakes National Park
Waterton ALTA
T0K 1M0 **SUMMER PHONE** Mobile in Pincher Crk.

WINTER ADDRESS c/o Canyon Church Camp Association
1011 4th Avenue S.
Lethbridge ALTA
T1J 0P7 **WINTER PHONE** 403-327-4454

CONTACT PERSON Jane De Coste

ACCREDITATION

AFFILIATION YM-YWCA, Canyon Church Camp Association

YEARS IN OPERATION 45

DATES OPEN CCCA in July and YMCA in August.

FEES CCCA $140 per session; YMCA $125-$165 per session.

SCHOLARSHIPS No

ACCOMODATION Cabins, showers, main lodge.

SPECIALTY Traditional

OBJECTIVES To provide youth with a deep appreciation of their environment, & a fun learning experience emphasizing growth & development in body, mind & spirit.

ACTIVITIES Horseback riding, hiking, swimming, acclimatization, crafts, nature walks, creek crawling, campfires.

EVALUATIONS No

MEDICAL FACILITIES Infirmary on site with nurse or doctor on duty.

VISITORS Not encouraged.

SPECIAL NEEDS FACILITIES Unspecified

DESCRIPTION Located in scenic Waterton Lakes National Park, nestled beside Pass Creek at the foot of Crandell Mountain.

NEAREST CITY/TOWN Pincher Creek

AGE SPREAD 8 to 16 years

CAMPERS PER SESSION Maximum 70

STAFF PER SESSION 3

COUNSELLOR:CAMPER RATIO CCCA 1 to 5 / YMCA 1 to 3

BOYS OR GIRLS ☐ Boys only ☐ Girls only ☒ Co-ed

NOTES The camp is jointly owned & operated by the Lethbridge YMCA and the CCCA (run by United Church members). YMCA address is: 515 Stafford Drive S., Lethbridge, Alberta T1J 2L3 Phone 403-327-9622.

CENTRE DE PLEIN AIR LUSSON

SUMMER ADDRESS #100, 8925 82nd Avenue

Edmonton ALTA
T6C 0Z2 **SUMMER PHONE** 403-348-5280

WINTER ADDRESS As above

WINTER PHONE 403-469-3997

CONTACT PERSON José Roberge
ACCREDITATION ACA
AFFILIATION Association Canadienne-Française d'Alberta
YEARS IN OPERATION 6
DATES OPEN July through August
FEES $150 per one-week session.
SCHOLARSHIPS No
ACCOMODATION Tents with wooden floors, main dining lodge, showers.
SPECIALTY French Immersion
OBJECTIVES To provide Francophones & Francophiles with outdoor education opportunities.

ACTIVITIES Canoeing, orienteering, field & co-operative games, hiking, campfires, environmental awareness.

EVALUATIONS No
MEDICAL FACILITIES First aid station; hospital 14 km away.
VISITORS Allowed
SPECIAL NEEDS FACILITIES Unspecified
DESCRIPTION Please enquire for details.

NEAREST CITY/TOWN Clyde
AGE SPREAD 5 to 17 years
CAMPERS PER SESSION 24
STAFF PER SESSION 4
COUNSELLOR:CAMPER RATIO 1 to 6
BOYS OR GIRLS ☐ Boys only ☐ Girls only ☒ Co-ed
NOTES Camp is operated by the Association Canadienne - Française d'Alberta, regionale d'Edmonton (ACFA).

DINOSAUR COUNTRY SCIENCE CAMP

SUMMER ADDRESS	PO Box 516
	East Coulee ALTA
	T0J 1B0
SUMMER PHONE	403-823-2030
WINTER ADDRESS	As above
WINTER PHONE	
CONTACT PERSON	Robin Digby
ACCREDITATION	ACA
AFFILIATION	Drumheller Regional Science Council
YEARS IN OPERATION	4
DATES OPEN	July through August
FEES	$348 per one-week session.
SCHOLARSHIPS	Bursaries available to those with financial need.
ACCOMODATION	High School residence & cafeteria.
SPECIALTY	Science: Natural Science
OBJECTIVES	To "uncover science & discover fun." To foster an understanding & appreciation of natural science through hands-on experience.
ACTIVITIES	Field experiments in ecology, archaeological site mapping, fossil prospecting, ice cream making, hiking, canoeing, swimming, animal tracking, bird-watching, star-gazing, flint-knapping, campfires.
EVALUATIONS	No
MEDICAL FACILITIES	Staff trained in emergency procedures; hospital 2 km away.
VISITORS	Allowed
SPECIAL NEEDS FACILITIES	Unspecified
DESCRIPTION	Please enquire for details.
NEAREST CITY/TOWN	Drumheller
AGE SPREAD	9 to 17 years
CAMPERS PER SESSION	32
STAFF PER SESSION	7
COUNSELLOR:CAMPER RATIO	1 to 5
BOYS OR GIRLS	☐ Boys only ☐ Girls only ☒ Co-ed
NOTES	There is also a 5-day canoe trip offered and some camps are available for girls only, please enquire.

FOOTHILLS

SUMMER ADDRESS	National Camps for the Blind PO Box 3190 Olds ALTA T0H 1P0
SUMMER PHONE	403-556-6767
WINTER ADDRESS	As above
WINTER PHONE	604-860-6319
CONTACT PERSON	John Reitor
ACCREDITATION	CCA, CCI
AFFILIATION	Christian (nondenominational)
YEARS IN OPERATION	20
DATES OPEN	One week in July
FEES	Free to all legally blind persons aged 9 & up.
SCHOLARSHIPS	
ACCOMODATION	Cabins, showers, dining hall.
SPECIALTY	Special Needs: Blind / Visually Impaired
OBJECTIVES	To allow the blind participant to discover undeveloped potential, increase self-confidence, improve physical vigour & develop an appreciation for God's love & care.
ACTIVITIES	Archery, boating, camp council, canoeing, crafts, hiking, horseback riding, rock climbing, sailing, swimming, rappelling, waterskiing, campfires.
EVALUATIONS	No
MEDICAL FACILITIES	Infirmary with medical staff on duty 24 hours.
VISITORS	Allowed on talent night.
SPECIAL NEEDS FACILITIES	Yes
DESCRIPTION	Please enquire for details.
NEAREST CITY/TOWN	Red Deer
AGE SPREAD	9 years & up.
CAMPERS PER SESSION	40
STAFF PER SESSION	Varies
COUNSELLOR:CAMPER RATIO	1 to 2
BOYS OR GIRLS	☐ Boys only ☐ Girls only ☒ Co-ed
NOTES	Special needs refers to blind or visually impaired campers. This program is designed to place emphasis on ability rather than the disability of the visually impaired individual.

FOOTHILLS CAMP

SUMMER ADDRESS Box 5007

Red Deer ALTA
T4N 6A1 **SUMMER PHONE** 403-342-5044

WINTER ADDRESS RR #3, Site 6, Box 12

Olds ALTA
T4H 1P4 **WINTER PHONE** 403-343-1523

CONTACT PERSON Bryan Lee
ACCREDITATION ACA, CCI
AFFILIATION Seventh Day Adventists
YEARS IN OPERATION 20
DATES OPEN July through August
FEES Please enquire.
SCHOLARSHIPS Available; church subsidizes half of fee.
ACCOMODATION Cabins, showers, washrooms, dining hall, swimming pool.
SPECIALTY Traditional
OBJECTIVES To provide an activity & skill-developing environment to help campers develop self-worth. Also to demonstrate the importance of God.
ACTIVITIES Horsemanship, trail riding, swimming, waterskiing, canoeing, gymnastics, crafts, mountain biking, campfires.

EVALUATIONS No
MEDICAL FACILITIES Nurse's station.
VISITORS Allowed
SPECIAL NEEDS FACILITIES Yes
DESCRIPTION Please enquire for details.

NEAREST CITY/TOWN Red Deer
AGE SPREAD 7 to 17 years
CAMPERS PER SESSION 75
STAFF PER SESSION 32
COUNSELLOR:CAMPER RATIO 1 to 3
BOYS OR GIRLS ☐ Boys only ☐ Girls only ☒ Co-ed
NOTES Special needs refers to wheelchair accessibility .

FRONTIER LODGE

SUMMER ADDRESS Box 1449

Rocky Mountain House ALTA
T0M 1T0 **SUMMER PHONE** 403-721-2202

WINTER ADDRESS As above

WINTER PHONE

CONTACT PERSON Steve Johnson
ACCREDITATION ACA, CCI
AFFILIATION Christian (nondenominational)
YEARS IN OPERATION 33
DATES OPEN July through August
FEES $33.50 per day.
SCHOLARSHIPS No
ACCOMODATION Heated cabins, central washrooms with running water.
SPECIALTY Wilderness Training
OBJECTIVES To promote personal growth (physically, mentally, emotionally, spiritually & socially) through Christian values; skill & leadership development in a wilderness setting.
ACTIVITIES Hiking, backpacking, rock climbing, canoeing, mountain biking, campfires.

EVALUATIONS No
MEDICAL FACILITIES Nurse on site; all staff trained in first aid.
VISITORS Allowed
SPECIAL NEEDS FACILITIES Unspecified
DESCRIPTION Please enquire for details.

NEAREST CITY/TOWN Rocky Mountain House
AGE SPREAD 12 years & up.
CAMPERS PER SESSION 15-20
STAFF PER SESSION 4
COUNSELLOR:CAMPER RATIO 1 to 5
BOYS OR GIRLS ☐ Boys only ☐ Girls only ☒ Co-ed
NOTES

KIEV'S K-HI UKRAINIAN YOUTH CAMP

SUMMER ADDRESS	PO Box 2		
	Glendon		ALTA
	T0A 1P0	**SUMMER PHONE**	403-635-3879
WINTER ADDRESS	PO Box 253		
	Elk Point		ALTA
	T0A 1A0	**WINTER PHONE**	403-724-2910

CONTACT PERSON Marshall Kachmar
ACCREDITATION ACA
AFFILIATION Ukrainian Orthodox Church
YEARS IN OPERATION 26
DATES OPEN July through August
FEES Please enquire.
SCHOLARSHIPS
ACCOMODATION Dormitories, shower house, dining hall.
SPECIALTY Ukrainian Development
OBJECTIVES To teach Ukrainian culture, art, language & religion.

ACTIVITIES Swimming, paddle boating, canoeing, arts & crafts, devotions, sports, Ukrainian language, Ukrainian cooking.

EVALUATIONS No
MEDICAL FACILITIES Medical facilities nearby.
VISITORS Allowed
SPECIAL NEEDS FACILITIES Unspecified
DESCRIPTION Located on Moose Lake.

NEAREST CITY/TOWN Bonnyville
AGE SPREAD 6 to 14 years
CAMPERS PER SESSION 45-75
STAFF PER SESSION 15
COUNSELLOR:CAMPER RATIO 1 to 7
BOYS OR GIRLS ☐ Boys only ☐ Girls only ☒ Co-ed
NOTES Family camping is an option; please enquire.

LONG LAKE JUNIOR FOREST WARDEN CAMP

SUMMER ADDRESS Box 2340

Athabasca ALTA
T0G 0B0 **SUMMER PHONE** 403-675-2276

WINTER ADDRESS 9920 108th Street
10th Floor
Edmonton ALTA
T5K 2M4 **WINTER PHONE** 403-427-2545

CONTACT PERSON Bill Bresnahan

ACCREDITATION

AFFILIATION Alberta Forest Service

YEARS IN OPERATION 12

DATES OPEN July through September

FEES None

SCHOLARSHIPS No

ACCOMODATION Tents, cabins, showers, dining hall.

SPECIALTY Forest Education

OBJECTIVES To develop an awareness of, and appreciation & respect for our forest environment. Also to teach responsible use of that environment.

ACTIVITIES Environmental education, kayaking, canoeing, rock climbing, fishing, campfires.

EVALUATIONS No

MEDICAL FACILITIES Staff trained in emergency medical procedures.

VISITORS Not allowed

SPECIAL NEEDS FACILITIES No

DESCRIPTION Situated in a natural forest surrounded by plants, trees, rivers & animals of the wilderness.

NEAREST CITY/TOWN Edmonton

AGE SPREAD 6 to 18 years

CAMPERS PER SESSION 60

STAFF PER SESSION 35

COUNSELLOR:CAMPER RATIO 1 to 7

BOYS OR GIRLS ☐ Boys only ☐ Girls only ☒ Co-ed

NOTES

MOONLIGHT BAY CAMP

SUMMER ADDRESS	Bissell Centre 10527 96th Street Edmonton T5H 2H6	**SUMMER PHONE**	ALTA 403-423-2285
WINTER ADDRESS	As above	**WINTER PHONE**	

CONTACT PERSON Marnie Law
ACCREDITATION ACA
AFFILIATION United Church
YEARS IN OPERATION 72
DATES OPEN July through August
FEES $145 per 5-day session.
SCHOLARSHIPS Camperships are available.
ACCOMODATION Cabins, showers, dining lodge, recreation hall.
SPECIALTY Disadvantaged Youth
OBJECTIVES To provide a camping experience to those in the inner city of Edmonton & elsewhere who might not otherwise be able to have one.
ACTIVITIES Swimming, canoeing, boating, hiking, crafts, field sports, co-operative games, campfires.

EVALUATIONS Yes; achievement certificates may also be awarded.
MEDICAL FACILITIES Yes
VISITORS Allowed
SPECIAL NEEDS FACILITIES Yes
DESCRIPTION Situated on Lake Wabamun.

NEAREST CITY/TOWN Edmonton
AGE SPREAD All ages
CAMPERS PER SESSION Approximately 45
STAFF PER SESSION 7
COUNSELLOR:CAMPER RATIO 1 to 5
BOYS OR GIRLS ☐ Boys only ☐ Girls only ☒ Co-ed
NOTES Camp is intended for socially & economically disadvantaged inner-city residents. Physically & emotionally challenged campers are also welcome.

PINE LAKE CAMP

SUMMER ADDRESS	PO Box 101		
	Pine Lake		ALTA
	T0M 1S0	**SUMMER PHONE**	403-886-4838
WINTER ADDRESS	10171 107th Street		
	Edmonton		ALTA
	T5J 1J5	**WINTER PHONE**	403-465-4348

CONTACT PERSON Captain Everett Barrow
ACCREDITATION ACA
AFFILIATION Salvation Army
YEARS IN OPERATION 55
DATES OPEN July through August
FEES $60 - $110 per session.
SCHOLARSHIPS Please enquire.
ACCOMODATION Cabins with bathrooms & showers, dining hall, pool.
SPECIALTY Christian Development
OBJECTIVES Character building & spiritual growth through wholesome activities & interpersonal relationships. Also to help youth put Christ in every phase of life.
ACTIVITIES Swimming, crafts, canoeing, Bible study, chapel, miniature golf, archery, music, chapel, campfires.

EVALUATIONS No
MEDICAL FACILITIES Hospital on site with nurse on duty 24 hours.
VISITORS Allowed
SPECIAL NEEDS FACILITIES Unspecified
DESCRIPTION Located on Pine Lake.

NEAREST CITY/TOWN Red Deer
AGE SPREAD 7 to 19 years
CAMPERS PER SESSION Approximately 170
STAFF PER SESSION Approximately 20-40
COUNSELLOR:CAMPER RATIO 1 to 6
BOYS OR GIRLS ☐ Boys only ☐ Girls only ☒ Co-ed
NOTES Family camping is an option; please enquire.

PIONEER RANCH

SUMMER ADDRESS PO Box 600

Rocky Mountain House ALTA
T0M 1T0 **SUMMER PHONE** 403-845-6777

WINTER ADDRESS #305-4209 99th Street

Edmonton ALTA
T6E 5V7 **WINTER PHONE** 403-462-4208

CONTACT PERSON Duane Dobson
ACCREDITATION ACA
AFFILIATION Inter Varsity Christian Fellowship
YEARS IN OPERATION 40
DATES OPEN July through August
FEES Please enquire.
SCHOLARSHIPS Available
ACCOMODATION Dorms, cabins, showers, dining hall, main lodge, pool.
SPECIALTY Christian Development
OBJECTIVES To provide campers with an atmosphere that challenges their personal growth & promotes Jesus in all aspects of life.

ACTIVITIES Horseback riding, canoeing, kayaking, swimming, archery, camp-wide games, ropes course, Bible study, hiking, crafts, campfires.

EVALUATIONS No
MEDICAL FACILITIES Infirmary with camp nurse.
VISITORS Allowed during scheduled Visitors Day.
SPECIAL NEEDS FACILITIES Unspecified
DESCRIPTION Located on Crimson Lake.

NEAREST CITY/TOWN Rocky Mountain House
AGE SPREAD 12 to 17 years
CAMPERS PER SESSION 40-100
STAFF PER SESSION 10-30
COUNSELLOR:CAMPER RATIO 1 to 6
BOYS OR GIRLS ☒ Boys only ☒ Girls only ☒ Co-ed
NOTES

SURPRISE LAKE CAMP

SUMMER ADDRESS	Box 5152		
	Edson		ALTA
	T7E 1T4	**SUMMER PHONE**	403-723-2159
WINTER ADDRESS	10645 79th Avenue		
	Edmonton		ALTA
	T6E 1S2	**WINTER PHONE**	403-439-4238

CONTACT PERSON Andriel Stoeckel
ACCREDITATION ACA
AFFILIATION United Church
YEARS IN OPERATION 43
DATES OPEN July through August
FEES $75 - $125 per session.
SCHOLARSHIPS Camperships are available.
ACCOMODATION Cabins, outhouses and wash-houses, dining hall, rec hall.
SPECIALTY Christian Development
OBJECTIVES To encourage growth in the camper's relationship with God, nature, and one another.

ACTIVITIES Swimming, hiking, canoeing, singing, drama, games, crafts, environmental education, worship, Bible study, leadership training, campfires.

EVALUATIONS No
MEDICAL FACILITIES Nurse's cabin.
VISITORS Allowed
SPECIAL NEEDS FACILITIES Unspecified
DESCRIPTION Situated in a semi-wilderness setting.

NEAREST CITY/TOWN Edmonton
AGE SPREAD 7 years to adult
CAMPERS PER SESSION Approximately 36-50
STAFF PER SESSION 24
COUNSELLOR:CAMPER RATIO 1 to 5
BOYS OR GIRLS ☐ Boys only ☐ Girls only ☒ Co-ed
NOTES Family camping is an option; please enquire.

SYLVAN LAKE SUMMER HOCKEY CAMP LTD.

SUMMER ADDRESS Box 274

Sylvan Lake ALTA
T0M 1Z0 **SUMMER PHONE** 403-887-2575

WINTER ADDRESS As above

WINTER PHONE

CONTACT PERSON Graham Parsons
ACCREDITATION
AFFILIATION None
YEARS IN OPERATION 20
DATES OPEN July through Labour Day
FEES Approx $360 per 10-day session.
SCHOLARSHIPS No
ACCOMODATION Dormitory, cafeteria, showers.
SPECIALTY Hockey
OBJECTIVES To provide each camper with a positive hockey experience by combining hockey fundamentals with summer fun.

ACTIVITIES Hockey, on-ice work-outs, dryland training, games, swimming, classroom time, educational videos.

EVALUATIONS Yes
MEDICAL FACILITIES Trainer on site.
VISITORS Allowed
SPECIAL NEEDS FACILITIES No
DESCRIPTION Please enquire for details.

NEAREST CITY/TOWN Red Deer
AGE SPREAD 6 to 18 years
CAMPERS PER SESSION 150 total; accomodation for 45 boys only.
STAFF PER SESSION 24
COUNSELLOR:CAMPER RATIO 1 to 8
BOYS OR GIRLS ☐ Boys only ☐ Girls only ☒ Co-ed
NOTES While both boys and girls are welcome, the residential facilities are available only for boys up to a maximum of 45. Thus for the majority of campers, this is a day camp.

TEEN TIME RANCH

SUMMER ADDRESS	RR #1		
	Dapp		ALTA
	T0G 0S0	**SUMMER PHONE**	403-954-2432
WINTER ADDRESS	8724 - 51st Avenue		
	Edmonton		ALTA
	T6E 5E8	**WINTER PHONE**	403-466-8530

CONTACT PERSON Greg Wiens
ACCREDITATION ACA, CCI
AFFILIATION Christian (nondenominational)
YEARS IN OPERATION 30
DATES OPEN July through August
FEES $130 - $280 per session.
SCHOLARSHIPS Limited sponsorship is available.
ACCOMODATION Cabins, main lodge with dining hall.
SPECIALTY Traditional
OBJECTIVES To provide a balanced program encouraging campers to develop physically, socially, mentally & spiritually.

ACTIVITIES Hay rides, horseback riding, canoeing, archery, swimming, sports, trampoline, orienteering, arts & crafts, campfires, camp-wide games.

EVALUATIONS No, but records are kept; trophies & badges are awarded.
MEDICAL FACILITIES First aid room.
VISITORS Allowed with prior arrangements.
SPECIAL NEEDS FACILITIES Yes
DESCRIPTION Located on the shores of Makewin Lake on a spacious 500 acre ranch.

NEAREST CITY/TOWN Edmonton
AGE SPREAD 8 to 17 years
CAMPERS PER SESSION 84
STAFF PER SESSION 30
COUNSELLOR:CAMPER RATIO 1 to 7
BOYS OR GIRLS ☐ Boys only ☐ Girls only ☒ Co-ed
NOTES Lodge facilities are wheelchair accessible. Family camping is an option; please enquire.

BRITISH COLUMBIA

ATLIN CENTRE FOR THE ARTS

SUMMER ADDRESS			
	Atlin		BC
	V0W 1A0	**SUMMER PHONE**	604-651-9693
WINTER ADDRESS	19 Elm Grove Avenue		
	Toronto		ONT
	M6K 2H9	**WINTER PHONE**	416-536-7971

CONTACT PERSON Dick Gernot
ACCREDITATION
AFFILIATION None
YEARS IN OPERATION
DATES OPEN Mid-June through August
FEES $550 to $980 per session.
SCHOLARSHIPS Some scholarships may be available.
ACCOMODATION 4-person units with fridge, stove, kitchen & running water.
SPECIALTY Arts
OBJECTIVES To awaken creative potential in practising artists, serious students, & art educators.

ACTIVITIES All areas of visual art, design, & creative writing.

EVALUATIONS No
MEDICAL FACILITIES None nearby
VISITORS Not applicable
SPECIAL NEEDS FACILITIES Unspecified
DESCRIPTION An isolated location in the landscape of forest, mountains, & lakes of northern British Columbia.

NEAREST CITY/TOWN Whitehorse (150 km)
AGE SPREAD Mature students, teachers & artists of all ages.
CAMPERS PER SESSION 20
STAFF PER SESSION 5 (plus one artist in residence)
COUNSELLOR:CAMPER RATIO Not applicable
BOYS OR GIRLS ☐ Boys only ☐ Girls only ☒ Co-ed
NOTES Fees do not include food. Students must buy & prepare their own meals. A minimum food expense of $50 per week is expected. Editor's note: Unsuited for young campers; late teens & older.

BLUE LAKE FORESTRY CENTRE

SUMMER ADDRESS	BC Forestry Association PO Box 845 Cranbrook BC V1C 4J6
SUMMER PHONE	604-489-1113
WINTER ADDRESS	As above
WINTER PHONE	
CONTACT PERSON	Kootenay Region Office
ACCREDITATION	
AFFILIATION	BC Forestry Association
YEARS IN OPERATION	
DATES OPEN	July to mid-August
FEES	$177 per 5-day session.
SCHOLARSHIPS	Please enquire.
ACCOMODATION	Cabins, wash-house with showers, rec & dining halls.
SPECIALTY	Forest Education
OBJECTIVES	To teach respect & understanding of the forest environment & forest management. To develop a well informed public & encourage a "forest ethic" in British Columbia.
ACTIVITIES	Canoeing, hiking, eco fun, swimming, fishing, arts & crafts, games, campfires.
EVALUATIONS	No
MEDICAL FACILITIES	Qualified industrial first aid attendant.
VISITORS	No
SPECIAL NEEDS FACILITIES	Unspecified
DESCRIPTION	Situated on Blue Lake, located deep in the Purcell Mountains, west of Canal Flats.
NEAREST CITY/TOWN	Cranbrook
AGE SPREAD	8 to 14 years
CAMPERS PER SESSION	72
STAFF PER SESSION	One leader per 6 campers
COUNSELLOR:CAMPER RATIO	1 to 6
BOYS OR GIRLS	☐ Boys only ☐ Girls only ☒ Co-ed
NOTES	

CAMP ALEXANDRA

SUMMER ADDRESS 2916 McBride Avenue

Surrey BC
V4A 3G2 **SUMMER PHONE** 604-535-0015

WINTER ADDRESS As above

WINTER PHONE

CONTACT PERSON Joan Lucas
ACCREDITATION BCCA
AFFILIATION Association of Neighbourhood Houses
YEARS IN OPERATION 76
DATES OPEN June through August
FEES $180 per one-week session.
SCHOLARSHIPS Please enquire.
ACCOMODATION Cabins, showers, main dining hall, fireplace.
SPECIALTY Special Needs & Disadvantaged Youth
OBJECTIVES To provide mentally handicapped adults & low income families with a camping experience emphasizing personal care & learning of new leisure skills.
ACTIVITIES Volleyball, shuffleboard, barbecues, swimming, nature walks, crafts, campfires.

EVALUATIONS No
MEDICAL FACILITIES Nurse on site.
VISITORS Allowed
SPECIAL NEEDS FACILITIES Yes
DESCRIPTION Located at Crescent Beach.

NEAREST CITY/TOWN Vancouver
AGE SPREAD All ages
CAMPERS PER SESSION Up to 100
STAFF PER SESSION Unspecified
COUNSELLOR:CAMPER RATIO Unspecified
BOYS OR GIRLS ☐ Boys only ☐ Girls only ☒ Co-ed
NOTES Special needs refers to mentally handicapped adults & low-income families.

CAMP COLUMBIA

SUMMER ADDRESS	North Cove Road
	Thetis Island BC
	V0R 2Y0 **SUMMER PHONE** 604-246-3751
WINTER ADDRESS	As above
	WINTER PHONE
CONTACT PERSON	Gregg Perry
ACCREDITATION	BCCA, CCI
AFFILIATION	Anglican Church
YEARS IN OPERATION	47
DATES OPEN	July through August
FEES	$210 per one-week session.
SCHOLARSHIPS	Bursaries are available.
ACCOMODATION	Cabins, separate washroom facilities, showers, dining hall.
SPECIALTY	Christian Development
OBJECTIVES	To foster the growth of the whole camper, mentally, socially, physically & spiritually.
ACTIVITIES	Quest, crafts, games, archery, canoeing, rowing, swimming, boating, field sports, singing, Christian education, drama, campfires.
EVALUATIONS	No
MEDICAL FACILITIES	Infirmary equipped for emergencies & regular medical care.
VISITORS	Not encouraged
SPECIAL NEEDS FACILITIES	Yes
DESCRIPTION	Located on over 70 acres of oceanfront property.
NEAREST CITY/TOWN	Victoria
AGE SPREAD	8 to 18 years
CAMPERS PER SESSION	75
STAFF PER SESSION	18
COUNSELLOR:CAMPER RATIO	1 to 4
BOYS OR GIRLS	☐ Boys only ☐ Girls only ☒ Co-ed
NOTES	Special needs refers to partial wheelchair accessibility. May also accommodate learning disabilities & blind campers; please enquire.

CAMP DEKA

SUMMER ADDRESS	c/o Hathaway Lake Resort		
	Lone Butte		BC
	V0K 1X0	**SUMMER PHONE**	
WINTER ADDRESS	440 Hendry Avenue		
	North Vancouver		BC
	V7L 4C5	**WINTER PHONE**	604-251-1116

CONTACT PERSON Craig Sheather
ACCREDITATION BCCA
AFFILIATION YM-YWCA
YEARS IN OPERATION 3
DATES OPEN June to Labour Day
FEES $680 per 12-day session.
SCHOLARSHIPS Yes
ACCOMODATION Large platform tents, showers, outhouses, dining hall.
SPECIALTY Wilderness Training
OBJECTIVES To promote individual development of self-esteem & confidence, to teach outdoor skills and an appreciation for outdoor living.
ACTIVITIES Ropes course, first aid instruction, extended camping expeditions, hiking, canoeing, kayaking, rock climbing, mountaineering, white water rafting, ceramics, woodworking, drama.
EVALUATIONS Yes
MEDICAL FACILITIES Health centre
VISITORS Allowed
SPECIAL NEEDS FACILITIES Unspecified
DESCRIPTION Located in the rugged wilderness of the Cariboo.

NEAREST CITY/TOWN 100 Mile House
AGE SPREAD 11 to 16 years
CAMPERS PER SESSION 40
STAFF PER SESSION 18
COUNSELLOR:CAMPER RATIO 1 to 3
BOYS OR GIRLS ☐ Boys only ☐ Girls only ☒ Co-ed
NOTES

CAMP ELPHINSTONE

SUMMER ADDRESS	1760 YMCA Road RR #1, S19, C35 Gibsons V0N 1V0	**SUMMER PHONE**	BC
WINTER ADDRESS	440 Hendry Avenue North Vancouver V7L 4C5	**WINTER PHONE**	BC 604-251-1116

CONTACT PERSON R.L. Bowering
ACCREDITATION BCCA
AFFILIATION YM-YWCA
YEARS IN OPERATION 85
DATES OPEN July through August
FEES $680 per 14-day session.
SCHOLARSHIPS Yes
ACCOMODATION Cabins, main dining hall, recreation hall.
SPECIALTY Traditional
OBJECTIVES To provide a place for living simply & skillfully in the outdoors, and to strengthen spiritual values & heighten the appreciation of the natural world & its beauties.
ACTIVITIES Canoeing, sailing, kayaking, rowing, fishing, swimming, sailboarding, tennis, soccer, volleyball, crafts, music, outdoor education, outtripping, CPR training, campfires.

EVALUATIONS Issued on request.
MEDICAL FACILITIES Health centre on site, clinic nearby.
VISITORS Allowed
SPECIAL NEEDS FACILITIES No
DESCRIPTION Please enquire for details.

NEAREST CITY/TOWN Gibsons
AGE SPREAD 7 to 16 years
CAMPERS PER SESSION 176
STAFF PER SESSION 50
COUNSELLOR:CAMPER RATIO 1 to 8
BOYS OR GIRLS ☒ Boys only ☒ Girls only ☐ Co-ed
NOTES Sessions are 2, 4, 6 or 8 weeks in length. Family camping is an option; please enquire.

CAMP FIRCOM

SUMMER ADDRESS

Gambier Island BC
V0N 1V0 **SUMMER PHONE**

WINTER ADDRESS 320 East Hastings Street

Vancouver BC
V6A 1P4 **WINTER PHONE** 604-662-7756

CONTACT PERSON Diane Ransom
ACCREDITATION BCCA
AFFILIATION United Church
YEARS IN OPERATION 70
DATES OPEN July through August
FEES $240 per one-week session.
SCHOLARSHIPS Camperships are available.
ACCOMODATION Cabins with adjacent wash-houses, dining hall.
SPECIALTY Traditional
OBJECTIVES To provide an opportunity for campers to strengthen personal growth & sense of belonging in a positive & caring community in a natural setting.
ACTIVITIES Swimming, canoeing, outtripping, hiking, rowing, arts & crafts, theatre, sports, archery, group games, music, chapel, campfires.

EVALUATIONS No
MEDICAL FACILITIES Infirmary with nurse on site.
VISITORS Allowed with prior notice.
SPECIAL NEEDS FACILITIES Unspecified
DESCRIPTION Located on one of the well-wooded Gulf Islands bordering the Strait of Georgia.

NEAREST CITY/TOWN Victoria
AGE SPREAD 8 to 18 years
CAMPERS PER SESSION Capacity 140
STAFF PER SESSION 18-22
COUNSELLOR:CAMPER RATIO 1 to 8
BOYS OR GIRLS ☐ Boys only ☐ Girls only ☒ Co-ed
NOTES Family camping is an option; please enquire.

CAMP HATIKVAH

SUMMER ADDRESS	RR #1		
	Oyama		BC
	V0H 1W0	**SUMMER PHONE**	
WINTER ADDRESS	#16 - 5763 Oak Street		
	Vancouver		BC
	V6M 2V7	**WINTER PHONE**	604-263-1200

CONTACT PERSON Beverly Pinsky
ACCREDITATION BCCA
AFFILIATION Jewish
YEARS IN OPERATION 48
DATES OPEN July through August
FEES $1391 for July session; $1044 for 3-week August session.
SCHOLARSHIPS Yes
ACCOMODATION Cabins, showers, dining hall.
SPECIALTY Jewish Development
OBJECTIVES To create a healthy Jewish/Zionistic atmosphere in a camp setting. To provide campers with a rich educational, cultural, & recreational experience focusing on a good sense of self.
ACTIVITIES Swimming, sailing, water skiing, educational sports, arts & crafts, drama, canoeing, & kayaking.

EVALUATIONS No
MEDICAL FACILITIES Infirmary with nurses on staff.
VISITORS Not allowed
SPECIAL NEEDS FACILITIES Unspecified
DESCRIPTION Please enquire for details.

NEAREST CITY/TOWN Kelowna
AGE SPREAD 8 to 15 years
CAMPERS PER SESSION Approximately 200
STAFF PER SESSION Approximately 70
COUNSELLOR:CAMPER RATIO 1 to 5
BOYS OR GIRLS ☐ Boys only ☐ Girls only ☒ Co-ed
NOTES

CAMP IMADENE

SUMMER ADDRESS	9175 South Shore Road
	Mesachie Lake BC
	V0R 2M0 **SUMMER PHONE**
WINTER ADDRESS	PO Box 8
	Duncan BC
	V9L 3X1 **WINTER PHONE** 604-749-6606
CONTACT PERSON	Robert L. Burns
ACCREDITATION	BCCA
AFFILIATION	Christian (nondenominational)
YEARS IN OPERATION	68
DATES OPEN	June through August
FEES	$130 - $150 per 6-day session.
SCHOLARSHIPS	Available for those able to demonstrate need.
ACCOMODATION	Cabins, washrooms with showers, main dining hall.
SPECIALTY	Christian Development
OBJECTIVES	To present the truths of the Bible & Jesus Christ as Lord & Saviour.
ACTIVITIES	Water skiing, boating, canoeing, swimming (instruction), all field games, crafts, kayaking, nature discovery, archery.
EVALUATIONS	No
MEDICAL FACILITIES	Hospital cottage & first aid room with nurse.
VISITORS	Allowed
SPECIAL NEEDS FACILITIES	Yes
DESCRIPTION	Located on Maple Bay on Vancouver Island.
NEAREST CITY/TOWN	Duncan
AGE SPREAD	8 to 19 years
CAMPERS PER SESSION	120
STAFF PER SESSION	55-60
COUNSELLOR:CAMPER RATIO	1 to 6
BOYS OR GIRLS	☐ Boys only ☐ Girls only ☒ Co-ed
NOTES	Special needs refers to full wheelchair accessibility. Family camping is an option; please enquire.

CAMP KOOLAREE

SUMMER ADDRESS			
	Kootenay Lake		BC
		SUMMER PHONE	
WINTER ADDRESS	c/o 2429 10th Avenue		
	Castlegar		BC
	V1N 3A1	**WINTER PHONE**	604-365-3729

CONTACT PERSON Frank Crocket
ACCREDITATION BCCA
AFFILIATION United Church
YEARS IN OPERATION 33
DATES OPEN July through August
FEES $95 per one-week session.
SCHOLARSHIPS Yes
ACCOMODATION Cabins, dining hall, lodge, washrooms with running water.
SPECIALTY Traditional
OBJECTIVES To provide a camp for use by people of all denominations for spiritual, physical, & emotional growth, & to glorify God.

ACTIVITIES Boating, hiking, volleyball, baseball, canoeing, archery, swimming.

EVALUATIONS No
MEDICAL FACILITIES Hospital building on site with nurse or IFA-certified staff.
VISITORS Not encouraged
SPECIAL NEEDS FACILITIES No
DESCRIPTION 137 acres located on the west arm of Kootenay Lake in a true wilderness setting, with no electricity.

NEAREST CITY/TOWN Nelson
AGE SPREAD 9 to 16 years
CAMPERS PER SESSION 60
STAFF PER SESSION Average of 7
COUNSELLOR:CAMPER RATIO Varies
BOYS OR GIRLS ☐ Boys only ☐ Girls only ☒ Co-ed
NOTES

CAMP POTLATCH

SUMMER ADDRESS			
	Potlatch Creek		BC
		SUMMER PHONE	
WINTER ADDRESS	7595 Victoria Drive		
	Vancouver		BC
	V5P 3Z6	**WINTER PHONE**	604-321-5546

CONTACT PERSON Jason Haight
ACCREDITATION BCCA
AFFILIATION Boys' & Girls' Clubs of Greater Vancouver
YEARS IN OPERATION 49
DATES OPEN July through August
FEES The fees are negotiated with each family.
SCHOLARSHIPS
ACCOMODATION Cabins, dining hall.
SPECIALTY Traditional
OBJECTIVES To instill campers with an enthusiasm for living & a responsible attitude towards themselves & others.

ACTIVITIES Swimming, canoeing, kayaking, rowing, hiking, overnights, camping skills, outtrips, rock climbing, orienteering, nature lore, archery, fishing, arts & crafts, Indian lore, games, campfires, sing-songs.
EVALUATIONS No, but awards are given for attaining set skill levels.
MEDICAL FACILITIES Infirmary with nurse on site.
VISITORS Not encouraged
SPECIAL NEEDS FACILITIES Unspecified
DESCRIPTION Located on the northern shores of Howe Sound, with sandy beaches & unspoiled hiking and camping territory.

NEAREST CITY/TOWN Vancouver
AGE SPREAD 7 to 17 years
CAMPERS PER SESSION 80
STAFF PER SESSION 35
COUNSELLOR:CAMPER RATIO 1 to 6
BOYS OR GIRLS ☐ Boys only ☐ Girls only ☒ Co-ed
NOTES Leadership training & teen adventures are also offered; please enquire.

CAMP PUNTCHESAKUT

SUMMER ADDRESS	465 Kinchant Street
	Quesnel BC
	V2J 2R7 **SUMMER PHONE** 604-249-5423
WINTER ADDRESS	As above
	WINTER PHONE
CONTACT PERSON	Heather Sapergia
ACCREDITATION	BCCA
AFFILIATION	Anglican Church
YEARS IN OPERATION	36
DATES OPEN	July through August
FEES	$90 - $155 per 5-10 day session.
SCHOLARSHIPS	Yes
ACCOMODATION	Cabins, showers, dining hall.
SPECIALTY	Christian Development
OBJECTIVES	To create, in an outdoor setting, a lively Christian community.
ACTIVITIES	Swimming, crafts, sports, canoeing, campfires, sing-songs, chapel service, handicrafts, Quest, campfires.
EVALUATIONS	No
MEDICAL FACILITIES	Sick bay with nurse, doctor, &/or IFA-certified staff.
VISITORS	Allowed on first day.
SPECIAL NEEDS FACILITIES	Yes
DESCRIPTION	Located on beautiful Puntchesakut Lake.
NEAREST CITY/TOWN	Quesnel
AGE SPREAD	8 to 17 years
CAMPERS PER SESSION	33
STAFF PER SESSION	12
COUNSELLOR:CAMPER RATIO	1 to 10
BOYS OR GIRLS	☐ Boys only ☐ Girls only ☒ Co-ed
NOTES	Special needs refers to wheelchair accessibility. Will also provide a one-on-one companion for campers with special needs; please enquire.

CAMP SAGITAWA

SUMMER ADDRESS PO Box 61

Moberly Lake BC
V0C 1X0 **SUMMER PHONE** 604-788-2361

WINTER ADDRESS As above

WINTER PHONE

CONTACT PERSON Ed Thomas
ACCREDITATION BCCA, CCI
AFFILIATION Christian (nondenominational)
YEARS IN OPERATION 25
DATES OPEN July through August
FEES $134 - $193 per 7-10 day session.
SCHOLARSHIPS Yes
ACCOMODATION Cabins, showers, main dining hall.
SPECIALTY Christian Development
OBJECTIVES To teach the application of Biblical Christianity for a complete life.

ACTIVITIES Sailing, riflery, archery, drama, puppetry, canoeing, Bible study, chapel, fishing, camp-wide games, hiking, trail rides, backpacking, campfires, crafts, outdoor living.

EVALUATIONS No
MEDICAL FACILITIES First aid room with attendant.
VISITORS Allowed by appointment.
SPECIAL NEEDS FACILITIES Unspecified
DESCRIPTION Located on Moberly Lake, 24 km north of Chetwynd.

NEAREST CITY/TOWN Dawson Creek
AGE SPREAD 8 to 18 years
CAMPERS PER SESSION 63
STAFF PER SESSION 22
COUNSELLOR:CAMPER RATIO 1 to 5
BOYS OR GIRLS ☒ Boys only ☐ Girls only ☐ Co-ed
NOTES Camp is operated by Sagitawa Christian Camping Society. Family camping is an option; please enquire.

CAMP SQUEAH

SUMMER ADDRESS 27915 Trans Canada Highway
C-1, RR #3
Hope BC
V0X 1L0 **SUMMER PHONE** 604-863-2266

WINTER ADDRESS As above

WINTER PHONE

CONTACT PERSON Rudy Kehler
ACCREDITATION BCCA
AFFILIATION Mennonite Brethren
YEARS IN OPERATION 33
DATES OPEN July through August
FEES $150 per 7-day session.
SCHOLARSHIPS Yes
ACCOMODATION Cabins, main dining lodge.
SPECIALTY Christian Development
OBJECTIVES To provide campers with new friends, new experiences & a new understanding of God's love, His creations, & the way He wants us to live.
ACTIVITIES Bible discovery, challenge course, nature lore, field sports, trampoline, camp-wide games, bush craft, rapelling, swimming, canoeing, archery, chapel, drama, hiking, music.

EVALUATIONS No
MEDICAL FACILITIES Nurse on staff; 15 minutes to hospital.
VISITORS Allowed
SPECIAL NEEDS FACILITIES Unspecified
DESCRIPTION Located at the base of Squeah Mountain, along the rim of the Fraser Canyon.

NEAREST CITY/TOWN Hope
AGE SPREAD 7 to 16 years
CAMPERS PER SESSION 140
STAFF PER SESSION 45
COUNSELLOR:CAMPER RATIO 1 to 9
BOYS OR GIRLS ☐ Boys only ☐ Girls only ☒ Co-ed
NOTES Financial assistance will be given to any camper requiring it. Need should be indicated on registration form.

CAMP SUNRISE

SUMMER ADDRESS	RR #1, Site 21, C-30
	Gibsons BC
	V0N 1V0 **SUMMER PHONE**
WINTER ADDRESS	4727 East Hastings Street
	Burnaby BC
	V5C 2K8 **WINTER PHONE** 604-299-3908
CONTACT PERSON	Captain A. Brad Bent
ACCREDITATION	BCCA
AFFILIATION	Salvation Army
YEARS IN OPERATION	69
DATES OPEN	May to September
FEES	$120 - $170 per 7-day session.
SCHOLARSHIPS	Please enquire
ACCOMODATION	Cabins, showers, dining hall.
SPECIALTY	Christian Development
OBJECTIVES	To extend the kingdom of God.
ACTIVITIES	Sports, music, hiking, games, Bible times, canoeing, fishing, swimming, nature study, campfires.
EVALUATIONS	No
MEDICAL FACILITIES	Unspecified; please enquire.
VISITORS	Not allowed
SPECIAL NEEDS FACILITIES	Yes
DESCRIPTION	Located in Langdale on ocean frontage property.
NEAREST CITY/TOWN	West Vancouver
AGE SPREAD	7 years & up.
CAMPERS PER SESSION	Up to 180
STAFF PER SESSION	25
COUNSELLOR:CAMPER RATIO	Varies
BOYS OR GIRLS	☐ Boys only ☐ Girls only ☒ Co-ed
NOTES	Special needs refers to full wheelchair accessibility. Family camping is an option; please enquire.

CAMP TULAHEAD

SUMMER ADDRESS	PO Box 1272		
	Princeton		BC
	V0X 1W0	**SUMMER PHONE**	604-295-6233
WINTER ADDRESS	10642 100 Avenue		
	Surrey		BC
	V3V 2X7	**WINTER PHONE**	604-581-5488

CONTACT PERSON Carol Skinner
ACCREDITATION BCCA, CCI
AFFILIATION Christian (nondenominational)
YEARS IN OPERATION 16
DATES OPEN July through August
FEES Range from $125 - $130 per one-week session.
SCHOLARSHIPS Yes
ACCOMODATION Cabins, central washrooms, dining hall.
SPECIALTY Traditional
OBJECTIVES To provide an experience that will be fun, friendly, safe & exciting. Also to develop self-confidence, social skills, & moral character in each camper.
ACTIVITIES Sailing, canoeing, archery, crafts, games, swimming, hiking, fishing, campfires, skits, theme nights, chapel, mini golf, team sports, moon ball.

EVALUATIONS No
MEDICAL FACILITIES Unspecified.
VISITORS Not allowed
SPECIAL NEEDS FACILITIES Unspecified
DESCRIPTION Located on the south end of Laird Lake, rangeland, mountains & over 600 feet of lakeshore comprise the property.

NEAREST CITY/TOWN Princeton
AGE SPREAD 7 to 18 years
CAMPERS PER SESSION 70
STAFF PER SESSION 27
COUNSELLOR:CAMPER RATIO 1 to 7
BOYS OR GIRLS ☐ Boys only ☐ Girls only ☒ Co-ed
NOTES

CHAWUTHEN

SUMMER ADDRESS	National Camps for the Blind PO Box 369 Hope BC V0X 1L0
SUMMER PHONE	604-869-2615
WINTER ADDRESS	As above
WINTER PHONE	604-860-6319
CONTACT PERSON	John Reitor
ACCREDITATION	CCA, CCI
AFFILIATION	Christian (nondenominational)
YEARS IN OPERATION	20
DATES OPEN	One week in late June or early July.
FEES	Free to all legally blind persons aged 9 & up.
SCHOLARSHIPS	
ACCOMODATION	Cabins, showers, dining hall.
SPECIALTY	Special Needs: Blind / Visually Impaired
OBJECTIVES	To allow the blind participant to discover undeveloped potential, increase self-confidence, improve physical vigour, & develop an appreciation for God's love & care.
ACTIVITIES	Archery, boating, camp council, canoeing, crafts, hiking, horseback riding, rock climbing, sailing, swimming, rappelling, water skiing, campfires.
EVALUATIONS	No
MEDICAL FACILITIES	Infirmary with medical staff on duty 24 hours.
VISITORS	Allowed on Talent Night.
SPECIAL NEEDS FACILITIES	Yes
DESCRIPTION	Please enquire for details.
NEAREST CITY/TOWN	Chilliwack
AGE SPREAD	9 years & up
CAMPERS PER SESSION	40
STAFF PER SESSION	Varies
COUNSELLOR:CAMPER RATIO	1 to 2
BOYS OR GIRLS	☐ Boys only ☐ Girls only ☒ Co-ed
NOTES	Special needs refers to blind or visually impaired campers. This program is designed to place emphasis on ability rather than the disability of the visually impaired individual.

CIRCLE SQUARE RANCH

SUMMER ADDRESS	Box 99		
	Armstrong		BC
	V0E 1B0	**SUMMER PHONE**	604-546-8877
WINTER ADDRESS	As above		
		WINTER PHONE	

CONTACT PERSON Don Bayne
ACCREDITATION BCCA
AFFILIATION Christian (nondenominational)
YEARS IN OPERATION 9
DATES OPEN July through August
FEES $215 per 6-day session.
SCHOLARSHIPS May be available with proof of need.
ACCOMODATION Bunkhouses with showers, main dining hall, lodge.
SPECIALTY Christian Development
OBJECTIVES To teach solid moral values & a healthy, balanced lifestyle; mentally, spiritually, physically & socially.

ACTIVITIES Horsemanship, archery, riflery, BMX biking, swimming, team sports, crafts, drama, mini golf, cookouts, campfires.

EVALUATIONS Crests and ribbons are awarded.
MEDICAL FACILITIES Industrial first aid person on staff; hospital 6 km away.
VISITORS Allowed
SPECIAL NEEDS FACILITIES Yes
DESCRIPTION Please enquire for details.

NEAREST CITY/TOWN Armstrong
AGE SPREAD 8 to 16 years
CAMPERS PER SESSION 70-85
STAFF PER SESSION 35-40
COUNSELLOR:CAMPER RATIO 1 to 7
BOYS OR GIRLS ☐ Boys only ☐ Girls only ☒ Co-ed
NOTES Special needs refers to limited wheelchair accessibility; please enquire. Operated by Crossroads Christian Communications Inc.

COLUMBIA BIBLE CAMP

SUMMER ADDRESS 44005 Watt Road

Lindell Beach BC
V0X 1P0 **SUMMER PHONE** 604-858-6845

WINTER ADDRESS As above

WINTER PHONE

CONTACT PERSON Henry Esau
ACCREDITATION BCCA, CCI
AFFILIATION Mennonite Brethren
YEARS IN OPERATION 35
DATES OPEN July through August
FEES $172 per one-week session.
SCHOLARSHIPS Some camperships are available.
ACCOMODATION Cabins, washrooms with showers, main dining hall.
SPECIALTY Christian Development
OBJECTIVES To present the gospel of Jesus Christ to campers & to develop their faith.

ACTIVITIES Chapel, water skiing, climbing, crafts, archery, sailing, canoeing, swimming, mountain biking, orienteering, Bible studies, camp-wide game, campfires.

EVALUATIONS No
MEDICAL FACILITIES Infirmary with nurse on staff.
VISITORS Not encouraged
SPECIAL NEEDS FACILITIES Unspecified
DESCRIPTION Located in the Columbia Valley, above Cultus Lake.

NEAREST CITY/TOWN Chilliwack
AGE SPREAD 9 to 18 years
CAMPERS PER SESSION 120
STAFF PER SESSION Approximately 30
COUNSELLOR:CAMPER RATIO 1 to 6
BOYS OR GIRLS ☐ Boys only ☐ Girls only ☒ Co-ed
NOTES Camp is owned & operated by the BC Conference of Mennonite Brethren Churches.

COURTENAY YOUTH MUSIC CENTRE

SUMMER ADDRESS PO Box 3056

Courtenay BC
V9N 5N3

SUMMER PHONE 604-338-7463

WINTER ADDRESS As above

WINTER PHONE

CONTACT PERSON Lucille Parsons
ACCREDITATION
AFFILIATION None
YEARS IN OPERATION 28
DATES OPEN July to August
FEES Please enquire.
SCHOLARSHIPS
ACCOMODATION Dormitory-style, cafeteria.
SPECIALTY Arts: Music
OBJECTIVES To provide intensive, personal study of music in a camp setting.

ACTIVITIES Individual & group lessons, performing opportunities & various recreational activities.

EVALUATIONS No
MEDICAL FACILITIES 10 minutes to hospital.
VISITORS Allowed
SPECIAL NEEDS FACILITIES Unspecified
DESCRIPTION Please enquire for details.

NEAREST CITY/TOWN Comox
AGE SPREAD 8 years to adult
CAMPERS PER SESSION Average 100
STAFF PER SESSION 50
COUNSELLOR:CAMPER RATIO 1 to 10
BOYS OR GIRLS ☐ Boys only ☐ Girls only ☒ Co-ed
NOTES

EASTER SEALS CAMP SHAWNIGAN

SUMMER ADDRESS RR #1
2180 East Shawnigan Lake Road
Shawnigan Lake BC
V0R 2W0 **SUMMER PHONE** 604-382-3171

WINTER ADDRESS #300 - 177 West 7th Avenue

Vancouver BC
V5Y 1K5 **WINTER PHONE** 604-873-1865

CONTACT PERSON Ray St. Dennis
ACCREDITATION BCCA
AFFILIATION BC Lions Society
YEARS IN OPERATION 15
DATES OPEN May through August
FEES Free to disabled children 18 & under/$335 disabled adults.
SCHOLARSHIPS Please enquire.
ACCOMODATION Dormitory, dining hall, showers, heated outdoor pool.
SPECIALTY Special Needs: Physical Disabilities
OBJECTIVES To boost disabled children's self-esteem through learning new skills & making new friends. Also to enable the experience of independence in a secure environment.
ACTIVITIES Nature lore, canoeing, arts & crafts, outtripping, dancing, aquatics, mini golf, campfires.

EVALUATIONS Yes
MEDICAL FACILITIES Infirmary supervised by nurse, doctor on call.
VISITORS Allowed
SPECIAL NEEDS FACILITIES Yes
DESCRIPTION Located on 20 acres of land, including some waterfront.

NEAREST CITY/TOWN Duncan
AGE SPREAD 6 years & up
CAMPERS PER SESSION 30-70
STAFF PER SESSION 7
COUNSELLOR:CAMPER RATIO 1 to 2
BOYS OR GIRLS ☐ Boys only ☐ Girls only ☒ Co-ed
NOTES

EASTER SEALS CAMP SQUAMISH

SUMMER ADDRESS	PO Box 730		
	Garibaldi Highlands		BC
	V0N 1T0	**SUMMER PHONE**	
WINTER ADDRESS	#300 - 177 West 7th Avenue		
	Vancouver		BC
	V5Y 1K5	**WINTER PHONE**	604-873-1865

CONTACT PERSON A.W. Connell
ACCREDITATION BCCA
AFFILIATION BC Lions Society
YEARS IN OPERATION 18
DATES OPEN June through August
FEES Free to campers up to 18 yrs; campers 19+ $335 for 6 days.
SCHOLARSHIPS
ACCOMODATION Dormitories, main dining hall.
SPECIALTY Special Needs: Mental & Physical Disabilities
OBJECTIVES To provide people with physical &/or mental disabilities with a positive, fun summer camp experience.

ACTIVITIES Swimming, arts & crafts, canoeing, horseback riding, fishing, camping, sports, games, dancing.

EVALUATIONS No
MEDICAL FACILITIES Nursing station with at least one nurse & assistant.
VISITORS Allowed during open house.
SPECIAL NEEDS FACILITIES Yes
DESCRIPTION Please enquire for details.

NEAREST CITY/TOWN Squamish
AGE SPREAD 5 years & up
CAMPERS PER SESSION Maximum 60
STAFF PER SESSION 30
COUNSELLOR:CAMPER RATIO 1 to 3
BOYS OR GIRLS ☐ Boys only ☐ Girls only ☒ Co-ed
NOTES Camp operated by The BC Lions Society for Children with Disabilities. Special needs refers to campers with mental &/or physical disabilities. Complete wheelchair accessibility.

EDUCO ADVENTURE SCHOOL

SUMMER ADDRESS PO Box 1978

100 Mile House BC
V0K 2E0 **SUMMER PHONE** 604-395-3388

WINTER ADDRESS As above

WINTER PHONE

CONTACT PERSON Ron Skene
ACCREDITATION BCCA
AFFILIATION None
YEARS IN OPERATION 25
DATES OPEN Unspecified; please enquire.
FEES $595 per 10-day session.
SCHOLARSHIPS Yes
ACCOMODATION Cabins, tents for outtrips, sauna.
SPECIALTY Wilderness Training
OBJECTIVES To lay a foundation of character that will allow campers to move into the future with assurance & stability. Emphasis is on discovery through challenging & exciting outdoor activity.
ACTIVITIES Canoeing, swimming, team games, saunas, campfires, kayaking, mountaineering, backpacking, rock climbing, rappelling, spelunking, cliff diving, ropes courses, life skills, journals.

EVALUATIONS A graduation certificate is issued upon completion.
MEDICAL FACILITIES First aid room.
VISITORS Allowed on the last day, parent participation day.
SPECIAL NEEDS FACILITIES Unspecified
DESCRIPTION The base camp is very remote, nestled between two Cariboo lakes. There is no electricity or running water.

NEAREST CITY/TOWN 100 Mile House
AGE SPREAD 9 years & up
CAMPERS PER SESSION 40
STAFF PER SESSION 12
COUNSELLOR:CAMPER RATIO 1 to 5
BOYS OR GIRLS ☐ Boys only ☐ Girls only ☒ Co-ed
NOTES Camp is operated by a non-profit society, Educo, & is affiliated with Renaissance Educational Associates (REA), an international network of educators and parents concerned with quality of character in education.

EVANS LAKE SUMMER CAMP

SUMMER ADDRESS BC Forestry Association, Coast Region
9800 A 140th Street
Surrey BC
V3T 4M5 **SUMMER PHONE** 604-582-0040

WINTER ADDRESS As above

WINTER PHONE

CONTACT PERSON Dave Campbell
ACCREDITATION BCCA
AFFILIATION BC Forestry Association
YEARS IN OPERATION 34
DATES OPEN July through August
FEES $185 per 6-day session; $235 per 8-day session.
SCHOLARSHIPS Yes
ACCOMODATION Cabins, hot showers, rec hall with fireplace, dining hall.
SPECIALTY Forest Education
OBJECTIVES To teach respect for & understanding of the forest environment & forest management. To develop a well informed public & encourage a "forest ethic" in BC.
ACTIVITIES Swimming, canoeing, archery, campfires, singing, hiking, group games, wildlife studies, paper-making, survival skills.

EVALUATIONS No
MEDICAL FACILITIES First aid attendant & first aid room; hospital 20 mins away.
VISITORS Allowed
SPECIAL NEEDS FACILITIES Unspecified
DESCRIPTION Located 14 km north of Squamish.

NEAREST CITY/TOWN Squamish
AGE SPREAD 8 to 15 years
CAMPERS PER SESSION 80
STAFF PER SESSION 13
COUNSELLOR:CAMPER RATIO 1 to 10
BOYS OR GIRLS ☐ Boys only ☐ Girls only ☒ Co-ed
NOTES

GAVIN LAKE

SUMMER ADDRESS BC Forestry Association
72 Seventh Avenue South
Williams Lake BC
V2G 4N5 **SUMMER PHONE** 604-392-2544

WINTER ADDRESS As above

WINTER PHONE

CONTACT PERSON Cariboo Region Office
ACCREDITATION
AFFILIATION BC Forestry Association
YEARS IN OPERATION 12
DATES OPEN July through August
FEES $95 per 3-day session; $175 per 5-day session.
SCHOLARSHIPS Yes
ACCOMODATION Cabins, main dining & recreation hall, hot showers.
SPECIALTY Forest Education
OBJECTIVES To teach respect for & understanding of the forest environment & forest management. To develop a well-informed public & encourage a "forest ethic" in BC.
ACTIVITIES Forestry studies & games, swimming, outtrips, wildlife studies, orienteering, campfires, canoeing, wilderness survival, field tours, fishing, soil studies.

EVALUATIONS No
MEDICAL FACILITIES Qualified first aid attendant
VISITORS Allowed during final day.
SPECIAL NEEDS FACILITIES Yes, the camp is wheelchair accessible.
DESCRIPTION Located 64 km northeast of Williams Lake.

NEAREST CITY/TOWN Williams Lake
AGE SPREAD 8 to 14 years
CAMPERS PER SESSION 50
STAFF PER SESSION 8
COUNSELLOR:CAMPER RATIO 1 to 6
BOYS OR GIRLS ☐ Boys only ☐ Girls only ☒ Co-ed
NOTES

GEORGE PRINGLE MEMORIAL CAMP

SUMMER ADDRESS	2520 West Shawnigan Lake Road RR #1 Shawnigan Lake V0R 2W0	**SUMMER PHONE**	BC
WINTER ADDRESS	619 David Street Victoria V8T 2E1	**WINTER PHONE**	BC 604-743-2189

CONTACT PERSON Edie Dibley
ACCREDITATION BCCA
AFFILIATION United Church
YEARS IN OPERATION 44
DATES OPEN July through August
FEES $139 per 5-day session.
SCHOLARSHIPS Bursaries are available.
ACCOMODATION Cabins, dining hall, washrooms with showers, lodge.
SPECIALTY Christian Development
OBJECTIVES To help campers develop mentally, socially, physically & spiritually. To provide the opportunity for extended periods of Christian experience, reflection, practice & enjoyment.
ACTIVITIES Crafts, archery, trampoline, hiking, swimming, canoeing, sailing, sailboarding, team sports, Bible study, windsurfing, singing, campfires.

EVALUATIONS No
MEDICAL FACILITIES Infirmary & nurse on site.
VISITORS Not encouraged
SPECIAL NEEDS FACILITIES Yes
DESCRIPTION Please enquire for details.

NEAREST CITY/TOWN Duncan
AGE SPREAD 7 to 18 years
CAMPERS PER SESSION 70
STAFF PER SESSION 10
COUNSELLOR:CAMPER RATIO 1 to 5
BOYS OR GIRLS ☐ Boys only ☐ Girls only ☒ Co-ed
NOTES Special needs refers to ability to accommodate campers with learning disabilities.

HABONIM DROR CAMP MIRIAM

SUMMER ADDRESS 835 Berry Point Road

Gabriola Island BC
V0R 1X0 **SUMMER PHONE**

WINTER ADDRESS 950 West 41st Avenue

Vancouver BC
V5Z 2N7 **WINTER PHONE** 604-263-6315

CONTACT PERSON Howard Robens
ACCREDITATION BCCA
AFFILIATION Jewish
YEARS IN OPERATION 46
DATES OPEN July through August
FEES $900 - $1150 per 2-3 week sessions.
SCHOLARSHIPS Available; please enquire.
ACCOMODATION Cabins, central dining hall, lodge.
SPECIALTY Jewish Development
OBJECTIVES To give campers a positive attitude about the Jewish people & the state of Israel. To create a kibbutz atmosphere emphasizing Jewish identity.
ACTIVITIES Hebrew, swimming, hiking, scouting, team sports, dancing, photography, crafts, Jewish values.

EVALUATIONS No
MEDICAL FACILITIES Infirmary with nurse on staff.
VISITORS Not allowed
SPECIAL NEEDS FACILITIES Unspecified
DESCRIPTION Please enquire for details.

NEAREST CITY/TOWN Nanaimo
AGE SPREAD 9 to 17 years
CAMPERS PER SESSION Approximately 120
STAFF PER SESSION 40
COUNSELLOR:CAMPER RATIO 1 to 6
BOYS OR GIRLS ☐ Boys only ☐ Girls only ☒ Co-ed
NOTES

JOHANNESEN INT'L SCHOOL OF THE ARTS

SUMMER ADDRESS c/o St. Michaels University School
3400 Richmond Road
Victoria BC
V8P 4P5 **SUMMER PHONE** 604-595-2626

WINTER ADDRESS #103 - 3737 Oak Street

Vancouver BC
V6H 2M4 **WINTER PHONE** 604-736-1611

CONTACT PERSON J.J. Johannesen

ACCREDITATION

AFFILIATION St. Michaels University School/University of Victoria

YEARS IN OPERATION 23

DATES OPEN July through August

FEES $1425 per 3-week program; $2020 per 6-week program.

SCHOLARSHIPS Limited scholarships based on merit & financial need.

ACCOMODATION Shared; each room has washroom with shower, sink & toilet.

SPECIALTY Arts: Music

OBJECTIVES The development of artistic expertise in gifted students; professional music development (strings, winds, keyboard, voice, chamber music).

ACTIVITIES Private lessons with master teachers, chamber & contemporary music, professional development seminars & some recreational facilities, weekly excursions on Vancouver Island.

EVALUATIONS No

MEDICAL FACILITIES Doctor on 24-hour call, hospital nearby.

VISITORS Allowed

SPECIAL NEEDS FACILITIES Unspecified

DESCRIPTION On the property of a world-renowned private boarding school which offers a large playing field, indoor swimming pool & tennis courts; close to beaches, Victoria & U of Victoria.

NEAREST CITY/TOWN Victoria

AGE SPREAD 16 years & up

CAMPERS PER SESSION

STAFF PER SESSION 30

COUNSELLOR:CAMPER RATIO Not applicable

BOYS OR GIRLS ☐ Boys only ☐ Girls only ☒ Co-ed

NOTES Non-boarding fees: $980/3-week session; $1425/6-week session. Exceptions to the age criteria are made for particularly gifted children. Access to many concerts. Most appropriate for mature young people.

JOHN MCINNIS FORESTRY CENTRE

SUMMER ADDRESS BC Forestry Association
#4 - 556 North Nechako Road
Prince George BC
V2K 1A1 **SUMMER PHONE** 604-563-0427

WINTER ADDRESS
BC
WINTER PHONE

CONTACT PERSON Michael Sanderson
ACCREDITATION BCCA, CCA
AFFILIATION BC Forestry Association
YEARS IN OPERATION 25
DATES OPEN July through August
FEES $160 per 6-day session.
SCHOLARSHIPS Yes
ACCOMODATION Cabins, washrooms with hot showers.
SPECIALTY Forest Education
OBJECTIVES To promote & develop a greater awareness & appreciation of our forest lands through the teaching of its use, value, management, tree identification, etc.
ACTIVITIES Forestry management, ecology / pond study, wildlife management, day hikes, canoeing, arts & crafts, water studies, campfires, drama, sports day.

EVALUATIONS No
MEDICAL FACILITIES First aid attendent.
VISITORS Allowed
SPECIAL NEEDS FACILITIES Yes
DESCRIPTION Located 57 km from Prince George on Tsitniz Lake.

NEAREST CITY/TOWN Prince George
AGE SPREAD 6 to 16 years
CAMPERS PER SESSION 40
STAFF PER SESSION 8-10
COUNSELLOR:CAMPER RATIO 1 to 10
BOYS OR GIRLS ☐ Boys only ☐ Girls only ☒ Co-ed
NOTES Special needs refers to wheelchair accessibility. Have offered 3-day camps for young children; please enquire.

KAWKAWA CAMP & CONFERENCE CENTRE

SUMMER ADDRESS	PO Box 1840		
	Hope		BC
	V0X 1L0	**SUMMER PHONE**	
WINTER ADDRESS	36074 Southridge Place		
	Abbotsford		BC
	V3G 1E2	**WINTER PHONE**	604-852-1111

CONTACT PERSON Ron Carter
ACCREDITATION BCCA, CCI
AFFILIATION Christian & Missionary Alliance
YEARS IN OPERATION 20
DATES OPEN July through August
FEES $198 per 6-day session.
SCHOLARSHIPS Please enquire.
ACCOMODATION Cottages & chalets, main dining hall.
SPECIALTY Christian Development
OBJECTIVES To encourage spiritual, social, mental, physical, & emotional growth based on the outdoors & the environment, with a Biblical emphasis.
ACTIVITIES Swimming, canoeing, hiking, games, hot tubbing, saunas, campfires, crafts, archery, riflery, Bible study, photography, ropes course, drama, campfires.

EVALUATIONS No
MEDICAL FACILITIES Nurse on site; hospital 3 km away.
VISITORS Allowed at beginning or end of sessions only.
SPECIAL NEEDS FACILITIES Unspecified
DESCRIPTION Located on Kawkawa Lake in the Coquihalla Valley between Mt. Ogilvie & Mt. Hope.

NEAREST CITY/TOWN Hope
AGE SPREAD 8 to 17 years
CAMPERS PER SESSION 80
STAFF PER SESSION 30
COUNSELLOR:CAMPER RATIO 1 to 8
BOYS OR GIRLS ☐ Boys only ☐ Girls only ☒ Co-ed
NOTES Family camping is an option; please enquire.

KEATS CAMP

SUMMER ADDRESS

Keats Island BC
SUMMER PHONE 604-886-7612

WINTER ADDRESS 234 Brooksbank Avenue

North Vancouver BC
V7J 2C1 **WINTER PHONE** 604-980-6799

CONTACT PERSON Kirk Potter
ACCREDITATION BCCA, CCI
AFFILIATION Baptist
YEARS IN OPERATION 68
DATES OPEN July through August
FEES $270 - $310 per one-week session.
SCHOLARSHIPS No
ACCOMODATION Cabins, washrooms with attached showers.
SPECIALTY Christian Development
OBJECTIVES To encourage new friendships, and the enjoyment of new experiences through Bible study & a relationship with Jesus Christ.
ACTIVITIES Windsurfing, sailing, canoeing, snorkeling, hiking, ropes course, field sports, drama, crafts, music, archery, Bible study, indoor games.

EVALUATIONS No
MEDICAL FACILITIES Nurse on site; hospital 20 minutes away.
VISITORS Allowed on Visitors Day, each Sunday.
SPECIAL NEEDS FACILITIES Unspecified
DESCRIPTION Situated on 400 acres of Keats Island, on the Sunshine Coast, with miles of waterfront.

NEAREST CITY/TOWN Sechelt
AGE SPREAD 8 to 18 years
CAMPERS PER SESSION 150
STAFF PER SESSION 80
COUNSELLOR:CAMPER RATIO 1 to 5
BOYS OR GIRLS ☐ Boys only ☐ Girls only ☒ Co-ed
NOTES

LATONA CATHOLIC CAMP

SUMMER ADDRESS	PO Box 98		
	Port Mellon		BC
	V0N 2S0	**SUMMER PHONE**	
WINTER ADDRESS	150 Robson Street		
	Vancouver		BC
	V6B 2A7	**WINTER PHONE**	604-683-0281

CONTACT PERSON Susan Stuart
ACCREDITATION BCCA
AFFILIATION Catholic Church
YEARS IN OPERATION 36
DATES OPEN Late June through August
FEES $225 - $275 per 5-7 day session.
SCHOLARSHIPS Please enquire
ACCOMODATION Cabins
SPECIALTY Christian Development
OBJECTIVES To encourage the physical, social, intellectual & spiritual growth which promotes strong Christian character, in an environment of community living.
ACTIVITIES Swimming, boating, canoeing, archery, arts & crafts, games & sports, campfires, outtrips, Mass, chaplain time.

EVALUATIONS No
MEDICAL FACILITIES First aid room with nurse on duty.
VISITORS Not allowed
SPECIAL NEEDS FACILITIES Unspecified
DESCRIPTION Located at the north end of Gambier Island in Howe Sound on 47 hectares of waterfront, accessible only by boat. An extraordinary wilderness site.
NEAREST CITY/TOWN Gibsons
AGE SPREAD 7 to 15 years
CAMPERS PER SESSION Maximum 112
STAFF PER SESSION 30-40
COUNSELLOR:CAMPER RATIO 1 to 8
BOYS OR GIRLS ☐ Boys only ☐ Girls only ☒ Co-ed
NOTES Family camping is an option; please enquire.

MOORECROFT CAMP

SUMMER ADDRESS	PO Box 4, RR #2, Stewart Road Nanoose Bay BC V0R 2R0
SUMMER PHONE	604-468-7511
WINTER ADDRESS	As above
WINTER PHONE	
CONTACT PERSON	Glen Kawahara
ACCREDITATION	BCCA
AFFILIATION	United Church
YEARS IN OPERATION	40
DATES OPEN	Mid-July through Labour Day
FEES	$60 - $175 per 3-7 day sessions.
SCHOLARSHIPS	Please enquire.
ACCOMODATION	Cabins, dining hall, lodge with fireplace, washrooms, showers.
SPECIALTY	Christian Development
OBJECTIVES	To give campers a chance to find new friends in a Christian atmosphere, and to develop & grow in tolerance & understanding through group living & Christian guidance.
ACTIVITIES	Nature study, field sports, treasure hunts, archery, riflery, crafts, rowboats & paddle boards, raft building, swimming, beachcombing, campfires, vespers.
EVALUATIONS	No
MEDICAL FACILITIES	Equipped first aid building with nurse or IFA.
VISITORS	Not encouraged
SPECIAL NEEDS FACILITIES	Unspecified
DESCRIPTION	Located on 90 acres, including tidal waterfront on Georgia Strait, forest, open field, & nature trails on Vancouver Island, 32 km north of Nanaimo.
NEAREST CITY/TOWN	Nanaimo
AGE SPREAD	9 to 18 years
CAMPERS PER SESSION	72 maximum
STAFF PER SESSION	Varies
COUNSELLOR:CAMPER RATIO	1 to 7
BOYS OR GIRLS	☐ Boys only ☐ Girls only ☒ Co-ed
NOTES	Family camping is an option; please enquire. A co-ed pack camp is offered for 15-18 year-olds.

NORTH VANCOUVER OUTDOOR SCHOOL

SUMMER ADDRESS PO Box 250

Brackendale BC
V0N 1H0 **SUMMER PHONE** 604-898-5422

WINTER ADDRESS As above

WINTER PHONE

CONTACT PERSON Victor Elderton
ACCREDITATION
AFFILIATION North Vancouver School District
YEARS IN OPERATION 24
DATES OPEN Year round
FEES $225 per 5-day session (based on 80 campers).
SCHOLARSHIPS Yes
ACCOMODATION Cabins, showers, dining hall.
SPECIALTY Science: Environmental Studies
OBJECTIVES The centre is a participatory one, offering a complex study approach based upon interactive experiences between people & a fish hatchery, coastal forest, & animal farm.
ACTIVITIES Each student spends 6 hours in field studies & 6 hours in integrated recreation.

EVALUATIONS No
MEDICAL FACILITIES Complete clinic on site with 24-hour first aid.
VISITORS Allowed
SPECIAL NEEDS FACILITIES Yes
DESCRIPTION In Paradise Valley, an environmental preserve, encompasses 165 hectares of the Cheakamus River watershed, 6 km from Alice Lake.
NEAREST CITY/TOWN Squamish
AGE SPREAD 7 years to adult
CAMPERS PER SESSION 80-90
STAFF PER SESSION 8
COUNSELLOR:CAMPER RATIO 1 to 9
BOYS OR GIRLS ☐ Boys only ☐ Girls only ☒ Co-ed
NOTES This is not a regular summer camp. A group of parents may get together & hire the school to design a program for their children. Call for further details.
Special needs refers to complete wheelchair accessibility.

OKANAGAN SUMMER SCHOOL OF THE ARTS

SUMMER ADDRESS	PO Box 22037 Penticton BC V2A 8L1
SUMMER PHONE	604-493-0390
WINTER ADDRESS	As above
WINTER PHONE	
CONTACT PERSON	Steven Philcox
ACCREDITATION	
AFFILIATION	None
YEARS IN OPERATION	35
DATES OPEN	July
FEES	Vary greatly depending upon the course; please enquire.
SCHOLARSHIPS	Yes
ACCOMODATION	Room & board can be arranged.
SPECIALTY	Arts
OBJECTIVES	To provide intensive teaching from the very best instructors in a broad spectrum of the arts to students of all ages & ability levels.
ACTIVITIES	Courses in music, visual arts, theatre, dance, children's programs, & special interests such as fibre arts, technology, & writing.
EVALUATIONS	No
MEDICAL FACILITIES	First aid station on site.
VISITORS	No
SPECIAL NEEDS FACILITIES	Yes
DESCRIPTION	Courses are held in the Penticton Secondary School, on the corner of Eckhardt & Main Street (unless otherwise stated).
NEAREST CITY/TOWN	Penticton
AGE SPREAD	All ages
CAMPERS PER SESSION	Varies
STAFF PER SESSION	Approximately 95
COUNSELLOR:CAMPER RATIO	
BOYS OR GIRLS	☐ Boys only ☐ Girls only ☒ Co-ed
NOTES	Bursaries are available based on talent & need. This is not a residential camp. Room & board in private homes may be arranged if requested well in advance of the course. Special needs refers to wheelchair accessibility. The Suzuki Violin Institute offers limited courses here as well.

OUTWARD BOUND

SUMMER ADDRESS #109 - 1367 West Broadway

Vancouver BC
V6H 4A9 **SUMMER PHONE** 604-737-3093

WINTER ADDRESS As above

WINTER PHONE

CONTACT PERSON Anne Hale or Andrew Orr
ACCREDITATION
AFFILIATION None
YEARS IN OPERATION 50
DATES OPEN June to October
FEES $1250 - $1950 per session.
SCHOLARSHIPS Yes
ACCOMODATION Tents (all equipment is provided).
SPECIALTY Wilderness Training
OBJECTIVES To encourage personal growth through taking risks, meeting challenges, building confidence & working with a group. Advocate minimum impact camping & environmental care.
ACTIVITIES Summer courses involve hiking, mountaineering, rock climbing.

EVALUATIONS No
MEDICAL FACILITIES All instructors have extensive training in wilderness first aid.
VISITORS Students are usually inaccessible during the course.
SPECIAL NEEDS FACILITIES No
DESCRIPTION Courses are held in the mountains around Pemberton.

NEAREST CITY/TOWN Pemberton
AGE SPREAD 15 to 70 years
CAMPERS PER SESSION Groups of 7-10
STAFF PER SESSION
COUNSELLOR:CAMPER RATIO 2 instructors per group
BOYS OR GIRLS ☐ Boys only ☐ Girls only ☒ Co-ed
NOTES This is not a camp, but a registered, non-profit educational organization taking people out into the wilderness on courses lasting 9-21 days. Financial aid may be available for those who can demonstrate need. Students must have a thorough medical check-up prior to a course. See also *Outward Bound, Ontario.*

PACIFIC MOUNTAIN GYMNASTICS CAMP

SUMMER ADDRESS	Pioneer Chehalis Lodge PO Box 127 Harrison Mills V0M 1L0	**SUMMER PHONE**	BC
WINTER ADDRESS	3214 West 10th Avenue Vancouver V6K 2L2	**WINTER PHONE**	BC 604-737-7693
CONTACT PERSON	Carla Bettor		
ACCREDITATION	BCCA		
AFFILIATION	None		
YEARS IN OPERATION	6		
DATES OPEN	July		
FEES	Approximately $450 per one-week session.		
SCHOLARSHIPS	Please enquire.		
ACCOMODATION	Bi-level dormitories, lodge, washrooms, showers, dining hall.		
SPECIALTY	Gymnastics		
OBJECTIVES	To provide a unique training experience for both recreational & competitive gymnasts.		
ACTIVITIES	Gymnastics training, horseback riding, dance, swimming, trampoline, crafts, games, hiking, volleyball.		
EVALUATIONS	No		
MEDICAL FACILITIES	First aid room		
VISITORS	Allowed on Parents Day.		
SPECIAL NEEDS FACILITIES	Yes		
DESCRIPTION	Located on the Chehalis River, 16 km from Harrison Hot Springs.		
NEAREST CITY/TOWN	Hope		
AGE SPREAD	6 to 18 years		
CAMPERS PER SESSION	80		
STAFF PER SESSION	36		
COUNSELLOR:CAMPER RATIO	1 to 8		
BOYS OR GIRLS	☐ Boys only ☒ Girls only ☐ Co-ed		
NOTES			

PIONEER CHEHALIS CAMP

SUMMER ADDRESS 16300 Morris Valley Road
PO Box 127
Harrison Mills BC
V0M 1L0 **SUMMER PHONE**

WINTER ADDRESS #202 - 8606 Fraser Street

Vancouver BC
V5X 3Y3 **WINTER PHONE** 604-325-1715

CONTACT PERSON Bill Enns
ACCREDITATION BCCA, CCI
AFFILIATION Inter Varsity Christian Fellowship of Canada
YEARS IN OPERATION 18
DATES OPEN July
FEES $225 - $580 per 4-14 day session.
SCHOLARSHIPS Yes
ACCOMODATION Lodge with rooms with individual washrooms, dining hall.
SPECIALTY Christian Development
OBJECTIVES To encourage skill development. Christian values are discussed to help campers clarify their own thinking about basic beliefs, & declare Jesus Christ as Saviour & Lord.
ACTIVITIES Horseback riding, team sports, cycling, hiking, crafts, campfires, skits, tubing (on the Chehalis River), hot tubbing, archery, ping pong, Bible study, swimming.

EVALUATIONS Achievement certificates are awarded for horseback riding.
MEDICAL FACILITIES Nurse on staff.
VISITORS Not encouraged
SPECIAL NEEDS FACILITIES Yes
DESCRIPTION Located on the Chehalis River, at the base of Hemlock Mountain.

NEAREST CITY/TOWN Mission
AGE SPREAD 6 to 18 years
CAMPERS PER SESSION 60
STAFF PER SESSION 20
COUNSELLOR:CAMPER RATIO 1 to 3
BOYS OR GIRLS ☐ Boys only ☒ Girls only ☒ Co-ed
NOTES Special needs refers to 2 bedrooms on the main floor designed for the physically disabled. The entire main floor is wheelchair accessible. Both boys & girls are accepted to age 13; girls alone may attend to age 18.

PIONEER PACIFIC CAMP

SUMMER ADDRESS

Thetis Island BC
V0R 2Y0 **SUMMER PHONE** 604-246-9613

WINTER ADDRESS #202 - 8606 Fraser Street

Vancouver BC
V5X 3Y3 **WINTER PHONE** 604-325-1715

CONTACT PERSON David Roycroft
ACCREDITATION BCCA, CCI
AFFILIATION Inter Varsity Christian Fellowship
YEARS IN OPERATION 40
DATES OPEN July through August
FEES $344 per one-week session; $584 per 2-week session.
SCHOLARSHIPS Yes
ACCOMODATION Lodge with rooms with individual washrooms, dining hall.
SPECIALTY Christian Development
OBJECTIVES To encourage skill development. To provide campers with an atmosphere that challenges their personal growth & invites them to experience God in creation.
ACTIVITIES Water skiing, sailing, canoeing, swimming, snorkeling, crafts, archery, field sports, orienteering, hiking, outtrips, Bible study, camp-wide games.

EVALUATIONS No, but badges & grades are awarded for swimming.
MEDICAL FACILITIES Infirmary with nurse or doctor on site; hospital nearby.
VISITORS Allowed, within certain guidelines.
SPECIAL NEEDS FACILITIES Unspecified
DESCRIPTION Located on Thetis Island, one of the northern Gulf Islands.

NEAREST CITY/TOWN Chemainus
AGE SPREAD 6 to 18 years
CAMPERS PER SESSION Up to 125
STAFF PER SESSION 50-70
COUNSELLOR:CAMPER RATIO 1 to 7
BOYS OR GIRLS ☐ Boys only ☐ Girls only ☒ Co-ed
NOTES Family camping is an option; please enquire.

S.A.L.T.S. VOYAGE

SUMMER ADDRESS	Box 5014, Station B		
	Victoria		BC
	V8R 6N3	**SUMMER PHONE**	604-383-6811
WINTER ADDRESS	As above		
		WINTER PHONE	

CONTACT PERSON Margaret Clark
ACCREDITATION
AFFILIATION Sail and Life Training Society (S.A.L.T.S.)
YEARS IN OPERATION 10
DATES OPEN June to September
FEES $650 per 10-day session.
SCHOLARSHIPS Yes, please enquire.
ACCOMODATION Berths, galley
SPECIALTY Sailing
OBJECTIVES To give young people the opportunity to develop physically, mentally and spiritually within the unique atmosphere of shipboard life.
ACTIVITIES Regular crew duties, raising and lowering sails, galley work, bosun's chores, steering, anchor watch at night. Also instruction in navigation, knots, history of sailing, small boat handling, shoreside excursions.
EVALUATIONS No
MEDICAL FACILITIES Medical kit on ship plus crew trained in first aid.
VISITORS N/A
SPECIAL NEEDS FACILITIES No
DESCRIPTION Sail out of Victoria to Desolation Sound.

NEAREST CITY/TOWN Varies
AGE SPREAD 13 to 25 years
CAMPERS PER SESSION 29 Maximum
STAFF PER SESSION 8
COUNSELLOR:CAMPER RATIO N/A
BOYS OR GIRLS ☐ Boys only ☐ Girls only ☒ Co-ed
NOTES

SASAMAT OUTDOOR CENTRE

SUMMER ADDRESS 3302 Senkler Road

Belcarra BC
V3H 4S3 **SUMMER PHONE** 604-939-2268

WINTER ADDRESS As above

WINTER PHONE

CONTACT PERSON Dave Stevens
ACCREDITATION BCCA
AFFILIATION Association of Neighbourhood Houses of Greater Vancouver.
YEARS IN OPERATION 32
DATES OPEN July through August
FEES $200 - $240 per 5-7 day session.
SCHOLARSHIPS Yes
ACCOMODATION Cabins, dining hall.
SPECIALTY Traditional
OBJECTIVES To offer challenging & exciting outdoor activities in a safe environment.

ACTIVITIES Sailing, hiking, canoeing, games, nature activities, full waterfront program, outdoor cooking, kayaking.

EVALUATIONS No
MEDICAL FACILITIES First aid room; hospital 10 minutes away.
VISITORS Not encouraged
SPECIAL NEEDS FACILITIES Yes
DESCRIPTION Situated overlooking Sasamat Lake, the forested site also features a sandy beach & small grass field.

NEAREST CITY/TOWN Vancouver
AGE SPREAD 6 to 16 years
CAMPERS PER SESSION 99
STAFF PER SESSION 20
COUNSELLOR:CAMPER RATIO 1 to 8
BOYS OR GIRLS ☐ Boys only ☐ Girls only ☒ Co-ed
NOTES Special needs may be accommodated with prior consultation. Also partially wheelchair accessible. Family camping is an option; please enquire.

SILVER LAKE FORESTRY CENTRE

SUMMER ADDRESS	BC Forestry Association #105 - 2417 Highway 97 N Kelowna BC V1X 4J2 **SUMMER PHONE** 604-860-6410
WINTER ADDRESS	As above
	WINTER PHONE
CONTACT PERSON	Heather Rice
ACCREDITATION	BCCA
AFFILIATION	BC Forestry Association
YEARS IN OPERATION	25
DATES OPEN	July through August
FEES	$180 per 6-day session.
SCHOLARSHIPS	Yes
ACCOMODATION	Log cabins with bunk beds, wash-houses, showers, lodge.
SPECIALTY	Forest Education
OBJECTIVES	To teach respect for & understanding of the forest environment & forest management. To develop a well-informed public & encourage a "forest ethic" in BC.
ACTIVITIES	"Eco-fun" program, canoeing, fishing, volleyball, swimming, orienteering, nature hikes, games, overnight campouts, campfires.
EVALUATIONS	No, but award certificates are issued.
MEDICAL FACILITIES	First aid cabin with an industrial first aid attendant.
VISITORS	Allowed
SPECIAL NEEDS FACILITIES	Yes
DESCRIPTION	Located in Peachland.
NEAREST CITY/TOWN	Kelowna
AGE SPREAD	7 to 14 years
CAMPERS PER SESSION	70
STAFF PER SESSION	5
COUNSELLOR:CAMPER RATIO	1 to 7
BOYS OR GIRLS	☐ Boys only ☐ Girls only ☒ Co-ed
NOTES	Special needs refers to limited wheelchair accessibility.

SOUTHERN BC CAMP CHERITH

SUMMER ADDRESS	11449 74A Avenue		
	Delta		BC
	V4C 1G3	**SUMMER PHONE**	604-596-2270
WINTER ADDRESS	As above		
		WINTER PHONE	

CONTACT PERSON	Erica Penner
ACCREDITATION	BCCA, CCI
AFFILIATION	Christian
YEARS IN OPERATION	32
DATES OPEN	August
FEES	$145 per one-week session.
SCHOLARSHIPS	No
ACCOMODATION	Cabins, showers, dining hall.
SPECIALTY	Christian Development
OBJECTIVES	To provide a Bible-based outdoor program that results in growth in the development of spiritual, intellectual, social, & physical skills in group-living experiences.
ACTIVITIES	Arts & crafts, nature, archery, swimming, canoeing, drama, campcraft, air riflery, hiking, Bible exploration.
EVALUATIONS	No
MEDICAL FACILITIES	Nurse on site as well as first aid trained staff.
VISITORS	Not allowed
SPECIAL NEEDS FACILITIES	Unspecified
DESCRIPTION	Located above Cultus Lake, at the Columbia Bible Camp.
NEAREST CITY/TOWN	Chilliwack
AGE SPREAD	8 to 18 years
CAMPERS PER SESSION	100
STAFF PER SESSION	40
COUNSELLOR:CAMPER RATIO	1 to 6
BOYS OR GIRLS	☐ Boys only ☒ Girls only ☐ Co-ed
NOTES	

STRATHCONA PARK LODGE WYLD

SUMMER ADDRESS PO Box 2160

Campbell River BC
V9W 5C9 **SUMMER PHONE** 604-286-8206

WINTER ADDRESS As above

WINTER PHONE

CONTACT PERSON Myrna Boulding
ACCREDITATION
AFFILIATION None
YEARS IN OPERATION 32
DATES OPEN July through August
FEES Approximately $59 - $69 per day.
SCHOLARSHIPS Please enquire.
ACCOMODATION Cabins, showers, dining hall.
SPECIALTY Wilderness Training
OBJECTIVES To develop outdoor skills, build confidence, strengthen bodies & encourage a sense of integration with nature.

ACTIVITIES Canoeing, kayaking, backpacking, survival lessons, overnight excursions, rock climbing, ropes course, hiking, sailing, environmental education, campcraft.

EVALUATIONS No
MEDICAL FACILITIES First aid room; all staff have basic or advanced first aid.
VISITORS Allowed
SPECIAL NEEDS FACILITIES Unspecified
DESCRIPTION The lodge is situated minutes away from Strathcona Provincial Park in the centre of Vancouver Island; a ruggedly beautiful wilderness location.
NEAREST CITY/TOWN Campell River
AGE SPREAD 11 to 18 years
CAMPERS PER SESSION Approximately 150
STAFF PER SESSION 45
COUNSELLOR:CAMPER RATIO 1 to 6
BOYS OR GIRLS ☐ Boys only ☐ Girls only ☒ Co-ed
NOTES There are various programs lasting 5, 6, 9, 10, 14 & 20 nights. Family camping is an option; please enquire.

SYLVAN ACRES BAPTIST CAMP

SUMMER ADDRESS PO Box 414

Chemainus BC
V0R 1K0 **SUMMER PHONE** 604-246-3714

WINTER ADDRESS As above

WINTER PHONE

CONTACT PERSON Wayne Stewart
ACCREDITATION BCCA, CCI
AFFILIATION Baptist Church
YEARS IN OPERATION 37
DATES OPEN Mid-July through Labour Day
FEES $109 - $140 per 6-7 day session.
SCHOLARSHIPS Yes
ACCOMODATION Dorm rooms, full shower facilities, main dining room.
SPECIALTY Christian Development
OBJECTIVES To nurture Christian living, encourage leadership & skill development, & provide recreation.

ACTIVITIES Swimming, diving, canoeing, war canoeing, sailing, water skiing, knee boarding, banana boating, arts & crafts, archery, photography, hiking, frisbee golf, drama, saunas, games, campfires, overnight campouts, devotions.

EVALUATIONS No
MEDICAL FACILITIES Nurse on site; hospital 30 minutes away.
VISITORS Not encouraged
SPECIAL NEEDS FACILITIES Yes
DESCRIPTION Located at Lake Cowichan on Vancouver Island.

NEAREST CITY/TOWN Duncan
AGE SPREAD 8 years & up.
CAMPERS PER SESSION 80
STAFF PER SESSION 40
COUNSELLOR:CAMPER RATIO 1 to 5
BOYS OR GIRLS ☐ Boys only ☐ Girls only ☒ Co-ed

NOTES Partial scholarships are available; please enquire. Special needs refers to partial wheelchair accessibility (dorms & lodge).

THUNDERBIRD OUTDOOR CENTRE

SUMMER ADDRESS 880 Courtney Street

Victoria BC
V8W 1C4 **SUMMER PHONE** 604-386-7511

WINTER ADDRESS As above

WINTER PHONE

CONTACT PERSON Jim Leggat
ACCREDITATION BCCA
AFFILIATION YM-YWCA
YEARS IN OPERATION 39
DATES OPEN July through August
FEES Wide range of rates according to programs; please enquire.
SCHOLARSHIPS Yes
ACCOMODATION Cabins and tent shelters, full washrooms, main dining hall.
SPECIALTY Traditional
OBJECTIVES To provide children with the opportunity to learn more about themselves while living & working in small groups, & to become more environmentally aware.
ACTIVITIES Canoeing, archery, orienteering, ropes course, arts & crafts, kayaking, climbing, camping skills, overnight backpacking trips, swimming, nature awareness, drama, campfires.

EVALUATIONS Issued on request.
MEDICAL FACILITIES Infirmary with nurse.
VISITORS Not allowed
SPECIAL NEEDS FACILITIES Unspecified
DESCRIPTION Situated on 1200 acres of wilderness nestled in the Sooke Hills.

NEAREST CITY/TOWN Victoria
AGE SPREAD 8 to 16 years
CAMPERS PER SESSION 152
STAFF PER SESSION 48
COUNSELLOR:CAMPER RATIO 1 to 4
BOYS OR GIRLS ☐ Boys only ☐ Girls only ☒ Co-ed
NOTES

VIC'S HOCKEY SCHOOLS

SUMMER ADDRESS 3431 Senkler Road

Belcarra BC
V3H 4S3 **SUMMER PHONE** 604-936-8427

WINTER ADDRESS As above

WINTER PHONE

CONTACT PERSON Vic LeMire
ACCREDITATION
AFFILIATION None
YEARS IN OPERATION 20
DATES OPEN August
FEES $189 to $210 per 4-day session; room & board $179.
SCHOLARSHIPS Please enquire.
ACCOMODATION This is a day camp but room & board can be arranged.
SPECIALTY Hockey
OBJECTIVES To teach hockey skills & tactics, & to improve self-confidence.

ACTIVITIES On-ice time, video classes, & dryland training.

EVALUATIONS Yes
MEDICAL FACILITIES Not specified; please enquire.
VISITORS Allowed
SPECIAL NEEDS FACILITIES No
DESCRIPTION Two BC locations:
1) In Vancouver, camp held at Britannia Ice Arena;
2) In Osoyoos, camp held at Sun Bowl Ice Rink.
NEAREST CITY/TOWN Vancouver / Osoyoos
AGE SPREAD 4 years & up
CAMPERS PER SESSION 20
STAFF PER SESSION 6
COUNSELLOR:CAMPER RATIO 1 to 3
BOYS OR GIRLS ☐ Boys only ☐ Girls only ☒ Co-ed
NOTES Separate camps for forwards & defensemen, and goaltenders.

WEBB'S HOLIDAY ACRES

SUMMER ADDRESS 1128 256 Street

Aldergrove BC
V0X 1A0 **SUMMER PHONE** 604-857-1712

WINTER ADDRESS As above

WINTER PHONE

CONTACT PERSON George & Barbara Getz
ACCREDITATION BCCA
AFFILIATION None
YEARS IN OPERATION 34
DATES OPEN July through August
FEES $136 per 4-day session; $271 per 7-day session.
SCHOLARSHIPS No
ACCOMODATION Dormitories, showers, dining hall.
SPECIALTY Horseback Riding
OBJECTIVES To give campers the most enjoyment from outdoor & country living & to teach western riding.

ACTIVITIES Instruction in riding & horsemanship, horseback & trail riding, swimming, gym, trampoline, hayrides, campfires, petting zoo, games, arts & crafts, tennis.

EVALUATIONS Weekly prizes for horsemanship & conduct are presented.
MEDICAL FACILITIES Hospital 10 minutes away.
VISITORS Allowed
SPECIAL NEEDS FACILITIES Unspecified
DESCRIPTION 55 acres of parkland in the beautiful Fraser Valley.

NEAREST CITY/TOWN Langley
AGE SPREAD 6 to 14 years
CAMPERS PER SESSION 80
STAFF PER SESSION 20
COUNSELLOR:CAMPER RATIO 1 to 5
BOYS OR GIRLS ☐ Boys only ☐ Girls only ☒ Co-ed
NOTES

MANITOBA

BREATHE FREE CAMP

SUMMER ADDRESS	Manitoba Lung Association 629 McDermot Avenue Winnipeg MAN R3A 1P6 **SUMMER PHONE** 204-774-5501
WINTER ADDRESS	As above
	WINTER PHONE
CONTACT PERSON	Sarah Young
ACCREDITATION	MCA
AFFILIATION	Manitoba Lung Association
YEARS IN OPERATION	8
DATES OPEN	July
FEES	$375 per 12-day session.
SCHOLARSHIPS	Yes
ACCOMODATION	Cabins, showers.
SPECIALTY	Special Needs: Lung Disease
OBJECTIVES	To provide opportunities to children with asthma or cystic fibrosis to learn & grow in the outdoors, and allow them to increase their skills in managing their breathing problems.
ACTIVITIES	Campouts, canoeing, kayaking, archery, rope climbing, nature studies, crafts, swimming, fishing, games, & mini-educational sessions on chronic lung disease management.
EVALUATIONS	No
MEDICAL FACILITIES	MD, nurse, & 2 physiotherapists on staff; 10 mins to hospital.
VISITORS	Not encouraged.
SPECIAL NEEDS FACILITIES	Yes
DESCRIPTION	The camp is situated on an island in beautiful Lake of the Woods.
NEAREST CITY/TOWN	Kenora
AGE SPREAD	8 to 15 years
CAMPERS PER SESSION	Maximum 45
STAFF PER SESSION	
COUNSELLOR:CAMPER RATIO	2 per cabin
BOYS OR GIRLS	☐ Boys only ☐ Girls only ☒ Co-ed
NOTES	Some financial assistance is available for those who require it; please enquire. Special Needs refers to campers with asthma, cystic fibrosis & other chronic lung disorders.

CADDY LAKE GIRL GUIDE CAMP

SUMMER ADDRESS	Girl Guides of Canada 210 - 1199 Nairn Avenue Winnipeg MAN R2L 0Y6
SUMMER PHONE	204-663-2970
WINTER ADDRESS	As above
WINTER PHONE	
CONTACT PERSON	Judy Shiels
ACCREDITATION	MCA
AFFILIATION	Girl Guides of Canada
YEARS IN OPERATION	45
DATES OPEN	July through August
FEES	Ranges from $83 - $247 per session.
SCHOLARSHIPS	Yes
ACCOMODATION	Platform tents with cots, washrooms, showers, dining hall.
SPECIALTY	Traditional
OBJECTIVES	To provide opportunities for girls to develop as individuals through rich experiences in outdoor living. A progressive program, with the Guide Promise & Law as its basis.
ACTIVITIES	Boating, canoeing, hiking, outdoor cooking, nature activities, crafts, swimming, archery, drama, games, backpacking.
EVALUATIONS	Interest badges are worked on & record sheets are mailed out.
MEDICAL FACILITIES	Fully equipped infirmary with nurse on duty, doctor on call.
VISITORS	Not encouraged
SPECIAL NEEDS FACILITIES	Yes
DESCRIPTION	Located in a rugged, wooded area on Caddy Lake in the beautiful Whiteshell Provincial Park, 8 km west of Hawk Lake.
NEAREST CITY/TOWN	Winnipeg
AGE SPREAD	7 to 15+ years
CAMPERS PER SESSION	100
STAFF PER SESSION	19
COUNSELLOR:CAMPER RATIO	1 to 4
BOYS OR GIRLS	☐ Boys only ☒ Girls only ☐ Co-ed
NOTES	Non-member campers are welcome. Financial assistance is available to members of the Girl Guides of Canada residing in the area of Winnipeg; please enquire. Special needs refers to the ability to integrate many disabilities into a regular camp. Each case is considered individually.

CAMP ASSINIBOIA

SUMMER ADDRESS	RR#1 Box 154 Headingly R0H 0C0	**SUMMER PHONE**	MAN 204-864-2159
WINTER ADDRESS	#200 - 600 Shaftesbury Blvd Winnipeg R3P 2J1	**WINTER PHONE**	MAN 204-896-1616

CONTACT PERSON Conference of Mennonites in Manitoba
ACCREDITATION MCA, CCI
AFFILIATION Mennonite Brethren
YEARS IN OPERATION 45
DATES OPEN July through August
FEES $124 - $140 per session.
SCHOLARSHIPS Yes
ACCOMODATION Cabins, showers, main lodge.
SPECIALTY Christian Development
OBJECTIVES To encourage the building of faith & community & an appreciation of God's creation.

ACTIVITIES Horseback riding, hayrides, swimming, archery, trampoline, ropes course, sports, Bible exploration, campfires, camp-wide games.

EVALUATIONS No
MEDICAL FACILITIES Infirmary
VISITORS Not allowed
SPECIAL NEEDS FACILITIES Yes
DESCRIPTION Situated in a forest of cottonwoods & elm, on the banks of the Assiniboine River.

NEAREST CITY/TOWN Winnipeg
AGE SPREAD 8 to 18 years
CAMPERS PER SESSION 80
STAFF PER SESSION 35
COUNSELLOR:CAMPER RATIO 1 to 4
BOYS OR GIRLS ☐ Boys only ☐ Girls only ☒ Co-ed
NOTES Family camping is an option.

CAMP BIRCHBARK

SUMMER ADDRESS c/o Camp Stephens

Lake of the Woods MAN

SUMMER PHONE

WINTER ADDRESS c/o Canadian Diabetes Association
283 Portage Avenue - 2nd Floor
Winnipeg MAN
R3B 2B5 **WINTER PHONE** 1-800-782-0715

CONTACT PERSON Julianna Gudbartson
ACCREDITATION MCA
AFFILIATION Canadian Diabetes Association
YEARS IN OPERATION 33
DATES OPEN Mid to late August
FEES Approx $500 per session.
SCHOLARSHIPS Limited camperships are available.
ACCOMODATION Cabins, showers, 2 large bathrooms.
SPECIALTY Special Needs: Diabetes
OBJECTIVES To encourage children with diabetes to become independent in their diabetes regime, to show them that they are not alone with diabetes.
ACTIVITIES Kayaking, canoeing, sailing, swimming, archery, rock climbing, nature lore, overnight camping, arts & crafts, camp-wide activities.

EVALUATIONS Yes; from the doctor, counsellor & diabetic intern.
MEDICAL FACILITIES Infirmary with a nurse, doctor & RD.
VISITORS Not allowed
SPECIAL NEEDS FACILITIES Yes
DESCRIPTION Located on Copeland Island.

NEAREST CITY/TOWN Kenora
AGE SPREAD 8 to 15 years
CAMPERS PER SESSION 64
STAFF PER SESSION 22
COUNSELLOR:CAMPER RATIO 1 per cabin
BOYS OR GIRLS ☐ Boys only ☐ Girls only ☒ Co-ed
NOTES Special Needs refers to campers with diabetes.
This camp is shared with campers at Camp Stephens which takes an additional 64 children.

CAMP BRERETON

SUMMER ADDRESS Lot 9, Block 7

Brereton Lake MAN

SUMMER PHONE

WINTER ADDRESS 308-885 Wilkes Ave

Winnipeg MAN
R3P 1J3 **WINTER PHONE** 204-489-7239

CONTACT PERSON Pat Finlayson

ACCREDITATION MCA, CCA

AFFILIATION Manitoba Canadian Girls in Training

YEARS IN OPERATION 57

DATES OPEN July

FEES $130 per one-week session.

SCHOLARSHIPS Available

ACCOMODATION Cabins, central washrooms with showers, dining & rec lodge.

SPECIALTY Christian Development

OBJECTIVES To provide an opportunity for campers to grow physically & spiritually, to learn new skills, & enjoy living outdoors in a Christian community.

ACTIVITIES Canoeing, swimming, crafts, Bible study, worship, outdoor skills, music, drama, hiking, morning energizers, cookouts, campfires.

EVALUATIONS No

MEDICAL FACILITIES Nurse or LPN on staff; hospital 30 minutes away.

VISITORS Not encouraged

SPECIAL NEEDS FACILITIES Yes

DESCRIPTION Located in the Whiteshell Provincial Park, the site offers rocky terrain & a beautiful lake.

NEAREST CITY/TOWN Winnipeg

AGE SPREAD 9 to 16 years

CAMPERS PER SESSION 40

STAFF PER SESSION 6-8

COUNSELLOR:CAMPER RATIO 1 to 4

BOYS OR GIRLS ☐ Boys only ☒ Girls only ☐ Co-ed

NOTES Financial assistance is available on request. Special needs refers to limited wheelchair accessibility.

CAMP KOINONIA

SUMMER ADDRESS	Box 312
	Boissevain MAN
	R0K 0E0 **SUMMER PHONE** 204-534-2504
WINTER ADDRESS	#200 - 600 Shaftesbury Blvd
	Winnipeg MAN
	R3P 2J1 **WINTER PHONE** 204-896-1616
CONTACT PERSON	Conference of Mennonites in Manitoba
ACCREDITATION	MCA, CCA
AFFILIATION	Mennonite Brethren
YEARS IN OPERATION	30
DATES OPEN	July through August
FEES	$124 - $140 per session.
SCHOLARSHIPS	Yes
ACCOMODATION	Cabins, showers, main lodge.
SPECIALTY	Christian Development
OBJECTIVES	To encourage the building of faith & community & an appreciation of God's creation.
ACTIVITIES	Archery, sports, canoeing, frisbee golf course, swimming, nature program, mountain biking, Bible exploration, camp-wide games, campfires.
EVALUATIONS	No
MEDICAL FACILITIES	Infirmary
VISITORS	Not allowed
SPECIAL NEEDS FACILITIES	Unspecified
DESCRIPTION	Situated in a boreal forest in the Turtle Mountain Provincial Park, with forest, lake, & marsh areas. 20 km sw of Boissevain.
NEAREST CITY/TOWN	Winnipeg
AGE SPREAD	8 to 18 years
CAMPERS PER SESSION	48
STAFF PER SESSION	20
COUNSELLOR:CAMPER RATIO	1 to 4
BOYS OR GIRLS	☐ Boys only ☐ Girls only ☒ Co-ed
NOTES	Mountain bike tripping offered.

CAMP MANITOU STARTER CAMP

SUMMER ADDRESS PO Box 2790

Winnipeg MAN
R3B 2N8 **SUMMER PHONE** 204-989-4180

WINTER ADDRESS As above

WINTER PHONE

CONTACT PERSON Camp Director
ACCREDITATION MCA
AFFILIATION YM-YWCA
YEARS IN OPERATION 3
DATES OPEN July
FEES $25 per 5-day session
SCHOLARSHIPS Yes
ACCOMODATION Cabins, central washrooms with showers, dining hall.
SPECIALTY Traditional
OBJECTIVES To allow independent youngsters to experience resident camping for the first time in a safe, structured environment close to home.
ACTIVITIES Swimming, play time, canoeing, archery, adventure & theme days, environmental & nature programs, drama, songs, stories, campfires.

EVALUATIONS No
MEDICAL FACILITIES Nurse on site, hospital 6 minutes away.
VISITORS Allowed on Parents' Night.
SPECIAL NEEDS FACILITIES Yes
DESCRIPTION Situated on over 30 acres of beautiful woodland, only one mile from the city.

NEAREST CITY/TOWN Winnipeg
AGE SPREAD 6 to 7 years
CAMPERS PER SESSION 28
STAFF PER SESSION 10
COUNSELLOR:CAMPER RATIO 1 to 6
BOYS OR GIRLS ☐ Boys only ☐ Girls only ☒ Co-ed
NOTES Special needs refers to full integration of campers with physical or mental handicaps, & social, emotional, or behavioral difficulties. Due to the site & program structure there are some limitations to the special needs that can be accommodated; please enquire.

CAMP MASSAD

SUMMER ADDRESS	Gimli Road & 10th Avenue Winnipeg Beach MAN R0C 3G0
SUMMER PHONE	204-389-5300
WINTER ADDRESS	#25 - 370 Hargrave Street Winnipeg MAN R3B 2K1
WINTER PHONE	204-943-2815
CONTACT PERSON	Linda Bloomfield
ACCREDITATION	MCA
AFFILIATION	None
YEARS IN OPERATION	43
DATES OPEN	July through August
FEES	$210/4 days; $695/2 weeks; $990/4 weeks; $1280/7 weeks.
SCHOLARSHIPS	Available
ACCOMODATION	Cabins, showers, dining hall.
SPECIALTY	Jewish Development
OBJECTIVES	To provide a total Jewish learning experience through a creative immersion program, use of the Hebrew language & observance of the dietary laws.
ACTIVITIES	Horseback riding, boating, swimming, tennis, team sports, tetherball, archery, arts & crafts, floor hockey, drama, orienteering, music, dancing, hiking, cook-outs, tefilah, maccabia, olympiada, yom sport.
EVALUATIONS	No
MEDICAL FACILITIES	Infirmary & nurse on site.
VISITORS	Not allowed
SPECIAL NEEDS FACILITIES	Unspecified
DESCRIPTION	Situated on the southern shore of Lake Winnipeg, just north of Winnipeg Beach. Tennis courts & baseball diamond on site.
NEAREST CITY/TOWN	Selkirk
AGE SPREAD	7 to 15 years
CAMPERS PER SESSION	Maximum 140
STAFF PER SESSION	22-28
COUNSELLOR:CAMPER RATIO	1 to 5
BOYS OR GIRLS	☐ Boys only ☐ Girls only ☒ Co-ed
NOTES	

CAMP MOOSE LAKE

SUMMER ADDRESS	Box 38		
	Sprague		MAN
	R0A 1Z0	**SUMMER PHONE**	1-437-2091
WINTER ADDRESS	#200 - 600 Shaftesbury Blvd		
	Winnipeg		MAN
	R3P 2J1	**WINTER PHONE**	204-896-1616

CONTACT PERSON Conference of Mennonites in Manitoba
ACCREDITATION MCA, CCI
AFFILIATION Mennonite Brethren
YEARS IN OPERATION 39
DATES OPEN July through August
FEES $124 - $140 per session.
SCHOLARSHIPS Yes
ACCOMODATION Cabins, showers, main lodge.
SPECIALTY Christian Development
OBJECTIVES To encourage the building of faith & community, & an appreciation of God's creation.

ACTIVITIES Canoeing, sailboarding, sports, archery, swimming, Bible exploration, camp-wide games, campfires.

EVALUATIONS No
MEDICAL FACILITIES Infirmary
VISITORS Not allowed
SPECIAL NEEDS FACILITIES Unspecified
DESCRIPTION Situated on the shores of Moose Lake in the Northwest Angle Provincial Forest, 38 km north of Sprague.

NEAREST CITY/TOWN Winnipeg
AGE SPREAD 8 to 18 years
CAMPERS PER SESSION 37
STAFF PER SESSION 18
COUNSELLOR:CAMPER RATIO 1 to 5
BOYS OR GIRLS ☐ Boys only ☐ Girls only ☒ Co-ed
NOTES Family & retreat camps available; please enquire.

CAMP STEPHENS

SUMMER ADDRESS	PO Box 2790
	Winnipeg MAN
	R3C 4B4 **SUMMER PHONE**
WINTER ADDRESS	#100 - 290 Vaughan Street
	Winnipeg MAN
	R3B 2N8 **WINTER PHONE** 204-989-4180
CONTACT PERSON	Ian Smith
ACCREDITATION	MCA
AFFILIATION	YM-YWCA
YEARS IN OPERATION	104
DATES OPEN	July through August
FEES	Unspecified; please enquire.
SCHOLARSHIPS	Yes
ACCOMODATION	Cabins, tents, washrooms, showers, main dining hall.
SPECIALTY	Traditional
OBJECTIVES	To develop leadership, understanding & appreciation for others. To instill a sense of responsibility & teach a wide range of physical & social skills.
ACTIVITIES	Canoeing, sailing, kayaking, rock climbing, archery, orienteering, crafts, environmental studies, group games, overnights, swimming, nature study.
EVALUATIONS	Yes
MEDICAL FACILITIES	Infirmary with nurse on site.
VISITORS	Allowed
SPECIAL NEEDS FACILITIES	Yes
DESCRIPTION	Situated on Copeland Island, on Lake of the Woods.
NEAREST CITY/TOWN	Kenora
AGE SPREAD	8 to 16 years
CAMPERS PER SESSION	136
STAFF PER SESSION	50-60
COUNSELLOR:CAMPER RATIO	1 to 7
BOYS OR GIRLS	☐ Boys only ☐ Girls only ☒ Co-ed
NOTES	Special needs refers to full integration of campers with physical or mental handicaps, & social, emotional, or behavioral difficulties. Due to the site & program structure, there are limitations to the special needs that can be accommodated. There are also wilderness adventure sailing or canoe trips which base themselves at Camp Stephens.

CAMP WANNAKUMBAC

SUMMER ADDRESS	Riding Mountain Conference Centre Box 125 Onanole MAN R0J 1N0
SUMMER PHONE	204-848-2380
WINTER ADDRESS	As above
WINTER PHONE	
CONTACT PERSON	Darren Gusdal
ACCREDITATION	MCA, CCA
AFFILIATION	None
YEARS IN OPERATION	55
DATES OPEN	July through August
FEES	$168 - $182 per one-week session.
SCHOLARSHIPS	Assistance may be available.
ACCOMODATION	Cabins, washrooms & showers, dining hall, recreation hall.
SPECIALTY	Traditional
OBJECTIVES	To provide a creative, educational experience in group living out-of-doors, using the resources of the natural environment to contribute to mental, physical, social & spiritual growth.
ACTIVITIES	Swimming, archery, canoeing, arts & crafts, photography, camp-wide games, drama, radio broadcasting, music, nature study, wilderness survival, camp outs, campfires.
EVALUATIONS	No (except as requested by Child and Family Services).
MEDICAL FACILITIES	Nurse on site, emergency facility 20 minutes away.
VISITORS	Not allowed
SPECIAL NEEDS FACILITIES	Unspecified
DESCRIPTION	Located on the western shore of Clear Lake in the Riding Mountain National Park.
NEAREST CITY/TOWN	Dauphin
AGE SPREAD	9 to 16 years
CAMPERS PER SESSION	77
STAFF PER SESSION	Approximately 14
COUNSELLOR:CAMPER RATIO	1 to 11
BOYS OR GIRLS	☐ Boys only ☐ Girls only ☒ Co-ed
NOTES	Scholarships may be provided by local organizations such as Manitoba Pool Elevators, United Grain Growers, Retail Co-ops, or Credit Unions; please enquire.

CAMP WASAGA

SUMMER ADDRESS			
	Onanole R0J 1N0	**SUMMER PHONE**	MAN 204-848-2268
WINTER ADDRESS	183 Canora Street		
	Winnipeg R3G 1T1	**WINTER PHONE**	MAN 204-775-6392

CONTACT PERSON Pat McCullough
ACCREDITATION MCA, CCA
AFFILIATION United Church
YEARS IN OPERATION 20
DATES OPEN July through August
FEES Adults $173; 4-16 yrs $126; under 4 yrs $63 per week.
SCHOLARSHIPS Yes
ACCOMODATION Cabins, dining hall, rec hall with fireplace, wash-house.
SPECIALTY Traditional
OBJECTIVES To provide a unique family camping vacation in a community atmosphere.

ACTIVITIES Canoeing, kayaking, swimming, hiking, fishing, orienteering, sports, arts & crafts, table games, star gazing, nature crafts, animal observation, bird-watching, drama & games.

EVALUATIONS No
MEDICAL FACILITIES Unspecified
VISITORS Yes
SPECIAL NEEDS FACILITIES Yes
DESCRIPTION Located on the south shore of Clear Lake in Riding Mountain National Park.

NEAREST CITY/TOWN Winnipeg
AGE SPREAD All ages
CAMPERS PER SESSION 14 families
STAFF PER SESSION Unspecified; please enquire.
COUNSELLOR:CAMPER RATIO Unspecified; please enquire.
BOYS OR GIRLS ☐ Boys only ☐ Girls only ☒ Co-ed
NOTES Bursaries are available; please enquire. Special needs refers to complete wheelchair accessibility.

CAMP WOODLANDS

SUMMER ADDRESS The Salvation Army Divisional Headquarters
301 - 400 Colony Street
Winnipeg MAN
R3B 2P4 **SUMMER PHONE** 204-744-1993

WINTER ADDRESS As above

WINTER PHONE

CONTACT PERSON Capt. & Mrs. Lee Graves
ACCREDITATION MCA, CCI
AFFILIATION Salvation Army
YEARS IN OPERATION 18
DATES OPEN July through August
FEES $115 per 5-day session.
SCHOLARSHIPS Yes
ACCOMODATION Cabins with washrooms & showers, dining hall.
SPECIALTY Christian Development
OBJECTIVES To serve the total personality & health needs of the camper through a creative, healthful experience in co-operative group living & outdoor settings.
ACTIVITIES Crafts, games, swimming, sports, campfires, Bible study, mini golf, ropes course, drama.

EVALUATIONS No
MEDICAL FACILITIES Infirmary with nurse on site; hospital 20 minutes away.
VISITORS Not encouraged
SPECIAL NEEDS FACILITIES Yes
DESCRIPTION Located just outside the town of Woodlands, north of Winnipeg.

NEAREST CITY/TOWN Winnipeg
AGE SPREAD 7 to 12 years
CAMPERS PER SESSION 70
STAFF PER SESSION
COUNSELLOR:CAMPER RATIO Unspecified
BOYS OR GIRLS ☐ Boys only ☐ Girls only ☒ Co-ed
NOTES Financial assistance is available to those in need; please enquire. Special needs refers to limited wheelchair accessibility.

CEDARWOOD

SUMMER ADDRESS	Box 1263
	Lac du Bonnet MAN
	R0E 1A0 **SUMMER PHONE** 204-345-8529
WINTER ADDRESS	325 Talbot Avenue
	Winnipeg MAN
	R2L 0P9 **WINTER PHONE** 204-669-4205
CONTACT PERSON	Tim Plett
ACCREDITATION	MCA, CCI
AFFILIATION	Christian (nondenominational)
YEARS IN OPERATION	10
DATES OPEN	July through August
FEES	$199 per 6-day session
SCHOLARSHIPS	Please enquire
ACCOMODATION	Lodge with bedrooms, washrooms, dining & rec halls.
SPECIALTY	Christian Development
OBJECTIVES	To provide balanced & exciting programs emphasizing Christian values. To encourage campers to examine Christian faith while enjoying the camp experience.
ACTIVITIES	Biking, climbing, swimming, kayaking, skateboarding, BMX.
EVALUATIONS	Yes
MEDICAL FACILITIES	Nurse on staff; hospital 15 minutes away.
VISITORS	Allowed
SPECIAL NEEDS FACILITIES	Yes
DESCRIPTION	On 65 acres of woods fronting on Lake Pinawa, near Lac du Bonnet.
NEAREST CITY/TOWN	Winnipeg
AGE SPREAD	12 years & up
CAMPERS PER SESSION	50
STAFF PER SESSION	27
COUNSELLOR:CAMPER RATIO	1 to 4
BOYS OR GIRLS	☐ Boys only ☐ Girls only ☒ Co-ed
NOTES	Special needs refers to full accessibility for physically challenged campers. There is also some learning disabled integration.

HILBRE BIBLE CAMP

SUMMER ADDRESS	General Delivery Hilbre MAN R0C 1L0 **SUMMER PHONE** 204-449-2293
WINTER ADDRESS	Shantyment International 6981 Millcreek Drive, Unit 17 Mississauga ONT L5N 6B8 **WINTER PHONE** 416-768-2136
CONTACT PERSON	Scott Kelusky
ACCREDITATION	MCA, CCI
AFFILIATION	Evangelical
YEARS IN OPERATION	30
DATES OPEN	July through mid-August
FEES	$42 per 5-day session.
SCHOLARSHIPS	Please enquire.
ACCOMODATION	Cabins, dormitories, lodge with showers, dining hall.
SPECIALTY	Christian Development
OBJECTIVES	To help campers begin & strengthen a personal relationship with God. To teach & model Godly principles in personal & social living.
ACTIVITIES	Volleyball, swimming, basketball, archery, cookouts, drama, games, canoeing, handicrafts, baseball, trampoline, hayrides, chapel, team sports.
EVALUATIONS	No
MEDICAL FACILITIES	Camp nurse & nursing station on site.
VISITORS	Allowed
SPECIAL NEEDS FACILITIES	Unspecified
DESCRIPTION	Located on the shore of Lake St. Martin, on 100 partially wooded acres.
NEAREST CITY/TOWN	Winnipeg
AGE SPREAD	8 to 16 years
CAMPERS PER SESSION	Approximately 300
STAFF PER SESSION	100-120
COUNSELLOR:CAMPER RATIO	1 to 4
BOYS OR GIRLS	☐ Boys only ☐ Girls only ☒ Co-ed
NOTES	

LAKE NUTIMIK BAPTIST CAMP

SUMMER ADDRESS	PO Seven Sisters
	Seven Sisters MAN
	R0E 1Y0 **SUMMER PHONE** 204-348-2551
WINTER ADDRESS	As above
	WINTER PHONE
CONTACT PERSON	John Wahl
ACCREDITATION	MCA, CCI
AFFILIATION	Baptist
YEARS IN OPERATION	40
DATES OPEN	July through August
FEES	$150 per one-week session; canoe trips $160.
SCHOLARSHIPS	Please enquire
ACCOMODATION	Cabins, dining hall, washrooms with showers.
SPECIALTY	Christian Development
OBJECTIVES	To help campers discover God & His purpose for their lives. To help them to experience a richer & fuller life, & enjoy & appreciate nature.
ACTIVITIES	Swimming, canoeing, windsurfing, water skiing, tubing, paddle boating, sports, archery, orienteering, hiking, mountain biking, cookouts, campfires, canoe trips.
EVALUATIONS	Yes
MEDICAL FACILITIES	Infirmary with nurse on site.
VISITORS	Not encouraged
SPECIAL NEEDS FACILITIES	Yes
DESCRIPTION	Situated in the middle of thousands of acres of forests, lakes, and rivers in Manitoba's Whiteshell Provincial Park. The camp is on the shore of Lake Nutimik.
NEAREST CITY/TOWN	Winnipeg
AGE SPREAD	7 to 16 years
CAMPERS PER SESSION	150
STAFF PER SESSION	Approximately 35
COUNSELLOR:CAMPER RATIO	1 to 8
BOYS OR GIRLS	☐ Boys only ☐ Girls only ☒ Co-ed
NOTES	New 3.5-day mini-camps are offered for 7-9 year olds. A 2-week challenging wilderness canoe trip is also offered.

RED ROCK BIBLE CAMP

SUMMER ADDRESS PO Box 790

Steinbach MAN
R0A 2A0 **SUMMER PHONE** 204-348-7267

WINTER ADDRESS As above

WINTER PHONE 204-326-9784

CONTACT PERSON Cliff Dirks
ACCREDITATION MCA
AFFILIATION Christian
YEARS IN OPERATION 47
DATES OPEN July through August
FEES $150 - $175 per 6-day session.
SCHOLARSHIPS Yes
ACCOMODATION Cabins or rooms in lodge, washrooms, showers, dining hall.
SPECIALTY Christian Development
OBJECTIVES To help campers discover God and His plan for their lives. To develop practical & recreational skills, & to experience companionship through group living & interaction.
ACTIVITIES Canoeing, rowing, sailing, boardsailing, waterskiing, archery, broomball, tubing, sports, fishing, crafts, orienteering, woodsmanship, music, drama, Bible memory, Sunday morning services.
EVALUATIONS No
MEDICAL FACILITIES Infirmary on site with nurse or doctor in attendance.
VISITORS Allowed on final day of camp.
SPECIAL NEEDS FACILITIES Yes
DESCRIPTION Located in the Whiteshell Provincial Park.

NEAREST CITY/TOWN Winnipeg
AGE SPREAD 8 to 17 years
CAMPERS PER SESSION 88
STAFF PER SESSION Approx 20
COUNSELLOR:CAMPER RATIO 1 to 4
BOYS OR GIRLS ☐ Boys only ☐ Girls only ☒ Co-ed
NOTES Camperships are available; call or write for a campership application form to be submitted with registration. Special needs refers to individual consideration of cases; integration of many non-physical disabilities is possible.

ROYAL WINNIPEG BALLET SCHOOL

SUMMER ADDRESS	380 Graham Avenue
	Winnipeg MAN
	R3C 4K2 **SUMMER PHONE** 204-956-0183
WINTER ADDRESS	As above
	WINTER PHONE
CONTACT PERSON	David Moroni
ACCREDITATION	
AFFILIATION	Royal Winnipeg Ballet
YEARS IN OPERATION	23
DATES OPEN	July through early August
FEES	Rates vary; please enquire.
SCHOLARSHIPS	Available for Atlantic Canada Residents.
ACCOMODATION	School residence dorms.
SPECIALTY	Arts: Ballet
OBJECTIVES	Introduction to rigour, discipline & standards required for development of a professional dancer. Assessment of successful auditionees for permanent school enrollment.
ACTIVITIES	Ballet classes & assessment of career potential.
EVALUATIONS	Yes
MEDICAL FACILITIES	City of Winnipeg facilities
VISITORS	Allowed
SPECIAL NEEDS FACILITIES	No
DESCRIPTION	Please enquire for details.
NEAREST CITY/TOWN	Winnipeg
AGE SPREAD	9 years & up
CAMPERS PER SESSION	
STAFF PER SESSION	
COUNSELLOR:CAMPER RATIO	Not applicable
BOYS OR GIRLS	☐ Boys only ☐ Girls only ☒ Co-ed
NOTES	A 3-week session is available to a limited number of students aged 9-12. Superior Propane Atlantic Canada Scholarship is a full scholarship available to one student in each of the 4 Atlantic provinces. Admission is by audition only. This is not a traditional camp; very strenuous.

UKRAINIAN PARK CAMP

SUMMER ADDRESS	100 Yale Avenue East		
	Winnipeg		MAN
	R2C 0H8	**SUMMER PHONE**	
WINTER ADDRESS	400 Day Street PO Box 247		
	Winnipeg		MAN
	R2C 2Z9	**WINTER PHONE**	204-222-4283

CONTACT PERSON Rev. Msgr. Michael Buyachok
ACCREDITATION MCA
AFFILIATION Catholic Church
YEARS IN OPERATION 30
DATES OPEN May through August
FEES $140 per one-week session.
SCHOLARSHIPS No; fees are subsidized by various parishes.
ACCOMODATION Cabins, showers, full washrooms, main dining hall.
SPECIALTY Christian Development
OBJECTIVES To foster cultural, religious, or ethnic activities encompassing youth for all faiths in an outdoor Christian camp setting.

ACTIVITIES Bible studies, sports, swimming, archery, hiking, crafts, music, prayers, competitive games, campfires.

EVALUATIONS No
MEDICAL FACILITIES Hospital 8 km away.
VISITORS Allowed on Sundays.
SPECIAL NEEDS FACILITIES Unspecified
DESCRIPTION 60 acres of lakefront property, with much preserved natural forest.

NEAREST CITY/TOWN Winnipeg
AGE SPREAD 7 to 14 years
CAMPERS PER SESSION 150
STAFF PER SESSION 10
COUNSELLOR:CAMPER RATIO 1 to 15
BOYS OR GIRLS ☐ Boys only ☐ Girls only ☒ Co-ed
NOTES

WINKLER BIBLE CAMP

SUMMER ADDRESS	Box 2340		
	Winkler		MAN
	R6W 4C1	**SUMMER PHONE**	204-325-9519
WINTER ADDRESS	As above		
		WINTER PHONE	
CONTACT PERSON	Paul Isaac		
ACCREDITATION	MCA, CCI		
AFFILIATION	Christian (nondenominational)		
YEARS IN OPERATION	45		
DATES OPEN	July through August		
FEES	$75 - $128 per one-week session.		
SCHOLARSHIPS	Please enquire.		
ACCOMODATION	Cabins, showers, dining hall.		
SPECIALTY	Christian Development		
OBJECTIVES	To provide each camper with a well-balanced program of recreation, camping instruction, & Bible teaching carried out by a committed Christian staff.		
ACTIVITIES	Team sports, ropes, archery, horsemanship, swimming, creative crafts, camp-craft, mini golf, devotions, chapel, Bible exploration.		
EVALUATIONS	No		
MEDICAL FACILITIES	Medical room with trained staff.		
VISITORS	Not encouraged		
SPECIAL NEEDS FACILITIES	Unspecified		
DESCRIPTION	Please enquire for details.		
NEAREST CITY/TOWN	Winnipeg		
AGE SPREAD	6 to 17 years		
CAMPERS PER SESSION	88		
STAFF PER SESSION	6		
COUNSELLOR:CAMPER RATIO	1 to 4		
BOYS OR GIRLS	☐ Boys only ☐ Girls only ☒ Co-ed		
NOTES			

NEW BRUNSWICK

CAMP BROOKWOOD

SUMMER ADDRESS			
	Bristol		NB
	E0J 1G0	**SUMMER PHONE**	506-392-6401
WINTER ADDRESS	RR #3		
	Woodstock		NB
	E0J 2B0	**WINTER PHONE**	506-328-3042

CONTACT PERSON Rev. Bill Morton
ACCREDITATION NBCA
AFFILIATION Anglican Church
YEARS IN OPERATION 27
DATES OPEN July to mid-August
FEES $80 per one-week session.
SCHOLARSHIPS Yes
ACCOMODATION Cabins, central wash-house, dining hall, main lodge.
SPECIALTY Christian Development
OBJECTIVES To offer children the opportunity to experience living in a community of faith.

ACTIVITIES Crafts, swimming (instruction), Bible study, sports, hiking, campfires, camping out under the stars, Red Cross instruction.

EVALUATIONS No
MEDICAL FACILITIES Staff trained in first aid; 7 minutes to hospital.
VISITORS Allowed
SPECIAL NEEDS FACILITIES Yes
DESCRIPTION Located on a hill surrounded by trees with a large playing field and pool.

NEAREST CITY/TOWN Bath
AGE SPREAD 8 to 17 years
CAMPERS PER SESSION 30
STAFF PER SESSION 10
COUNSELLOR:CAMPER RATIO 1 to 5
BOYS OR GIRLS ☐ Boys only ☒ Girls only ☒ Co-ed
NOTES Girls-only session are for campers aged 8-11; co-ed sessions encompass all campers aged 8-17 years.

CAMP ECTUS

SUMMER ADDRESS	PO Box 38		
	Petit-Rocher		NB
	E0B 2E0	**SUMMER PHONE**	506-783-2894
WINTER ADDRESS	As above		
			NB
		WINTER PHONE	506-783-8279

CONTACT PERSON Jean-Eudes Doucet
ACCREDITATION NBCA
AFFILIATION None
YEARS IN OPERATION 35
DATES OPEN June through August
FEES $165 for 5 days; $195 for 6 days; $225 for 7 days.
SCHOLARSHIPS No
ACCOMODATION Cabins, dining hall, wash-house.
SPECIALTY French Immersion
OBJECTIVES To encourage a healthy lifestyle & independence among campers. Children plan, organize & realize their own activity schedules.
ACTIVITIES Swimming, theatre, games, outings, crafts, campfires, picnics, canoeing, cooking, woodworking, sculpture.

EVALUATIONS Yes upon request.
MEDICAL FACILITIES Staff is first aid trained; hospital in Bathurst.
VISITORS Not allowed
SPECIAL NEEDS FACILITIES Unspecified
DESCRIPTION On 25 acres of wooded waterfront property.

NEAREST CITY/TOWN Bathurst
AGE SPREAD 7 to 12 years
CAMPERS PER SESSION Maximum 90
STAFF PER SESSION 1 per 3.5 campers
COUNSELLOR:CAMPER RATIO 1 to 4
BOYS OR GIRLS ☐ Boys only ☐ Girls only ☒ Co-ed
NOTES Camp is owned & operated by the Association Camp Ectus (non-profit). The camp is operated strictly in French.

CAMP ELM TREE

SUMMER ADDRESS			
	Petit-Rocher		NB
	E0B 2E0	**SUMMER PHONE**	506-783-4317
WINTER ADDRESS	309 St. Patrick Street		
	Bathurst		NB
	E2A 1E2	**WINTER PHONE**	506-546-3532
CONTACT PERSON	Blake & Mark Mullin		
ACCREDITATION	NBCA		
AFFILIATION	United Church		
YEARS IN OPERATION	49		
DATES OPEN	Late June through July		
FEES	Varied fee schedule; please enquire.		
SCHOLARSHIPS	No		
ACCOMODATION	Central lodge with dining hall & cabins, washrooms.		
SPECIALTY	Christian Development		
OBJECTIVES	To provide a Christian community in an outdoor setting.		
ACTIVITIES	Swimming, Bible study, mission, crafts, sports, nature, drama, campfires, ropes course.		
EVALUATIONS	No		
MEDICAL FACILITIES	Nurse on site.		
VISITORS	Allowed		
SPECIAL NEEDS FACILITIES	No		
DESCRIPTION	Situated on Chaleur Bay, with views of Quebec's Gaspé coast. The camp is nestled in a heavily wooded area with a sandy beach and rugged coastline.		
NEAREST CITY/TOWN	Bathurst		
AGE SPREAD	6 to13 years		
CAMPERS PER SESSION	Maximum 80		
STAFF PER SESSION	1 per 4 campers		
COUNSELLOR:CAMPER RATIO	1 to 4		
BOYS OR GIRLS	☐ Boys only ☐ Girls only ☒ Co-ed		
NOTES			

CAMP GLENBURN

SUMMER ADDRESS RR #2

Hampton NB
E0G 1Z0 **SUMMER PHONE** 506-832-5632

WINTER ADDRESS YM-YWCA Saint John
19-25 Hazen Avenue
Saint John NB
E2L 3G6 **WINTER PHONE** 506-634-4949

CONTACT PERSON Sherry Golding
ACCREDITATION NBCA
AFFILIATION YM-YWCA
YEARS IN OPERATION 66
DATES OPEN July through August
FEES $218 per one-week session; $436 per 2-week session.
SCHOLARSHIPS Yes
ACCOMODATION Cabins, dining hall, modern washrooms.
SPECIALTY Traditional
OBJECTIVES To provide a safe, caring environment, a value-centred learning experience for the development of youth through challenge & discovery, & to strive to be learners & leaders.
ACTIVITIES Canoeing, kayaking, board sailing, swimming, environmental studies, crafts, ropes course, outdoor leadership skills, campfires.

EVALUATIONS No
MEDICAL FACILITIES Nurse on site.
VISITORS Not allowed
SPECIAL NEEDS FACILITIES Yes
DESCRIPTION Located on 29 acres with a fresh water beach on Belleisle Bay and plenty of wooded area.

NEAREST CITY/TOWN Hampton
AGE SPREAD 7 to 15 years
CAMPERS PER SESSION Maximum 160
STAFF PER SESSION 1 per 3 campers
COUNSELLOR:CAMPER RATIO 1 to 4
BOYS OR GIRLS ☐ Boys only ☐ Girls only ☒ Co-ed
NOTES Camperships are available according to need. Special needs facilities refers to accomodation of all special needs campers excluding wheelchairs due to the terrain of the camp.

CAMP GOODTIME

SUMMER ADDRESS	Canadian Cancer Society P.O. Box 2089 St. John E2L 3T5	**SUMMER PHONE**	NB 506-634-6272
WINTER ADDRESS	As above	**WINTER PHONE**	
CONTACT PERSON	Director of Patient Services		
ACCREDITATION			
AFFILIATION	Canadian Cancer Society		
YEARS IN OPERATION	2		
DATES OPEN	Last week of June		
FEES	No cost to campers or accompanying friend or sibling.		
SCHOLARSHIPS	Unspecified.		
ACCOMODATION	Cabins, central dining hall, arts & crafts building.		
SPECIALTY	Special Needs: Cancer		
OBJECTIVES	To provide a positive camping experience for children living with cancer. To increase self-confidence and independence.		
ACTIVITIES	Swimming, boating, crafts, hiking, outtrips, high ropes course, kayaking, canoeing, earth education, drama, campfires.		
EVALUATIONS	Yes		
MEDICAL FACILITIES	Wellness centre with full medical staff on site.		
VISITORS	Not encouraged.		
SPECIAL NEEDS FACILITIES	Yes		
DESCRIPTION	Large wooded site with hiking trails and playing fields on the shore of Belleisle Bay.		
NEAREST CITY/TOWN	Saint John		
AGE SPREAD	7 to 13 years		
CAMPERS PER SESSION	50		
STAFF PER SESSION	24		
COUNSELLOR:CAMPER RATIO	1 to 3		
BOYS OR GIRLS	☐ Boys only ☐ Girls only ☒ Co-ed		
NOTES			

CAMP JEUNNESSE RICHELIEU

SUMMER ADDRESS Rue de la Chapelle
PO Box 1029
Tracadie NB
E0C 2B0 **SUMMER PHONE** 506-395-6880

WINTER ADDRESS As above
NB
WINTER PHONE 506-395-5079

CONTACT PERSON Claude Losier
ACCREDITATION NBCA
AFFILIATION None
YEARS IN OPERATION 4
DATES OPEN June through Labour Day
FEES $170 per 5-day session.
SCHOLARSHIPS Please enquire.
ACCOMODATION Cabins, main dining hall, wash-house, showers.
SPECIALTY Traditional
OBJECTIVES To offer a positive camping experience to youth.

ACTIVITIES Pottery, sculpting, theatre, games, sports, water activities, cycling, ecology, bird-watching, nature trails, environmental education.

EVALUATIONS Yes
MEDICAL FACILITIES Local Tracadie facilities.
VISITORS Not encouraged
SPECIAL NEEDS FACILITIES Yes
DESCRIPTION Located in the centre of Tracadie on 20 acres of land with shoreline.

NEAREST CITY/TOWN Tracadie
AGE SPREAD 9 to 12 years
CAMPERS PER SESSION Maximum 52
STAFF PER SESSION 1 per 2 campers
COUNSELLOR:CAMPER RATIO 1 to 4
BOYS OR GIRLS ☐ Boys only ☐ Girls only ☒ Co-ed
NOTES Special needs refers to integration of mentally or physically disabled children in the camps. Cases are considered individually. Fully wheelchair accessible. Camp is run solely in French.

CAMP LIBERTY

SUMMER ADDRESS	Canadian Cancer Society PO Box 2089 Saint John NB E2L 3T5 **SUMMER PHONE** 506-634-6272
WINTER ADDRESS	As above
	WINTER PHONE
CONTACT PERSON	Director of Patient Services
ACCREDITATION	
AFFILIATION	Canadian Cancer Society
YEARS IN OPERATION	5
DATES OPEN	5 days in July
FEES	No cost to campers or accompanying friend or sibling
SCHOLARSHIPS	
ACCOMODATION	Dormitory, central hall, washrooms.
SPECIALTY	Special Needs: Cancer
OBJECTIVES	To increase the self-esteem and confidence of teens diagnosed with cancer through a peer support program and a positive outdoor experience.
ACTIVITIES	Vary with each group. Can include dances, coping sessions, swimming, campfires, games, sand-sculpture competition, theme nights, hiking, sports.
EVALUATIONS	Yes
MEDICAL FACILITIES	2 nurses on site.
VISITORS	No
SPECIAL NEEDS FACILITIES	Yes
DESCRIPTION	Farm setting with playing fields, waterfall, amphitheatre, arts building.
NEAREST CITY/TOWN	Saint John
AGE SPREAD	14 to 19 years
CAMPERS PER SESSION	25 to 30
STAFF PER SESSION	15
COUNSELLOR:CAMPER RATIO	1 to 3
BOYS OR GIRLS	☐ Boys only ☐ Girls only ☒ Co-ed
NOTES	

CAMP MEDLEY

SUMMER ADDRESS	RR#1		
	Upper Gagetown E0G 1V0	**SUMMER PHONE**	NB 506-488-2874
WINTER ADDRESS	As above		
		WINTER PHONE	NB 506-674-1011

CONTACT PERSON Peter Irish
ACCREDITATION NBCA
AFFILIATION Anglican Church
YEARS IN OPERATION 49
DATES OPEN Late June through August.
FEES Unspecified; please enquire.
SCHOLARSHIPS Please enquire.
ACCOMODATION Cabins, main lodge, dining hall, wash-house.
SPECIALTY Christian Development
OBJECTIVES To provide a camping experience in a Christian environment, allowing campers to grow in their commitment to & relationship with Jesus.
ACTIVITIES Canoeing, swimming, crafts, archery, chapel, sports, ropes course, campfires.

EVALUATIONS No
MEDICAL FACILITIES Nurse on site.
VISITORS Not encouraged.
SPECIAL NEEDS FACILITIES Unspecified
DESCRIPTION Located on the St. John River surrounded by forest and woodlands.

NEAREST CITY/TOWN Oromocto
AGE SPREAD 8 to 16 years
CAMPERS PER SESSION Maximum 140
STAFF PER SESSION 35
COUNSELLOR:CAMPER RATIO 1 to 11
BOYS OR GIRLS ☒ Boys only ☒ Girls only ☒ Co-ed
NOTES Boys & girls have separate camps to age 11; co-ed sessions are offered to campers aged 12-16.

CAMP ROTARY

SUMMER ADDRESS	Canadian Rehabilitation Council for the Disabled PO Box 29 Chipman NB E0E 1C0 **SUMMER PHONE** 506-385-2147
WINTER ADDRESS	65 Brunswick Street Fredericton NB E3B 1G5 **WINTER PHONE** 506-386-8060
CONTACT PERSON	Shirley Hunt
ACCREDITATION	NBCA
AFFILIATION	None
YEARS IN OPERATION	40
DATES OPEN	Late June through August
FEES	$520 per one-week session.
SCHOLARSHIPS	Yes
ACCOMODATION	Cabins, recreation hall, dining hall, wash-house.
SPECIALTY	Special Needs
OBJECTIVES	Camp motto is "focus on ability".
ACTIVITIES	Canoeing, computers, archery, swimming, sports, earth education, crafts, theme days, campfires.
EVALUATIONS	Yes
MEDICAL FACILITIES	Infirmary with nurse & assistant nurse.
VISITORS	Allowed
SPECIAL NEEDS FACILITIES	Yes
DESCRIPTION	A 21-acre beachfront site with outdoor heated pool, playing court, wheelchair-accessible playground & nature trails. Situated on an old farm on the banks of Grand Lake.
NEAREST CITY/TOWN	Minto
AGE SPREAD	6 years to adult
CAMPERS PER SESSION	Maximum 125
STAFF PER SESSION	62
COUNSELLOR:CAMPER RATIO	1 to 4
BOYS OR GIRLS	☐ Boys only ☐ Girls only ☒ Co-ed
NOTES	Special needs refers to camps for disabled campers: diabetic, mentally, & physically handicapped sessions. Sponsorships are availabe through outside agencies.

CAMP SHICKTEHAWK

SUMMER ADDRESS PO Box 293

Bristol NB
E0J 1G0 **SUMMER PHONE** 506-392-6556

WINTER ADDRESS As above

NB
WINTER PHONE

CONTACT PERSON Kevin Matthews
ACCREDITATION NBCA, CCI
AFFILIATION Baptist
YEARS IN OPERATION 59
DATES OPEN Late June through August
FEES $90 - $130 per one-week session.
SCHOLARSHIPS No
ACCOMODATION Cabins, dining hall, washrooms.
SPECIALTY Christian Development
OBJECTIVES To encourage the development of the body, mind, & spirit through physical, mental, & spiritual challenges & discussions.

ACTIVITIES Swimming, crafts, sports, archery, Bible study, mission, ropes course, drama, computers, boating, music, campfires, hiking.

EVALUATIONS No
MEDICAL FACILITIES Health care centre with nurse on site.
VISITORS Allowed
SPECIAL NEEDS FACILITIES Unspecified
DESCRIPTION A 65-acre wooded site with waterfront, a pool & gymnasium.

NEAREST CITY/TOWN Bath
AGE SPREAD 7 years to adult
CAMPERS PER SESSION Maximum 140
STAFF PER SESSION 28
COUNSELLOR:CAMPER RATIO 1 to 4
BOYS OR GIRLS ☒ Boys only ☒ Girls only ☒ Co-ed
NOTES Family camping is an option. Some specialty (computer, swimming, basketball, music, craft, & swimming) camps are offered.

CAMP TALAKADIK

SUMMER ADDRESS	PO Box 217		
	Norton		NB
	E0G 2N0	**SUMMER PHONE**	506-839-2964
WINTER ADDRESS	PO Box 175		
	St. John		NB
	E2L 3X8	**WINTER PHONE**	506-696-1508

CONTACT PERSON Hollis Boyd
ACCREDITATION NBCA
AFFILIATION Baptist
YEARS IN OPERATION 33
DATES OPEN Late June through August
FEES $105 per one-week session.
SCHOLARSHIPS Please enquire.
ACCOMODATION Cabins, main lodge with dining hall, wash-house.
SPECIALTY Christian Development
OBJECTIVES To lead campers to the saving knowledge of Jesus.

ACTIVITIES Swimming, canoeing, archery, sports, Bible study, mission, crafts, nature trails, campfires.

EVALUATIONS No
MEDICAL FACILITIES Nurse on site.
VISITORS Allowed
SPECIAL NEEDS FACILITIES Yes
DESCRIPTION A site with beach waterfront, offering nature trails & an open field.

NEAREST CITY/TOWN Sussex
AGE SPREAD 6 to 18 years
CAMPERS PER SESSION Maximum 120
STAFF PER SESSION 60
COUNSELLOR:CAMPER RATIO 1 to 4
BOYS OR GIRLS ☒ Boys only ☒ Girls only ☒ Co-ed
NOTES Some 4-day camps are offered for $65; please enquire. Special needs refers to a 3-day mentally & physically handicapped camp offered. Camp can not accommodate wheelchairs, however; please enquire.

CAMP TAWASI

SUMMER ADDRESS

Murray Corner NB
SUMMER PHONE 506-538-2549

WINTER ADDRESS RR #6
71 Weston Dr.
Moncton NB
ELC 8Kl
WINTER PHONE 506-383-8083

CONTACT PERSON Dale Briggs
ACCREDITATION NBCA
AFFILIATION United Church
YEARS IN OPERATION 50+
DATES OPEN Late June through July
FEES Unspecified; please enquire.
SCHOLARSHIPS
ACCOMODATION Cabins, main dining hall.
SPECIALTY Christian Development
OBJECTIVES To provide a Christian camping experience for youth.

ACTIVITIES Bible study, crafts, sports, swimming, campfires, special events, canoeing.

EVALUATIONS No
MEDICAL FACILITIES Infirmary with nurse on site.
VISITORS Please call first.
SPECIAL NEEDS FACILITIES Nurse on site.
DESCRIPTION A beachfront location with nature trails. 25 acres surrounded by water on the shore of the Northumberland Strait.

NEAREST CITY/TOWN Sackville
AGE SPREAD 8 to 14 years
CAMPERS PER SESSION Maximum 70
STAFF PER SESSION 24
COUNSELLOR:CAMPER RATIO 1 to 5
BOYS OR GIRLS ☐ Boys only ☐ Girls only ☒ Co-ed
NOTES

CAMP WAWEIG

SUMMER ADDRESS

Waweig NB

SUMMER PHONE 506-466-4040

WINTER ADDRESS PO Box 363

St. Stephen NB
E3L 2X3

WINTER PHONE 506-466-1517

CONTACT PERSON Alan Halstead
ACCREDITATION NBCA
AFFILIATION Baptist
YEARS IN OPERATION 80 +
DATES OPEN Late June to early August
FEES Unspecified; please enquire.
SCHOLARSHIPS Yes. Please equire.
ACCOMODATION Cabins, dining hall, wash-house.
SPECIALTY Christian Development
OBJECTIVES To offer a Christian camping experience encouraging children to live in harmony with others.

ACTIVITIES Swimming, canoeing, sports, crafts, Bible study, mission, obstacle course, & campfires.

EVALUATIONS No
MEDICAL FACILITIES Nurse on site.
VISITORS Not encouraged.
SPECIAL NEEDS FACILITIES Limited wheelchair access.
DESCRIPTION On the Waweig River surrounded by woodlands and open space.

NEAREST CITY/TOWN St. Stephen
AGE SPREAD 9 to 17 years
CAMPERS PER SESSION Maximum 50
STAFF PER SESSION 10
COUNSELLOR:CAMPER RATIO 1 to 4
BOYS OR GIRLS ☒ Boys only ☒ Girls only ☒ Co-ed
NOTES Co-ed sessions are for campers aged 13-17 years only.

CAMP WEGESEGUM

SUMMER ADDRESS PO Box 29

Chipman NB
E0E 1C0 **SUMMER PHONE** 506-339-6545

WINTER ADDRESS As above

NB
WINTER PHONE 506-386-8060

CONTACT PERSON Shirley Hunt
ACCREDITATION NBCA
AFFILIATION Christian (nondenominational)
YEARS IN OPERATION 71
DATES OPEN July through August
FEES $125 per 6-day session.
SCHOLARSHIPS No
ACCOMODATION Cabins, dining lodge, wash-house & outhouses.
SPECIALTY Christian Development
OBJECTIVES The camp seeks to encourage loving relationships, foster the spirit of Jesus Christ, & celebrate God's presence in all life.

ACTIVITIES Swimming, canoeing, crafts, Bible study, nature trails, games, sports, campfires, chapel.

EVALUATIONS No
MEDICAL FACILITIES First aid trained staff on site; medical clinic 5 km away.
VISITORS Not encouraged
SPECIAL NEEDS FACILITIES Yes
DESCRIPTION Situated on the Salmon River, the site offers a pool, ball field, & outdoor chapel on its 50 acres of pine-forested land.

NEAREST CITY/TOWN Chipman
AGE SPREAD 6 to 17 years
CAMPERS PER SESSION Maximum 100
STAFF PER SESSION 25
COUNSELLOR:CAMPER RATIO 1 to 6
BOYS OR GIRLS ☒ Boys only ☒ Girls only ☒ Co-ed
NOTES Family camping is an option.

CAMP WILDWOOD

SUMMER ADDRESS

Bouctouche NB
E0A 1G0 **SUMMER PHONE** 506-743-2757

WINTER ADDRESS PO Box 564

Moncton NB
E1C 8L9 **WINTER PHONE** 506-387-7617

CONTACT PERSON Geoff Brace
ACCREDITATION NBCA
AFFILIATION Baptist
YEARS IN OPERATION 82
DATES OPEN June through August
FEES Approximately $112 per one-week session.
SCHOLARSHIPS Yes
ACCOMODATION Cabins, main lodge, wash-house.
SPECIALTY Christian Development.
OBJECTIVES To provide a Christian atmosphere & well-rounded program that encourages campers to personal growth & to experience God in His creation.
ACTIVITIES Swimming, canoeing, kayaking, nature studies, floor hockey, crafts, drama, archery, sports, outdoor skills.

EVALUATIONS Yes, for swimming.
MEDICAL FACILITIES Nurse on site.
VISITORS Not encouraged
SPECIAL NEEDS FACILITIES Yes
DESCRIPTION A well-forested waterfront property with a dock on Little Bouctouche River.

NEAREST CITY/TOWN Bouctouche
AGE SPREAD 6 to 19 years
CAMPERS PER SESSION Maximum 130
STAFF PER SESSION 32
COUNSELLOR:CAMPER RATIO 1 to 6
BOYS OR GIRLS ☒ Boys only ☒ Girls only ☒ Co-ed
NOTES Family camping is an option. Camperships are available through outside agencies or churches. Special needs refers to wheelchair-accessible buildings.

CAMP WOOLASTOOK

SUMMER ADDRESS RR #6

Perth-Andover NB
E0J 1V0 **SUMMER PHONE** 506-273-2443

WINTER ADDRESS As above

NB
WINTER PHONE 506-392-6534

CONTACT PERSON Sandra McIntosh
ACCREDITATION NBCA
AFFILIATION United Church
YEARS IN OPERATION 60+
DATES OPEN July to mid-August
FEES $60 per one-week session.
SCHOLARSHIPS No
ACCOMODATION Cabins, wash-house, modern washrooms, main dining hall.
SPECIALTY Christian Development
OBJECTIVES To provide opportunities for campers to experience God, joyful worship & Christian community in the uniqueness of an outdoor setting.
ACTIVITIES Swimming, crafts, Bible study, sports, trails, campfires, drama.

EVALUATIONS Yes
MEDICAL FACILITIES At least 1 first aid trained staff; hospital 14 km away.
VISITORS Not encouraged
SPECIAL NEEDS FACILITIES No
DESCRIPTION Located in Kincardine, in a deep valley with a stream flowing past the site. The camp offers a swimming pool & many trails.

NEAREST CITY/TOWN Perth-Andover
AGE SPREAD 6 to 18 years
CAMPERS PER SESSION Maximum 70
STAFF PER SESSION 24
COUNSELLOR:CAMPER RATIO 1 to 4
BOYS OR GIRLS ☐ Boys only ☐ Girls only ☒ Co-ed
NOTES

CIRCLE SQUARE RANCH

SUMMER ADDRESS PO Box 2120

Sussex NB
E0E 1P0 **SUMMER PHONE** 506-432-6362

WINTER ADDRESS As above

NB
WINTER PHONE 506-433-5953

CONTACT PERSON Dana Welner
ACCREDITATION NBCA, CCI
AFFILIATION Christian
YEARS IN OPERATION 13
DATES OPEN July through August
FEES $205 per one-week session.
SCHOLARSHIPS Yes
ACCOMODATION Main building with rooms, dining hall, rec hall, washrooms.
SPECIALTY Horseback Riding & Christian Development
OBJECTIVES There is a Biblical theme of "balanced living". The camp motto is "It's better to build a child than to repair a man".

ACTIVITIES Horseback riding, swimming, canoeing, archery, sports, crafts, ropes course, trails, orienteering, go-carting, BMX biking, games, trampoline, spiritual time, campfires.

EVALUATIONS No
MEDICAL FACILITIES Health centre & trained staff; emergency facility nearby.
VISITORS Not encouraged
SPECIAL NEEDS FACILITIES Unspecified.
DESCRIPTION Located atop Snider Mountain, the camp is a real ranch with wagons, a barn, pool, pond, 2 riding arenas, a sports field, and a go-cart track. There is also a man-made lake.
NEAREST CITY/TOWN Sussex
AGE SPREAD 6 to 16 years
CAMPERS PER SESSION Maximum 160
STAFF PER SESSION 80
COUNSELLOR:CAMPER RATIO 1 to 4
BOYS OR GIRLS ☒ Boys only ☒ Girls only ☒ Co-ed
NOTES Camperships are available according to need; please enquire.

GREEN HILL LAKE CAMP

SUMMER ADDRESS Green Hill Lake Road
RR #1
Lower Hainesville NB
E0H 1J0 **SUMMER PHONE** 506-463-2267

WINTER ADDRESS As above

WINTER PHONE

CONTACT PERSON Steven Alward
ACCREDITATION NBCA, CCI
AFFILIATION Baptist Church
YEARS IN OPERATION 34
DATES OPEN July through August
FEES Approximately $115 per one-week session.
SCHOLARSHIPS Yes
ACCOMODATION Cabins, main lodge, dining hall, modern washrooms.
SPECIALTY Christian Development
OBJECTIVES To provide a fun camping experience in which campers are encouraged to think about spiritual values & to apply them in practical ways, while enjoying wholesome activities.
ACTIVITIES Swimming, wilderness survival, canoeing, kayaking, archery, nature study, Bible study, missions, crafts, hiking, sports, drama, orienteering, campfires, games, first aid training.

EVALUATIONS No
MEDICAL FACILITIES Nurse on site.
VISITORS Not encouraged
SPECIAL NEEDS FACILITIES Unspecified.
DESCRIPTION Waterfront site on 22 acres of wilderness trails, surrounded by rolling hills in the province's midwestern region.

NEAREST CITY/TOWN Fredericton
AGE SPREAD 7 to 15 years
CAMPERS PER SESSION Maximum 130
STAFF PER SESSION 32
COUNSELLOR:CAMPER RATIO 1 to 5
BOYS OR GIRLS ☒ Boys only ☒ Girls only ☒ Co-ed
NOTES Co-ed camp sessions are for campers aged 13-15 years. Family camping is an option. Scholarships may be available through the church. Some specialized (sports or wilderness survival) camps are offered.

LIVINGSTON LAKE CAMP

SUMMER ADDRESS			
	Alma		NB
		SUMMER PHONE	506-887-2532
WINTER ADDRESS	15 Everett Street		
	Moncton		NB
	E1C 3Z6	**WINTER PHONE**	506-858-0949

CONTACT PERSON Hélène Riviére
ACCREDITATION NBCA
AFFILIATION Moncton Boys' & Girls' Club
YEARS IN OPERATION 24
DATES OPEN July through August
FEES Boys'/Girls' Club members $115/6 days; nonmembers $165.
SCHOLARSHIPS No
ACCOMODATION Cabins, main lodge, wash-house, showers.
SPECIALTY Traditional
OBJECTIVES To provide a camp experience filled with outdoor activities, emphasizing an understanding, concern & appreciation of our wilderness & natural environment.
ACTIVITIES Swimming, canoeing, arts & crafts, trails, outings, outdoor skills, cooking, sports, camp-wide games, hiking, drama, campfires.

EVALUATIONS Yes
MEDICAL FACILITIES Health station, with all staff first aid trained; hospital nearby.
VISITORS Not encouraged
SPECIAL NEEDS FACILITIES Unspecified.
DESCRIPTION A waterfront site with an open playing field.

NEAREST CITY/TOWN Moncton
AGE SPREAD 6 to 12 years
CAMPERS PER SESSION Maximum 80
STAFF PER SESSION 40
COUNSELLOR:CAMPER RATIO 1 to 4
BOYS OR GIRLS ☐ Boys only ☐ Girls only ☒ Co-ed
NOTES Camp is bilingual.

SAINT JOHN VALLEY BIBLE CAMP

SUMMER ADDRESS	PO Box 355		
	Hartland		NB
	E0J 1N0	**SUMMER PHONE**	506-375-6673
WINTER ADDRESS	As above		
			NB
		WINTER PHONE	506-375-6953

CONTACT PERSON Wilmot Smith
ACCREDITATION NBCA
AFFILIATION Baptist
YEARS IN OPERATION 46
DATES OPEN July to early August
FEES Unspecified; please enquire.
SCHOLARSHIPS Yes.
ACCOMODATION Cabins, washrooms, dining hall, recreation hall.
SPECIALTY Christian Development
OBJECTIVES To teach youth about the Lord.

ACTIVITIES Swimming, sports, Bible study, outtrips, crafts, campfires, hiking, games, paddle boats, picnics.

EVALUATIONS No.
MEDICAL FACILITIES Unspecified; please enquire.
VISITORS Allowed.
SPECIAL NEEDS FACILITIES Yes.
DESCRIPTION On the St. John River surrounded by woods.

NEAREST CITY/TOWN Hartland
AGE SPREAD 4 to 18 years
CAMPERS PER SESSION Maximum 120
STAFF PER SESSION 40
COUNSELLOR:CAMPER RATIO 1 to 5
BOYS OR GIRLS ☒ Boys only ☒ Girls only ☒ Co-ed
NOTES Co-ed sessions are for campers aged 4-9 & 13-18 years. Family camping is an option; please enquire.

SANDY COVE BIBLE CAMP

SUMMER ADDRESS			
	Dumfries		NB
		SUMMER PHONE	506-575-2628
WINTER ADDRESS	PO Box 104		
	Prince William		NB
	E0H 1S0	**WINTER PHONE**	506-433-6792

CONTACT PERSON Albert Dean
ACCREDITATION NBCA
AFFILIATION Baptist
YEARS IN OPERATION
DATES OPEN July through August
FEES Unspecified; please enquire.
SCHOLARSHIPS Please enquire.
ACCOMODATION Cabins, main lodge, washrooms.
SPECIALTY Christian Development
OBJECTIVES To expose children to Christ in an outdoor camping experience.

ACTIVITIES Canoeing, archery, crafts, swimming (instruction), Bible study, chapel time, sports, waterskiing, hiking, campfires.

EVALUATIONS No
MEDICAL FACILITIES Nurse on site.
VISITORS Please enquire.
SPECIAL NEEDS FACILITIES Unspecified
DESCRIPTION The camp offers 65 acres of woodland, as well as a sports field & various sports courts.

NEAREST CITY/TOWN Fredericton
AGE SPREAD 7 to 17 years
CAMPERS PER SESSION Maximum 135
STAFF PER SESSION 45
COUNSELLOR:CAMPER RATIO 1 to 3
BOYS OR GIRLS ☐ Boys only ☐ Girls only ☒ Co-ed
NOTES Family camping is an option; please enquire.

NEWFOUNDLAND AND LABRADOR

BROTHER BRENNAN CENTRE

SUMMER ADDRESS	Environmental Education Commission PO Box 2265 St. John's NFLD A1C 6E6
SUMMER PHONE	709-753-8530
WINTER ADDRESS	As above
WINTER PHONE	
CONTACT PERSON	Dick Coombs
ACCREDITATION	NLCA
AFFILIATION	None
YEARS IN OPERATION	9
DATES OPEN	Year round
FEES	N/A
SCHOLARSHIPS	N/A
ACCOMODATION	Cabins, showers, dining hall.
SPECIALTY	Science: Natural Science
OBJECTIVES	To create an increased, meaningful awareness & appreciation of nature.
ACTIVITIES	Hiking, swimming, orienteering, canoeing, botanical & zoological observation, woodlot management, geological exploration, general ecological education, environmental issues.
EVALUATIONS	No
MEDICAL FACILITIES	Unspecified; please enquire.
VISITORS	Not encouraged
SPECIAL NEEDS FACILITIES	Unspecified
DESCRIPTION	Located in the Deer Park/Salmonier wilderness area.
NEAREST CITY/TOWN	St. John's
AGE SPREAD	13 to 15 years
CAMPERS PER SESSION	Maximum 50
STAFF PER SESSION	3
COUNSELLOR:CAMPER RATIO	1 to 10
BOYS OR GIRLS	☐ Boys only ☐ Girls only ☒ Co-ed
NOTES	Program run in conjunction with the Newfoundland school district; available to school groups & local organizations. This is not a regular summer camp program.

CAMP DOUWANA

SUMMER ADDRESS	c/o Max Simms Memorial Camp PO Box 760 Bishop's Falls NFLD A0H 1C0
SUMMER PHONE	
WINTER ADDRESS	Canadian Diabetes Assn—Nfld & Labrador Division 103 Le Marchant Road St. John's NFLD A1C 2H1
WINTER PHONE	709-754-0953
CONTACT PERSON	Heidi Windsor
ACCREDITATION	NLCA
AFFILIATION	Canadian Diabetes Foundation
YEARS IN OPERATION	20
DATES OPEN	July to August
FEES	Unspecified; please enquire.
SCHOLARSHIPS	
ACCOMODATION	Dormitory rooms, showers, main dining hall.
SPECIALTY	Special Needs: Diabetes
OBJECTIVES	To give children the opportunity to meet others with diabetes and learn about their condition while enjoying traditional summer camp fun.
ACTIVITIES	Swimming, hiking, boating, sports day, movies, education sessions.
EVALUATIONS	No
MEDICAL FACILITIES	Infirmary on site with a doctor, 3 nurses & 2 dieticians.
VISITORS	Allowed
SPECIAL NEEDS FACILITIES	Yes
DESCRIPTION	Situated on 25 acres of grassy meadows surrounded by forests.
NEAREST CITY/TOWN	Gander
AGE SPREAD	7 to 17 years
CAMPERS PER SESSION	40-50
STAFF PER SESSION	9
COUNSELLOR:CAMPER RATIO	1 to 4
BOYS OR GIRLS	☐ Boys only ☐ Girls only ☒ Co-ed
NOTES	Special needs refers to diabetic campers.

CAMP STARRIGAN

SUMMER ADDRESS General Delivery

Musgravetown NFLD
A0C 1Z0 **SUMMER PHONE**

WINTER ADDRESS 21 Adams Avenue

St. John's NFLD
A1C 4Z1 **WINTER PHONE** 709-726-2273

CONTACT PERSON Captain Eddie Vincent
ACCREDITATION NLCA
AFFILIATION Salvation Army
YEARS IN OPERATION 15
DATES OPEN May to October
FEES Unspecified; please enquire.
SCHOLARSHIPS No
ACCOMODATION Cabins, tents, showers, dining hall.
SPECIALTY Christian Development
OBJECTIVES To teach Christian values & provide a good climate for relaxation, learning & fun.

ACTIVITIES Arts & crafts, Bible study, campfires, games, sports.

EVALUATIONS No
MEDICAL FACILITIES Nurse on staff.
VISITORS Not encouraged
SPECIAL NEEDS FACILITIES Unspecified
DESCRIPTION Please enquire for details.

NEAREST CITY/TOWN Gander
AGE SPREAD All ages
CAMPERS PER SESSION Unspecified
STAFF PER SESSION 12
COUNSELLOR:CAMPER RATIO 20
BOYS OR GIRLS ☐ Boys only ☐ Girls only ☒ Co-ed
NOTES

LAVROCK

SUMMER ADDRESS 19 Kings Bridge Road

St. John's NFLD
A1C 3R4 **SUMMER PHONE** 709-579-9227

WINTER ADDRESS As above

WINTER PHONE

CONTACT PERSON Ron Lee
ACCREDITATION NLCA
AFFILIATION Anglican Church
YEARS IN OPERATION 6
DATES OPEN July through August
FEES $125 per one-week session.
SCHOLARSHIPS Yes
ACCOMODATION Cabins, showers, dining hall.
SPECIALTY Christian Development
OBJECTIVES To create a Christian environment where young people can grow together in love & fellowship as a community.

ACTIVITIES Arts & crafts, campfires, games, sports.

EVALUATIONS No
MEDICAL FACILITIES Nurse on staff.
VISITORS Not encouraged
SPECIAL NEEDS FACILITIES Yes
DESCRIPTION Please enquire for details.

NEAREST CITY/TOWN St. John's
AGE SPREAD 8 to 18 years
CAMPERS PER SESSION 80-100
STAFF PER SESSION 10
COUNSELLOR:CAMPER RATIO 1 to 9
BOYS OR GIRLS ☐ Boys only ☐ Girls only ☒ Co-ed
NOTES Special needs refers to wheelchair accessibility.

LION MAX SIMMS MEMORIAL CAMP

SUMMER ADDRESS PO Box 760

Bishop's Falls NFLD
A0H 1C0 **SUMMER PHONE** 709-258-5862

WINTER ADDRESS As above

WINTER PHONE

CONTACT PERSON Phil Lingard
ACCREDITATION NLCA
AFFILIATION Christian (nondenominational)
YEARS IN OPERATION 12
DATES OPEN May through August
FEES Approx $20 per day.
SCHOLARSHIPS Please enquire.
ACCOMODATION Main building with dorms, washrooms & dining room.
SPECIALTY Special Needs
OBJECTIVES To provide special needs individuals with an accessible camping program.

ACTIVITIES Arts & crafts, hiking, sports, archery, swimming, campfires, dances, movies, scavenger hunts, talent shows, off-site trips, bowling, hayrides, boat rides, horseback & buggy rides.

EVALUATIONS No
MEDICAL FACILITIES First aid station with nurse on duty.
VISITORS Allowed
SPECIAL NEEDS FACILITIES Yes
DESCRIPTION Situated on 25 acres of grassy meadow surrounded by fir, spruce, & old pine trees.

NEAREST CITY/TOWN Gander
AGE SPREAD All ages
CAMPERS PER SESSION 50-70
STAFF PER SESSION 10-15
COUNSELLOR:CAMPER RATIO 1 to 6
BOYS OR GIRLS ☐ Boys only ☐ Girls only ☒ Co-ed
NOTES From May through August special needs camps are held on behalf of various groups. Please enquire to determine the types of special needs & their times. Camps for physical & mental disabilities are offered.

WEST HAVEN LODGE

SUMMER ADDRESS PO Box 626

Baie Verte NFLD
A0K 1B0

SUMMER PHONE 709-754-0386

WINTER ADDRESS As above

WINTER PHONE

CONTACT PERSON Marion Ronalds
ACCREDITATION NLCA
AFFILIATION United Church
YEARS IN OPERATION 30
DATES OPEN June through August
FEES $12 per day up to 12 yrs; $15 per day ages 12 & up.
SCHOLARSHIPS Please enquire.
ACCOMODATION Bunkhouses, showers, dining hall, recreational building.
SPECIALTY Christian Development
OBJECTIVES To help children have fun while they grow spiritually, experience the love of God & the fellowship of friends & leaders, and gain respect for themselves & others.
ACTIVITIES Arts & crafts, Bible study, campfires, canoeing, films, nature study, sports & games, swimming, singing, reflection & discussion groups, hiking.

EVALUATIONS No
MEDICAL FACILITIES Infirmary with nurse on staff; hospital 20 minutes away.
VISITORS Not encouraged
SPECIAL NEEDS FACILITIES Unspecified
DESCRIPTION Situated on the shore of Deer Lake at Pasadena.

NEAREST CITY/TOWN Corner Brook
AGE SPREAD 8 to 18 years
CAMPERS PER SESSION Approximately 50
STAFF PER SESSION 8-10
COUNSELLOR:CAMPER RATIO 1 to 5
BOYS OR GIRLS ☐ Boys only ☐ Girls only ☒ Co-ed
NOTES

NOVA SCOTIA

BIG COVE (A.D.D.) CAMP

SUMMER ADDRESS RR# 1

Thorburn NS
B0K 1W0 **SUMMER PHONE** 902-922-2224

WINTER ADDRESS

1565 South Park St.
Halifax NS
B3J 2L2 **WINTER PHONE** 902-423-9622

CONTACT PERSON Megan Jentz
ACCREDITATION CANS
AFFILIATION YM-YWCA
YEARS IN OPERATION 2
DATES OPEN 1 week in August
FEES $275 per one-week session.
SCHOLARSHIPS Please enquire.
ACCOMODATION Cabins, central wash-house & dining hall.
SPECIALTY Special Needs: Attention Deficit Disorder
OBJECTIVES To provide campers with a positive camping experience.

ACTIVITIES Swimming, nature crafts, canoeing, backpacking, outtrips, archery, kayaking, camp-wide games, campfires.

EVALUATIONS No
MEDICAL FACILITIES Nurse on site; 15 minutes to hospital.
VISITORS No
SPECIAL NEEDS FACILITIES Please enquire.
DESCRIPTION Located by the ocean on 1000 acres of forest, marsh and fields.

NEAREST CITY/TOWN New Glasgow
AGE SPREAD 7 to 17 years
CAMPERS PER SESSION 60
STAFF PER SESSION 35
COUNSELLOR:CAMPER RATIO 1 to 2 for ages 7-11 / 1 to 3 for ages 12 & up
BOYS OR GIRLS ☐ Boys only ☐ Girls only ☒ Co-ed
NOTES

BIG COVE CAMP

SUMMER ADDRESS	RR# 1		
	Thorburn		NS
	B0K 1W0	**SUMMER PHONE**	902-922-2224
WINTER ADDRESS			
	1565 South Park St.		
	Halifax		NS
	B3J 2L2	**WINTER PHONE**	902-423-9622

CONTACT PERSON Megan Jentz

ACCREDITATION CANS

AFFILIATION YM-YWCA

YEARS IN OPERATION 105 (This is the oldest camp in Canada)

DATES OPEN July through August

FEES $580 per 2-week session.

SCHOLARSHIPS Camperships are available, please enquire.

ACCOMODATION Cabins, central dining hall, central wash-house.

SPECIALTY Traditional

OBJECTIVES To provide children with opportunities for individual growth based on democratic small-group living.

ACTIVITIES Swimming, nature crafts, snorkeling, ocean canoe tripping, backpacking, outtrips, archery, kayaking, camp-wide games, campfires.

EVALUATIONS No

MEDICAL FACILITIES Nurse on site; 15 minutes to hospital.

VISITORS No

SPECIAL NEEDS FACILITIES Campers with special needs considered on individual basis.

DESCRIPTION Located by the ocean on 1000 acres of forest, marsh and fields.

NEAREST CITY/TOWN New Glasgow

AGE SPREAD 7 to 17 years

CAMPERS PER SESSION 112

STAFF PER SESSION 41

COUNSELLOR:CAMPER RATIO 1 to 4

BOYS OR GIRLS ☐ Boys only ☐ Girls only ☒ Co-ed

NOTES 15-17 year-olds participate in leadership development programs.

CAMP ATLANTIC

SUMMER ADDRESS Canadian Diabetes Association
6080 Young St., Suite 101
Halifax NS
B3L 5K2 **SUMMER PHONE** 902-453-4232

WINTER ADDRESS As above

WINTER PHONE

CONTACT PERSON Loren Abramson
ACCREDITATION CANS
AFFILIATION Canadian Diabetes Association
YEARS IN OPERATION 20
DATES OPEN 1 week in August.
FEES $125 per one-week session.
SCHOLARSHIPS Yes, please enquire
ACCOMODATION Cabins, central dining hall, recreation hall.
SPECIALTY Special Needs: Diabetes
OBJECTIVES To help children with diabetes learn to work with their disease by establishing confidence and security by meeting and interacting with other children with diabetes.
ACTIVITIES Soccer, volleyball, swimming, campcraft, canoeing, hiking, nature studies, overnights, arts & crafts, scavenger hunt, skits, sailboards, talent show.

EVALUATIONS No
MEDICAL FACILITIES Infirmary with medical staff.
VISITORS Not encouraged.
SPECIAL NEEDS FACILITIES Yes
DESCRIPTION A large wooded site with hiking trails and playing fields, located on the shore of Lake Fanning. This is the Camp Wopomeo site.
NEAREST CITY/TOWN Yarmouth.
AGE SPREAD 8 to 12 years
CAMPERS PER SESSION 56
STAFF PER SESSION 30
COUNSELLOR:CAMPER RATIO 1 to 4
BOYS OR GIRLS ☐ Boys only ☐ Girls only ☒ Co-ed
NOTES Junior and senior 4-day adventure camps are also offered by the Canadian Diabetes Association.

CAMP GOODTIME

SUMMER ADDRESS Canadian Cancer Society
5826 South St., Suite 1
Halifax NS
B3H 1S6 **SUMMER PHONE** 902-423-0222

WINTER ADDRESS As above

WINTER PHONE 1-800-639-0222

CONTACT PERSON Judy Pinkerton
ACCREDITATION CANS
AFFILIATION Canadian Cancer Society
YEARS IN OPERATION 10
DATES OPEN 1 week in August
FEES $50 per one-week session.
SCHOLARSHIPS Yes, please enquire.
ACCOMODATION Cabins, central dining hall, recreation hall.
SPECIALTY Special Needs: Cancer
OBJECTIVES To encourage the independence and self-confidence of children with cancer by providing them with a fun and active camp experience.
ACTIVITIES Swimming, canoeing, arts & crafts, drama, archery, hiking, basketball, tetherball, theme days, outtrips, campfires.

EVALUATIONS No
MEDICAL FACILITIES Yes, see below.
VISITORS No.
SPECIAL NEEDS FACILITIES Yes.
DESCRIPTION A large wooded site with hiking trails and playing fields, located on the shore of Lake Fanning.

NEAREST CITY/TOWN Yarmouth
AGE SPREAD 7 to 15 years
CAMPERS PER SESSION 100
STAFF PER SESSION 15-20
COUNSELLOR:CAMPER RATIO 1 to 5
BOYS OR GIRLS ☐ Boys only ☐ Girls only ☒ Co-ed
NOTES Infirmary with doctor, oncology nurse, RN, hemophilia nurse, pharmacist; hospital 30 minutes away.

CAMP KADIMAH

SUMMER ADDRESS Barss Corner

Lunenburg County NS
B0R 1A0 **SUMMER PHONE** 902-644-2313

WINTER ADDRESS 1515 South Park St., Suite 305

Halifax NS
B3J 2L2 **WINTER PHONE** 902-422-7491

CONTACT PERSON Atlantic Jewish Council
ACCREDITATION
AFFILIATION Atlantic Jewish Council
YEARS IN OPERATION 51
DATES OPEN July through August.
FEES $2450 for 6 weeks/$2640 for Counsellor-in-training session.
SCHOLARSHIPS Yes, please enquire.
ACCOMODATION Cabins, central dining hall & wash-house, gym, kosher food.
SPECIALTY Jewish Development
OBJECTIVES Provide children with the best camp experience; to be sensitive to the needs of the individual within a Jewish context.

ACTIVITIES Swimming, water skiing, arts & crafts, canoeing, archery, hiking, sailing, windsurfing, tennis, basketball, campfires. Counsellors-in-training also have outtrips to different cities.

EVALUATIONS No
MEDICAL FACILITIES Infirmary with doctor and nurse; hospital nearby.
VISITORS Allowed on visiting day.
SPECIAL NEEDS FACILITIES Unspecified.
DESCRIPTION Large wooded site with sports fields on Lake William.

NEAREST CITY/TOWN Bridgewater
AGE SPREAD 7 to 16 years
CAMPERS PER SESSION 230
STAFF PER SESSION 75-80
COUNSELLOR:CAMPER RATIO Included in above number.
BOYS OR GIRLS ☐ Boys only ☐ Girls only ☒ Co-ed

NOTES

CAMP TREASURE CHEST

SUMMER ADDRESS Lung Association
17 Alma Crescent
Halifax NS
B3N 3E6 **SUMMER PHONE** 902-443-8141

WINTER ADDRESS As above

WINTER PHONE

CONTACT PERSON Michael McDonald
ACCREDITATION
AFFILIATION Lung Association
YEARS IN OPERATION 6
DATES OPEN 1 week in August
FEES No cost to campers
SCHOLARSHIPS
ACCOMODATION Cabins, central dining hall, recreation hall.
SPECIALTY Special Needs: Asthma / Lung Disease
OBJECTIVES To provide a fun camp experience for children with asthma, and teach them that there are no limits to what they can do.

ACTIVITIES Swimming, canoeing, kayaking, asthma education, arts & crafts, camp-wide games, skit night, team-building, soccer, baseball, campfires.

EVALUATIONS Yes.
MEDICAL FACILITIES Infirmary with doctors, therapist, nurses, dietician.
VISITORS Visits can be arranged.
SPECIAL NEEDS FACILITIES Yes
DESCRIPTION Site for this year had not been chosen at print time; please enquire.

NEAREST CITY/TOWN See above.
AGE SPREAD 8 to 12 years
CAMPERS PER SESSION 80
STAFF PER SESSION 18 plus counsellors.
COUNSELLOR:CAMPER RATIO 1 to 6
BOYS OR GIRLS ☐ Boys only ☐ Girls only ☒ Co-ed
NOTES

CAMP WOPOMEO

SUMMER ADDRESS	YM-YWCA of Yarmouth P.O Box 86 Yarmouth NS B5A 4B1
SUMMER PHONE	902-761-2000
WINTER ADDRESS	As above
WINTER PHONE	902-742-7181
CONTACT PERSON	Krista Moore
ACCREDITATION	CANS
AFFILIATION	YW-YMCA
YEARS IN OPERATION	70+
DATES OPEN	July through August
FEES	$180 per one-week session.
SCHOLARSHIPS	Camperships are available; please enquire.
ACCOMODATION	Cabins, leaders' lodge, central dining hall, recreation hall.
SPECIALTY	Traditional
OBJECTIVES	To allow children to learn about the outdoors, make new friends and have fun.
ACTIVITIES	Swimming, canoeing, windsurfing, drama, outtrips, arts & crafts, archery, hiking, outdoor education, theme days, basketball, baseball, volleyball, campfires, camp-wide games.
EVALUATIONS	No
MEDICAL FACILITIES	Infirmary with nurse on site.
VISITORS	Yes, on Visitors Day.
SPECIAL NEEDS FACILITIES	Unspecified; please enquire.
DESCRIPTION	A large wooded site with hiking trails and playing fields located on Lake Fanning.
NEAREST CITY/TOWN	Yarmouth
AGE SPREAD	7 to 15 years
CAMPERS PER SESSION	80
STAFF PER SESSION	12
COUNSELLOR:CAMPER RATIO	1 to 5
BOYS OR GIRLS	☐ Boys only ☐ Girls only ☒ Co-ed
NOTES	

JUNIOR CHOIR CAMP

SUMMER ADDRESS Nova Scotia Choral Federation
1809 Barrington St., Suite 901
Halifax NS
B3J 3K8

SUMMER PHONE 902-423-4688

WINTER ADDRESS As above

WINTER PHONE

CONTACT PERSON Tim Cross

ACCREDITATION

AFFILIATION Nova Scotia Choral Federation

YEARS IN OPERATION 16

DATES OPEN 1 week in August.

FEES $230 per one-week session.

SCHOLARSHIPS Yes, please enquire.

ACCOMODATION Cabins, central washrooms, dining hall, rehearsal pavillion.

SPECIALTY Music: Choral Singing

OBJECTIVES To provide nourishment and encouragement to children who want to sing. No prior experience is necessary.

ACTIVITIES Rehearsal 3 times a day, art & drama classes, games, crafts, scavenger hunts, talent night, sing-songs.

EVALUATIONS Yes.

MEDICAL FACILITIES Nurse on site; 2 minutes to hospital.

VISITORS Not encouraged.

SPECIAL NEEDS FACILITIES Considered on individual basis.

DESCRIPTION Beautifully situated in a hemlock forest in Berwick.

NEAREST CITY/TOWN Berwick

AGE SPREAD 8 to 13 years

CAMPERS PER SESSION 90

STAFF PER SESSION 3

COUNSELLOR:CAMPER RATIO 1 to 5

BOYS OR GIRLS ☐ Boys only ☐ Girls only ☒ Co-ed

NOTES The same program is offered in July at a camp in Glace Bay.

PUGWASH

SUMMER ADDRESS National Camps for the Blind
RR #4, Gulf Shore Road
Pugwash NS
B0K 1L0 **SUMMER PHONE** 902-243-2097

WINTER ADDRESS As above

WINTER PHONE 519-369-6692

CONTACT PERSON Chris Risk
ACCREDITATION CCA, CCI
AFFILIATION Christian (nondenominational)
YEARS IN OPERATION 20
DATES OPEN One week in July
FEES Free to all legally blind persons aged 9 & up.
SCHOLARSHIPS
ACCOMODATION Cabins, showers, dining hall.
SPECIALTY Special Needs: Blind / Visually Impaired
OBJECTIVES To allow the blind participant to discover undeveloped potential, increase self-confidence, improve physical vigour, & develop an appreciation for God's love & care.
ACTIVITIES Archery, boating, camp council, canoeing, crafts, hiking, horseback riding, rock climbing, sailing, swimming, rappelling, waterskiing, campfires.

EVALUATIONS No
MEDICAL FACILITIES Infirmary with medical staff on duty 24 hours.
VISITORS Allowed on Talent Night.
SPECIAL NEEDS FACILITIES Yes
DESCRIPTION Please enquire for details.

NEAREST CITY/TOWN Amherst
AGE SPREAD 9 years & up.
CAMPERS PER SESSION 40
STAFF PER SESSION Varies
COUNSELLOR:CAMPER RATIO 1 to 2
BOYS OR GIRLS ☐ Boys only ☐ Girls only ☒ Co-ed
NOTES Special needs refers to blind or visually impaired campers. This program is designed to place emphasis on ability rather than the disability of the visually impaired individual.

SCHOLÉ

SUMMER ADDRESS	Forest Glen PO Box 10, RR #1 Margaree Valley B0E 2C0	**SUMMER PHONE**	NS 902-248-2601
WINTER ADDRESS	As above	**WINTER PHONE**	

CONTACT PERSON Lorna Green

ACCREDITATION

AFFILIATION Native American Lore Camp

YEARS IN OPERATION 8

DATES OPEN Mid-June through August

FEES NALC $250 per week; SW USA tours $1600 for 34 days.

SCHOLARSHIPS Yes

ACCOMODATION Tipis, outhouse, main log cabin.

SPECIALTY Environmental Studies and Native Culture

OBJECTIVES To teach co-operation among young people, promote friendships cross-Canada, teach respect & love for Mother Earth, & encourage craft skills related to earth & survival.

ACTIVITIES NALC: making bow & arrow, peace pipe, drum & rattle, and survival shelters, hide-tanning, tipi living, swimming, whale cruise, sweat lodge, tracking, fishing, camouflage.
SW Tour: Hiking, bike riding, camping, & sight seeing.

EVALUATIONS No

MEDICAL FACILITIES Staff trained in first aid & CPR (St. John's Ambulance).

VISITORS Allowed

SPECIAL NEEDS FACILITIES Unspecified

DESCRIPTION Located on beautiful Cape Breton Island, surrounded by the sea, inland mountains, river valleys, & highland bogs & barrens.

NEAREST CITY/TOWN Sydney

AGE SPREAD 8 to 16 years

CAMPERS PER SESSION NALC 10-12; SW Tour 6-8.

STAFF PER SESSION 3

COUNSELLOR:CAMPER RATIO 1 to 3

BOYS OR GIRLS ☐ Boys only ☐ Girls only ☒ Co-ed

NOTES SW Tour Activities: sight-seeing & visiting national parks & sites of Native American activities. Morning hike or bike, free time in afternoon, campfires each evening. A combination of the full summer programme (6 weeks) at the Native American Lore Camp & the Southwest Tour is available for a combined discounted price of $2700.

SCOTIAN GLEN CAMP

SUMMER ADDRESS RR#1

Thorburn NS
B0K 1W0 **SUMMER PHONE** 902-421-1717

WINTER ADDRESS Salvation Army
1329 Barrington St.
Halifax NS
B3J 1Y9 **WINTER PHONE** 902-421-1717

CONTACT PERSON Captain Wally Simpson
ACCREDITATION
AFFILIATION Salvation Army
YEARS IN OPERATION 60+
DATES OPEN June through mid-September
FEES $68-80 per 5-day session.
SCHOLARSHIPS Yes, please enquire.
ACCOMODATION Cabins, central dining hall, showers.
SPECIALTY Christian Development
OBJECTIVES To serve the spiritual, social and recreational needs of campers through creative experiences in co-operative group living in the natural setting of God's creation.
ACTIVITIES Swimming, canoeing, music, hiking, concerts, arts & crafts, Bible study, games, campfires.

EVALUATIONS Only for music camp.
MEDICAL FACILITIES Infirmary, nurse on site, 20 minutes to hospital.
VISITORS Yes
SPECIAL NEEDS FACILITIES Yes
DESCRIPTION 164 wooded acres of spacious grassland, nature trails through wooded areas on Sutherlands River, swimming pool.

NEAREST CITY/TOWN New Glasgow
AGE SPREAD 7 to 18 years
CAMPERS PER SESSION 60-120
STAFF PER SESSION 20
COUNSELLOR:CAMPER RATIO 1 to 4
BOYS OR GIRLS ☐ Boys only ☐ Girls only ☒ Co-ed
NOTES

SHERBROOKE LAKE CAMP

SUMMER ADDRESS	New Ross		
			NS
	B0J 2M0	**SUMMER PHONE**	902-644-2479
WINTER ADDRESS	P.O. Box 80		
	Coldbrook		NS
	B4R 1B6	**WINTER PHONE**	902-678-9829

CONTACT PERSON Stephen Franey
ACCREDITATION
AFFILIATION United Church
YEARS IN OPERATION 30
DATES OPEN July through August
FEES $85-95 per 6-day session.
SCHOLARSHIPS Please enquire
ACCOMODATION Cabins, latrines, dining hall.
SPECIALTY Traditional
OBJECTIVES To rejuvenate and instill in campers a respect and love for creation, the land and ecosystem around them.

ACTIVITIES Swimming, canoeing, windsurfing, archery, camp-wide games, crafts, hiking, river walks, treasure hunts, mini-Olympics, vespers, campfires.

EVALUATIONS No
MEDICAL FACILITIES Nurse on site
VISITORS Not encouraged.
SPECIAL NEEDS FACILITIES No
DESCRIPTION A lovely wooded setting with ball fields and 1000 feet of sandy beach.

NEAREST CITY/TOWN New Ross
AGE SPREAD 8 to 17 years
CAMPERS PER SESSION 60
STAFF PER SESSION 8
COUNSELLOR:CAMPER RATIO 1 to 4
BOYS OR GIRLS ☐ Boys only ☐ Girls only ☒ Co-ed
NOTES

YOUTH CHOIR CAMP

SUMMER ADDRESS Nova Scotia Choral Federation
1809 Barrington St., Suite 901
Halifax NS
B3J 3K8 **SUMMER PHONE** 902-423-4685

WINTER ADDRESS As above

WINTER PHONE

CONTACT PERSON Tim Cross
ACCREDITATION
AFFILIATION Nova Scotia Choral Federation
YEARS IN OPERATION 17
DATES OPEN 1 week in July.
FEES $275 per one-week session.
SCHOLARSHIPS Yes, please enquire.
ACCOMODATION Cabins, central washrooms, dining hall, rehearsal pavillion.
SPECIALTY Music: Choral Singing
OBJECTIVES To provide nourishment and encouragement to teens who want to sing. No prior experience is necessary.

ACTIVITIES Rehearsal 3 times a day, voice lessons, individual practice and free time.

EVALUATIONS Yes.
MEDICAL FACILITIES Nurse on site; 2 minutes to hospital.
VISITORS Not encouraged.
SPECIAL NEEDS FACILITIES Considered on individual basis.
DESCRIPTION Beautifully situated in a hemlock forest in Berwick.

NEAREST CITY/TOWN Berwick
AGE SPREAD 13 to 17 years
CAMPERS PER SESSION 50
STAFF PER SESSION 12
COUNSELLOR:CAMPER RATIO 1 to 5
BOYS OR GIRLS ☐ Boys only ☐ Girls only ☒ Co-ed
NOTES

ONTARIO

ARROWHEAD CAMP

SUMMER ADDRESS RR #1

Dwight ONT
P0A 1H0 **SUMMER PHONE** 705-635-1600

WINTER ADDRESS 115 Larkin Drive

Nepean ONT
K2J 1C2 **WINTER PHONE** 613-825-4426

CONTACT PERSON Pam Richardson
ACCREDITATION OCA
AFFILIATION None
YEARS IN OPERATION 22
DATES OPEN July to mid-August
FEES $850 per 2-week session.
SCHOLARSHIPS Please enquire.
ACCOMODATION Cabins equipped with washrooms, showers.
SPECIALTY Traditional
OBJECTIVES To provide a positive, fun, safe camping experience in a family atmosphere.

ACTIVITIES Waterskiing, swimming, sailing, windsufing, canoeing, archery, tennis.

EVALUATIONS No
MEDICAL FACILITIES Nurse on site; hospital 20 minutes away.
VISITORS Allowed for campers staying more than one session.
SPECIAL NEEDS FACILITIES Unspecified.
DESCRIPTION Please enquire for details.

NEAREST CITY/TOWN Huntsville
AGE SPREAD 6 to 16 years
CAMPERS PER SESSION 90
STAFF PER SESSION 32
COUNSELLOR:CAMPER RATIO 1 to 4
BOYS OR GIRLS ☐ Boys only ☐ Girls only ☒ Co-ed
NOTES

BARK LAKE LEADERSHIP CENTRE

SUMMER ADDRESS

Irondale ONT
K0M 1X0 **SUMMER PHONE** 1-800-668-6638

WINTER ADDRESS As above

WINTER PHONE

CONTACT PERSON Rob Heming
ACCREDITATION OCA, CCA
AFFILIATION Ontario Ministry of Culture, Tourism and Recreation
YEARS IN OPERATION 45
DATES OPEN Late June through August
FEES From $210 per 1-week session to $360 per 2-week session.
SCHOLARSHIPS Please enquire.
ACCOMODATION Shared occupancy accomodation, modern dining hall.
SPECIALTY Leadership Development
OBJECTIVES To improve the community, outdoor, recreation, tourism & environmental leadership base by providing accessible, individual, & collaborative educational & training initiatives.
ACTIVITIES Canoeing, swimming, kayaking, snorkeling, archery, crafts, hiking, table tennis, horseshoes, ropes & walls course, orienteering.

EVALUATIONS No
MEDICAL FACILITIES Staff have first aid certificates; hospital 40 km away.
VISITORS No
SPECIAL NEEDS FACILITIES Unspecified
DESCRIPTION Set in the hills & sparkling lakes of the Haliburton Highlands, specifically on Bark Lake, on a 2500-hectare wilderness reserve.
NEAREST CITY/TOWN Haliburton
AGE SPREAD 15 to 24 years
CAMPERS PER SESSION Unspecified; please enquire.
STAFF PER SESSION Unspecified; please enquire.
COUNSELLOR:CAMPER RATIO Unspecified; please enquire.
BOYS OR GIRLS ☐ Boys only ☐ Girls only ☒ Co-ed
NOTES

BLUE MOUNTAIN CAMP

SUMMER ADDRESS	RR #3 Collingwood ONT L9Y 3Z2
SUMMER PHONE	705-445-3941
WINTER ADDRESS	Easter Seals Society 250 Ferrand Drive, Suite #200 Don Mills ONT M3C 3P2
WINTER PHONE	416-421-8377
CONTACT PERSON	Mark Sack
ACCREDITATION	OCA, CCA
AFFILIATION	Easter Seals Society
YEARS IN OPERATION	59
DATES OPEN	July through August
FEES	$925 per one-week session.
SCHOLARSHIPS	Yes; assistance available on request.
ACCOMODATION	Cabins with showers, dining hall, recreation hall.
SPECIALTY	Special Needs: Physical Disabilities
OBJECTIVES	To provide oportunities & challenges for campers to develop independence, build self-esteem & develop creative expression skills.
ACTIVITIES	Astronomy, horseback riding, campcraft, music, drama, canoeing, sailing, swimming, computers, archery, fishing, sports.
EVALUATIONS	Yes
MEDICAL FACILITIES	3 nurses on staff; hospital nearby.
VISITORS	Not encouraged
SPECIAL NEEDS FACILITIES	Yes
DESCRIPTION	Waterfront location with wooded nature trails.
NEAREST CITY/TOWN	Barrie
AGE SPREAD	7 to 19 years
CAMPERS PER SESSION	72
STAFF PER SESSION	Maximum 50
COUNSELLOR:CAMPER RATIO	1 to 2
BOYS OR GIRLS	☐ Boys only ☐ Girls only ☒ Co-ed
NOTES	One of 5 Ontario Easter Seal Camps dedicated to offering warm, accessible environments & camping fun to physically disabled young people. Family camping is also an option.

CAMP AKOMAK

SUMMER ADDRESS

Ahmic Harbour ONT
P0A 1A0 **SUMMER PHONE** 705-387-3810

WINTER ADDRESS 3631 Mandarin Woods Drive N.

Jacksonville Florida
32223 **WINTER PHONE** 1-800-368-4152

CONTACT PERSON Carl Williams
ACCREDITATION OCA
AFFILIATION None
YEARS IN OPERATION 66
DATES OPEN July through August
FEES $1750 per 28-day session; $2450 per 49-day session.
SCHOLARSHIPS No
ACCOMODATION Cabins, showers, dining hall.
SPECIALTY Swimming
OBJECTIVES To develop campers as athletes & as people, to help them grow in self-esteem & learn techniques for success that will last a lifetime.
ACTIVITIES Swimming, canoeing, kayaking, tennis, golf, softball, soccer, basketball, lacrosse, field hockey, volleyball, track & field, numerous other sports.

EVALUATIONS No
MEDICAL FACILITIES Nurse on duty at all times.
VISITORS Allowed
SPECIAL NEEDS FACILITIES No
DESCRIPTION A beautiful, wooded setting on Ahmic Lake, surrounded by rivers, lakes, waterfalls & hiking trails.

NEAREST CITY/TOWN Parry Sound
AGE SPREAD 8 to 17 years
CAMPERS PER SESSION Unspecified; please enquire.
STAFF PER SESSION Unspecified; please enquire.
COUNSELLOR:CAMPER RATIO Unspecified; please enquire.
BOYS OR GIRLS ☐ Boys only ☒ Girls only ☐ Co-ed
NOTES The camp offers an all-sports program for overall fitness as well as the competitive swimming program.

CAMP ALLSAW

SUMMER ADDRESS	P.O. Box 75 RR #2 Haliburton K0M 1S0	**SUMMER PHONE**	ONT 705-457-1738
WINTER ADDRESS	9 Calais Ave. Downsview M3M 1N3	**WINTER PHONE**	ONT 416-766-4204

CONTACT PERSON Kate Moore
ACCREDITATION OCA
AFFILIATION None
YEARS IN OPERATION 32
DATES OPEN July
FEES $650 - $700 per 2-week session.
SCHOLARSHIPS Please enquire.
ACCOMODATION Cabins, platform tents, wash-houses, showers, rec hall.
SPECIALTY Traditional
OBJECTIVES To develop self-esteem in each camper, foster a positive attitude towards health, physical fitness, ethics & morality, and an awareness of the environment.
ACTIVITIES Archery, drama, fitness, campcraft, windsurfing, kayaking, swimming, canoeing, arts & crafts, ecology & conservation, ropes course.

EVALUATIONS No
MEDICAL FACILITIES Health centre with nurse on site.
VISITORS Not allowed
SPECIAL NEEDS FACILITIES Unspecified
DESCRIPTION Located in the Haliburton Highlands on Soyers Lake, offering 119 acres of land with a varied landscape, eco-centre, & organic gardens.
NEAREST CITY/TOWN Haliburton
AGE SPREAD 7 to 16 years
CAMPERS PER SESSION 75
STAFF PER SESSION 25
COUNSELLOR:CAMPER RATIO 1 to 4
BOYS OR GIRLS ☐ Boys only ☐ Girls only ☒ Co-ed
NOTES

CAMP AROWHON

SUMMER ADDRESS	
	Algonquin Park ONT
	P0A 1B0 **SUMMER PHONE** 705-633-5651
WINTER ADDRESS	72 Lyndhurst Ave.
	Toronto ONT
	M5R 2Z7 **WINTER PHONE** 416-975-9060
CONTACT PERSON	Joanne Kates
ACCREDITATION	OCA, American Camping Association
AFFILIATION	None
YEARS IN OPERATION	61
DATES OPEN	July through August
FEES	$1550 - $4000 per session.
SCHOLARSHIPS	Please enquire.
ACCOMODATION	Cabins with indoor plumbing, dining hall.
SPECIALTY	Sports
OBJECTIVES	To simultaneously nurture & challenge children by offering intense teaching as well as close individual attention to each camper.
ACTIVITIES	Tennis, drama, arts & crafts, hiking, windsurfing, archery, sports, sailing, canoeing, horseback riding, & swimming (compulsory).
EVALUATIONS	Yes
MEDICAL FACILITIES	Infirmary with doctor & 2 nurses on site.
VISITORS	Allowed
SPECIAL NEEDS FACILITIES	See Notes below.
DESCRIPTION	Situated on a private lake in the Algonquin Park wilderness.
NEAREST CITY/TOWN	Huntsville
AGE SPREAD	7 to 16 years
CAMPERS PER SESSION	215
STAFF PER SESSION	85
COUNSELLOR:CAMPER RATIO	1 to 4
BOYS OR GIRLS	☐ Boys only ☐ Girls only ☒ Co-ed
NOTES	There are no special facilities, but special needs campers can be integrated into the camp.

CAMP AWAKENING (BOYS)

SUMMER ADDRESS c/o Kilcoo Camp

Minden ONT
K0M 2K0 **SUMMER PHONE** 705-286-1091

WINTER ADDRESS 150 Eglinton Avenue E
Suite #204
Toronto ONT
M4P1E8 **WINTER PHONE** 416-487-8400

CONTACT PERSON Melinda Evans
ACCREDITATION OCA
AFFILIATION None
YEARS IN OPERATION 12
DATES OPEN July through August
FEES $945 per 2-week session.
SCHOLARSHIPS Yes
ACCOMODATION Cabins with washroooms modified for physical disabilities.
SPECIALTY Special Needs: Physical Disabilities
OBJECTIVES To enable teenage boys with physical disabilities to discover their strengths & abilities.

ACTIVITIES Canoe tripping, swimming, kayaking, sailing, windsurfing, archery, crafts, riding, riflery, sports.

EVALUATIONS Yes
MEDICAL FACILITIES Doctor & nurse on site.
VISITORS Not allowed
SPECIAL NEEDS FACILITIES Yes
DESCRIPTION Located in the Haliburton Highlands.

NEAREST CITY/TOWN Haliburton
AGE SPREAD 12 to 18 years
CAMPERS PER SESSION 14
STAFF PER SESSION 70 (regular staff of Kilcoo Camp)
COUNSELLOR:CAMPER RATIO 1 to 2
BOYS OR GIRLS ☒ Boys only ☐ Girls only ☐ Co-ed

NOTES This camp operates in conjunction with the Kilcoo Camp program for able-bodied boys. See next page for the girls' camp.

CAMP AWAKENING (GIRLS)

SUMMER ADDRESS c/o Camp Gay Venture

Haliburton ONT
K0M 1S0 **SUMMER PHONE** 705-286-1799

WINTER ADDRESS

87 Inglewood Drive
Toronto ONT
M4T 1H4 **WINTER PHONE** 416-487-8400

CONTACT PERSON Melinda Evans
ACCREDITATION OCA
AFFILIATION None
YEARS IN OPERATION 6
DATES OPEN July to August
FEES $945 per 2-week session.
SCHOLARSHIPS Yes
ACCOMODATION Cabins with washroooms modified for physical disabilities.
SPECIALTY Special Needs: Physical Disabilities
OBJECTIVES To enable teenage girls with physical disabilities to discover their strengths & abilities.

ACTIVITIES Swimming, canoeing, sailing, drama, pottery, horseback riding, kayaking, crafts, environmental education.

EVALUATIONS Yes
MEDICAL FACILITIES Infirmary with 2 nurses on site.
VISITORS Not allowed.
SPECIAL NEEDS FACILITIES Yes
DESCRIPTION Please enquire for details.

NEAREST CITY/TOWN Haliburton
AGE SPREAD 12 to 18 years
CAMPERS PER SESSION 14
STAFF PER SESSION 70 (regular staff of Camp Gay Venture)
COUNSELLOR:CAMPER RATIO 1 to 2
BOYS OR GIRLS ☐ Boys only ☒ Girls only ☐ Co-ed
NOTES This camp operates in conjunction with the Camp Gay Venture program for able-bodied girls. See previous page for the boys' camp.

CAMP BIG CANOE

SUMMER ADDRESS	R.R. #5		
	Bracebridge		ONT
	P1L 1X3	**SUMMER PHONE**	705-645-4963
WINTER ADDRESS	31 Blake Street		
	Stouffville		ONT
	L4A 4H7	**WINTER PHONE**	905-640-2638

CONTACT PERSON Barbara Hendren
ACCREDITATION OCA
AFFILIATION United Church
YEARS IN OPERATION 28
DATES OPEN July through August
FEES $517 per 12-day session; please enquire for further rates.
SCHOLARSHIPS Yes
ACCOMODATION Raised tents, cabins, showers, dining & recreation lodge.
SPECIALTY Christian Development
OBJECTIVES To allow campers to experience the challenges & rewards of outdoor living & appreciate the natural environment. Also to promote physical, intellectual & spiritual development.
ACTIVITIES Environmental awareness, swimming, kayaking, earth studies, archery, outtripping, canoeing, crafts, volleyball, hiking, campfires, sing-songs, vespers, worship.

EVALUATIONS General assessment letter & certificates of skill attainment.
MEDICAL FACILITIES Nurse on site; doctor on call.
VISITORS Not encouraged
SPECIAL NEEDS FACILITIES See Notes below.
DESCRIPTION A 225-acre wooded site surrounding Hart Lake in the Muskoka District.

NEAREST CITY/TOWN Richmond Hill
AGE SPREAD 6 to 15 years
CAMPERS PER SESSION 72
STAFF PER SESSION 25
COUNSELLOR:CAMPER RATIO 1 to 5
BOYS OR GIRLS ☐ Boys only ☐ Girls only ☒ Co-ed
NOTES No special needs facilities, but able to integrate special needs campers.

CAMP CHERITH

SUMMER ADDRESS PO Box 142

Walkerton ONT
N0G 2V0 **SUMMER PHONE** 519-881-2448

WINTER ADDRESS 1282 Radom Street

Pickering ONT
L1W 1J4 **WINTER PHONE** 905-831-9293

CONTACT PERSON Anne Worts
ACCREDITATION OCA, CCI
AFFILIATION Christian (nondenominational)
YEARS IN OPERATION 42
DATES OPEN June through August
FEES $199 per one-week session.
SCHOLARSHIPS No
ACCOMODATION Cabins, flush toilets, showers, dining hall, recreation hall.
SPECIALTY Christian Development
OBJECTIVES To help boys & girls find Christ by developing the whole person.

ACTIVITIES Archery, riflery, crafts, music, drama, swimming, canoeing, kayaking, rowing, orienteering, horsemanship, outdoor cookery, sports, Bible exploration, campfires.

EVALUATIONS No
MEDICAL FACILITIES Medical centre with nurse on site.
VISITORS Allowed on Saturdays.
SPECIAL NEEDS FACILITIES Unspecified
DESCRIPTION Please enquire for details.

NEAREST CITY/TOWN Owen Sound
AGE SPREAD 5 to 17 years
CAMPERS PER SESSION 98
STAFF PER SESSION 35
COUNSELLOR:CAMPER RATIO 1 to 7
BOYS OR GIRLS ☐ Boys only ☒ Girls only ☒ Co-ed

NOTES

CAMP EKON

SUMMER ADDRESS RR #1

Rosseau ONT
P0C 1J0 **SUMMER PHONE** 705-732-2222

WINTER ADDRESS 1190 Danforth Avenue

Toronto ONT
M4J 1M6 **WINTER PHONE** 416-778-1505

CONTACT PERSON Gordon Rixon
ACCREDITATION OCA, CCA
AFFILIATION Catholic Church
YEARS IN OPERATION 24
DATES OPEN July through August
FEES $270 - $1020 per 2-4 week session.
SCHOLARSHIPS Yes
ACCOMODATION Cabins for 8-13 yrs; platform tents for older campers.
SPECIALTY Traditional
OBJECTIVES To foster holistic growth in a recreational environment.

ACTIVITIES Sailing, windsurfing, Red Cross training, canoeing, kayaking, drama, crafts, campfires, tripping, optional daily mass, literature program, swimming.

EVALUATIONS No
MEDICAL FACILITIES Dispensary with staff nurse; doctor on call.
VISITORS Allowed
SPECIAL NEEDS FACILITIES Yes
DESCRIPTION Please enquire for details.

NEAREST CITY/TOWN Parry Sound
AGE SPREAD 8 to 17 years
CAMPERS PER SESSION 85
STAFF PER SESSION 40
COUNSELLOR:CAMPER RATIO 1 to 2
BOYS OR GIRLS ☒ Boys only ☒ Girls only ☐ Co-ed
NOTES Special needs refers to limited wheelchair accessibility.

CAMP GAY VENTURE

SUMMER ADDRESS			
	Haliburton		ONT
	K0M 1S0	**SUMMER PHONE**	705-286-1799
WINTER ADDRESS	87 Inglewood Drive		
	Toronto		ONT
	M4T 1H4	**WINTER PHONE**	416-481-7322

CONTACT PERSON Janet Adamson
ACCREDITATION OCA
AFFILIATION None
YEARS IN OPERATION 49
DATES OPEN July through August
FEES $1930 per 4-week session; $980 per 2-week session.
SCHOLARSHIPS No
ACCOMODATION Cabins, showers, main dining hall.
SPECIALTY Traditional
OBJECTIVES Development of the individual through leisure skill development & friendships.

ACTIVITIES Swimming, canoeing, waterskiing, sailing, windsurfing, tennis, drama , pottery, horseback riding, land sports, tripping, environmental awareness, kayaking, ropes course, crafts.

EVALUATIONS Yes
MEDICAL FACILITIES Infirmary with 2 nurses on site.
VISITORS Allowed
SPECIAL NEEDS FACILITIES Yes
DESCRIPTION Please enquire for details.

NEAREST CITY/TOWN Haliburton
AGE SPREAD 7 to 15 years
CAMPERS PER SESSION 150
STAFF PER SESSION 70
COUNSELLOR:CAMPER RATIO 1 to 5
BOYS OR GIRLS ☐ Boys only ☒ Girls only ☐ Co-ed
NOTES Special needs campers welcome.

CAMP HOLLYBURN

SUMMER ADDRESS PO Box 99

Rosseau ONT
P0C 1J0 **SUMMER PHONE** 705-732-4389

WINTER ADDRESS As above

WINTER PHONE 705-645-2074

CONTACT PERSON Mr. & Mrs. Ted Yard
ACCREDITATION OCA, CCA
AFFILIATION None
YEARS IN OPERATION 28
DATES OPEN July through August
FEES $450 - $2000 per 1-5 week session.
SCHOLARSHIPS Please enquire.
ACCOMODATION Cabins, central shower & toilet facilities.
SPECIALTY Traditional
OBJECTIVES To focus on social & physical skill development, personal achievement & developing an appreciation for nature & outdoor living.
ACTIVITIES Canoeing, rowing, lifesaving training, tennis, wood craft, orienteering, hiking, arts & crafts, games, campfires, leadership training, swimming, sailing, kayaking, archery.

EVALUATIONS No
MEDICAL FACILITIES Nurse on staff & doctor on call.
VISITORS Not encouraged
SPECIAL NEEDS FACILITIES Unspecified
DESCRIPTION 400 acres including the clear, warm waters of Tiley Lake, in the heart of Muskoka.

NEAREST CITY/TOWN Huntsville
AGE SPREAD 7 to 15 years
CAMPERS PER SESSION 110
STAFF PER SESSION 50
COUNSELLOR:CAMPER RATIO 1 to 3
BOYS OR GIRLS ☐ Boys only ☐ Girls only ☒ Co-ed
NOTES Offers a canoe trip for ages 16 & up; please enquire.

CAMP IAWAH

SUMMER ADDRESS	RR #2		
	Godfrey		ONT
	K0H 1T0	**SUMMER PHONE**	613-273-5621
WINTER ADDRESS	As above		
		WINTER PHONE	
CONTACT PERSON	A. Doornekamp		
ACCREDITATION	OCA, CCA		
AFFILIATION	None		
YEARS IN OPERATION	39		
DATES OPEN	July through August		
FEES	Unspecified; please enquire.		
SCHOLARSHIPS	Yes		
ACCOMODATION	Cabins, central washroom & showers, recreation hall.		
SPECIALTY	Christian Development		
OBJECTIVES	To present Jesus Christ as "The Way, The Truth, & The Life". Also to exemplify Christian principles & to promote a holistic outdoor experience for campers.		
ACTIVITIES	Swimming, sailing, boating, waterskiing, soccer, volleyball, basketball, orienteering, hiking, survival training, ecological studies, handcrafts, campfires.		
EVALUATIONS	No		
MEDICAL FACILITIES	Infirmary with nurse on site.		
VISITORS	Allowed on Visitors Day.		
SPECIAL NEEDS FACILITIES	Unspecified		
DESCRIPTION	A 205-acre site with 2.5 km of shoreline.		
NEAREST CITY/TOWN	Kingston		
AGE SPREAD	7 to 15 years		
CAMPERS PER SESSION	100		
STAFF PER SESSION	40		
COUNSELLOR:CAMPER RATIO	1 to 3		
BOYS OR GIRLS	☒ Boys only ☒ Girls only ☒ Co-ed		
NOTES	Family camp is an option.		

CAMP KAHQUAH

SUMMER ADDRESS RR #1

Magnetawan ONT
P0A 1P0 **SUMMER PHONE** 705-387-3923

WINTER ADDRESS As above

ONT
WINTER PHONE

CONTACT PERSON Phillip Miller
ACCREDITATION OCA, CCI
AFFILIATION None
YEARS IN OPERATION 32
DATES OPEN July through Labour Day
FEES Unspecified; please enquire.
SCHOLARSHIPS
ACCOMODATION Cabins, communal showers, toilets, dining facilities, rec hall.
SPECIALTY Christian Development
OBJECTIVES To provide an experience that will foster the spiritual, social, physical, & educational development of children & teens, emphasizing God's plan for each individual's life.
ACTIVITIES Swimming, waterskiing, windsurfing, canoeing, worship, Bible studies, music, drama, hiking, campfires.

EVALUATIONS No
MEDICAL FACILITIES Nurse on duty.
VISITORS Allowed
SPECIAL NEEDS FACILITIES Yes
DESCRIPTION Overlooking Ahmic Lake, near Magnetawan. The camp is situated among birch, maple & pine trees.

NEAREST CITY/TOWN Hamilton
AGE SPREAD 8 to 19 years
CAMPERS PER SESSION 85
STAFF PER SESSION 35-40
COUNSELLOR:CAMPER RATIO 1 to 6
BOYS OR GIRLS ☐ Boys only ☐ Girls only ☒ Co-ed
NOTES Special needs refers to accomodation of mentally challenged campers.

CAMP KAKEKA

SUMMER ADDRESS	PO Box 436		
	Haliburton		ONT
	K0M 1S0	**SUMMER PHONE**	
WINTER ADDRESS	PO Box 5099, Station LCD 1		
	Burlington		ONT
	L7R 3Y8	**WINTER PHONE**	905-319-0789

CONTACT PERSON John Miller
ACCREDITATION OCA, CCA
AFFILIATION None
YEARS IN OPERATION 44
DATES OPEN July through August
FEES Approximately $240 - $455 per 1-2 week session.
SCHOLARSHIPS No
ACCOMODATION Cabins, tents, central washroom, dining hall, large games room.
SPECIALTY Christian Development
OBJECTIVES To focus on skill development & leadership training through a well-rounded program where staff & campers are challenged to live consistent, dedicated Christian lives.
ACTIVITIES Archery, Bible study, campfires, canoeing, nature lore, swimming, sports, water activities.

EVALUATIONS No, but achievement awards are given.
MEDICAL FACILITIES Infirmary with nurse on site.
VISITORS Not encouraged
SPECIAL NEEDS FACILITIES Yes
DESCRIPTION Located on 207 acres of woodland & shoreline situated on Basshaunt Lake.

NEAREST CITY/TOWN Haliburton
AGE SPREAD 8 to 18 years
CAMPERS PER SESSION 130
STAFF PER SESSION 40
COUNSELLOR:CAMPER RATIO 1 to 7
BOYS OR GIRLS ☒ Boys only ☐ Girls only ☐ Co-ed
NOTES Limited facilities for special needs campers; please enquire. Father & son weekends are offered; please enquire.

CAMP KAWARTHA

SUMMER ADDRESS RR #4

Lakefield ONT
K0L 2H0 **SUMMER PHONE** 705-652-3860

WINTER ADDRESS As above

WINTER PHONE

CONTACT PERSON Rudy Massimo
ACCREDITATION OCA
AFFILIATION None
YEARS IN OPERATION 73
DATES OPEN July through August
FEES $380 per 1-week session; $650 per 2-week session.
SCHOLARSHIPS Subsidies are available.
ACCOMODATION Cabins, washrooms & showers, main dining hall.
SPECIALTY Traditional
OBJECTIVES To emphasize individual development in recreational leadership, social interaction & personal values, and to encourage awareness & appreciation of the environment.
ACTIVITIES Archery, arts & crafts, drama, eco-skills, land sports, canoeing, sailing, swimming, windsurfing, kayaking, camp fires.

EVALUATIONS Issued upon request.
MEDICAL FACILITIES Infirmary with nurse on site; doctor on call.
VISITORS Allowed during Open House days.
SPECIAL NEEDS FACILITIES Unspecified
DESCRIPTION Located on the south shore of Clear Lake on 180 acres of land with wooded & open areas.

NEAREST CITY/TOWN Peterborough
AGE SPREAD 8 to 16 years
CAMPERS PER SESSION 78
STAFF PER SESSION 28
COUNSELLOR:CAMPER RATIO 1 to 5
BOYS OR GIRLS ☐ Boys only ☐ Girls only ☒ Co-ed
NOTES

CAMP KEEWAYTAN

SUMMER ADDRESS RR #3

Wellandport ONT
L0R 2J0 **SUMMER PHONE** 416-386-6205

WINTER ADDRESS As above

WINTER PHONE

CONTACT PERSON Diane Wiber
ACCREDITATION OCA
AFFILIATION Creative Centre for Learning & Development
YEARS IN OPERATION 21
DATES OPEN July through August
FEES Approximately $1350 per 26-day session.
SCHOLARSHIPS No
ACCOMODATION Dorm rooms with washrooms, showers, dining hall, gym.
SPECIALTY Special Needs: Learning Disabilities
OBJECTIVES To provide positive experiences to children with particular difficulties; to improve campers' self-confidence & self-esteem.

ACTIVITIES Remedial, arts & crafts, woodworking, rhythmics, drama, music, canoeing, swimming, life skills.

EVALUATIONS Yes; with a focus on identified areas of improvement.
MEDICAL FACILITIES Nurse on premises; hospital 15 km away.
VISITORS Not allowed
SPECIAL NEEDS FACILITIES Yes
DESCRIPTION Please enquire for details.

NEAREST CITY/TOWN Welland
AGE SPREAD 7 to 17 years
CAMPERS PER SESSION 50-60
STAFF PER SESSION 27
COUNSELLOR:CAMPER RATIO 1 to 3
BOYS OR GIRLS ☐ Boys only ☐ Girls only ☒ Co-ed
NOTES Special needs refers to education & remedial for children with learning disabilities, hyperactivity, & Praeder Willi Syndrome. Not wheelchair accessible.

CAMP KENNEBEC

SUMMER ADDRESS	RR #2		
	Arden		ONT
	K0H 1B0	**SUMMER PHONE**	613-335-2114
WINTER ADDRESS	As above		
		WINTER PHONE	

CONTACT PERSON Steve Hannon
ACCREDITATION OCA
AFFILIATION None
YEARS IN OPERATION 29
DATES OPEN July through August
FEES $2175 - $4275 per session
SCHOLARSHIPS Yes
ACCOMODATION Cabins, showers, dining hall.
SPECIALTY Special Needs: Learning Disabilities
OBJECTIVES For children with learning disabilities to gain self esteem & improve their academic abilities.

ACTIVITIES Academic tutoring by teaching staff, computers, water sports, band, archery, riflery, rocketry, photography, drama, sports, hiking, tripping.

EVALUATIONS Yes
MEDICAL FACILITIES Infirmary with a doctor & nurse.
VISITORS Allowed on Visitors Day (one per session).
SPECIAL NEEDS FACILITIES Yes
DESCRIPTION Please enquire for details.

NEAREST CITY/TOWN Kingston
AGE SPREAD 6 to 18 years
CAMPERS PER SESSION 120
STAFF PER SESSION 80
COUNSELLOR:CAMPER RATIO 1 to 2
BOYS OR GIRLS ☐ Boys only ☐ Girls only ☒ Co-ed
NOTES Special needs refers to children with learning disabilities. General campers are also accepted.

CAMP KINTAIL

SUMMER ADDRESS	RR #3		
	Goderich		ONT
	N7A 3X9	**SUMMER PHONE**	519-529-7317
WINTER ADDRESS	Box 2418		
	Exeter		ONT
	N0M 1S7	**WINTER PHONE**	519-235-3701

CONTACT PERSON Gwen Brown
ACCREDITATION OCA
AFFILIATION Presbyterian Church
YEARS IN OPERATION 65
DATES OPEN Late June through Labour Day
FEES $206 per 7-day session; $260 per 10-day session.
SCHOLARSHIPS Yes
ACCOMODATION Cabins, showers in the main lodge.
SPECIALTY Christian Development
OBJECTIVES To challenge & develop campers physically, mentally, spiritually, emotionally & socially.

ACTIVITIES Swimming, canoeing, Bible discovery, choir, arts & crafts, nature study, campfires.

EVALUATIONS No
MEDICAL FACILITIES New health care centre on site.
VISITORS Allowed
SPECIAL NEEDS FACILITIES Yes
DESCRIPTION Please enquire for details.

NEAREST CITY/TOWN Goderich
AGE SPREAD 5 to 16 years
CAMPERS PER SESSION 72
STAFF PER SESSION 17
COUNSELLOR:CAMPER RATIO 1 to 4
BOYS OR GIRLS ☐ Boys only ☐ Girls only ☒ Co-ed
NOTES Special needs facilities refers to wheelchair accessibility.

CAMP KITCHIKEWANA

SUMMER ADDRESS

Honey Harbour ONT
P0E 1E0 **SUMMER PHONE**

WINTER ADDRESS c/o Midland YMCA
Box 488
Midland ONT
L4R 4L3 **WINTER PHONE** 705-526-7828

CONTACT PERSON Krystie Elsdon
ACCREDITATION OCA
AFFILIATION YM-YWCA
YEARS IN OPERATION 75
DATES OPEN Late June through August
FEES $352 per one-week session; $705 per 2-week session.
SCHOLARSHIPS Yes; sponsorship is available.
ACCOMODATION Cabins, showers, dining hall, recreation halls, craftshop.
SPECIALTY Traditional
OBJECTIVES To offer safe & educational experiences encouraging fun & a healthy lifestyle through outdoor skills & activities, recognizing interdependence & celebrating individuality.
ACTIVITIES Swimming, water sports, land sports, drama, environmental education, crafts, outtripping.

EVALUATIONS Yes
MEDICAL FACILITIES Doctor or nurse on duty.
VISITORS Allowed with prior arrangements.
SPECIAL NEEDS FACILITIES Yes
DESCRIPTION Located on Beausoleil Island, in the Georgian Bay Islands National Park, with lots of trees & sandy beaches.

NEAREST CITY/TOWN Toronto
AGE SPREAD 7 to 15 years
CAMPERS PER SESSION 158
STAFF PER SESSION 60
COUNSELLOR:CAMPER RATIO 1 to 4
BOYS OR GIRLS ☐ Boys only ☐ Girls only ☒ Co-ed
NOTES The one-week sessions are introductory camps for children aged 7-10; two-week programs are for those 8-15 yrs. Learning disabled campers can be accommodated. Family camping is an option.

CAMP KWASIND

SUMMER ADDRESS	RR #1		
	Utterson		ONT
	P0B 1M0	**SUMMER PHONE**	705-769-3751
WINTER ADDRESS	103 Yorkview Drive		
	North York		ONT
	M2R 1J9	**WINTER PHONE**	416-512-0760

CONTACT PERSON Susan Murphy
ACCREDITATION OCA
AFFILIATION Baptist
YEARS IN OPERATION 50
DATES OPEN Late June through early September
FEES $124 - $224 per week; please enquire.
SCHOLARSHIPS No
ACCOMODATION Cabins, showers, main dining lodge.
SPECIALTY Christian Development
OBJECTIVES To help people to nurture their faith & find God in a natural setting. To lead people in the Christian way of living.

ACTIVITIES Land & water sports, music, crafts, swimming, canoe trips, Bible & nature study, campfires.

EVALUATIONS No
MEDICAL FACILITIES Medical centre with nurse or doctor attending.
VISITORS Allowed on change-over days.
SPECIAL NEEDS FACILITIES Unspecified
DESCRIPTION Located on a picturesque bay on Skeleton Lake in the Muskoka District, just north of Bracebridge.

NEAREST CITY/TOWN Bracebridge
AGE SPREAD 7 to 19 years
CAMPERS PER SESSION 100
STAFF PER SESSION 30-35
COUNSELLOR:CAMPER RATIO 1 to 8
BOYS OR GIRLS ☐ Boys only ☐ Girls only ☒ Co-ed
NOTES Year-round camping is available for church-affiliated & outside groups holding meetings & retreats both during the week & on weekends from mid-September through June. Family camping is an option.

CAMP MEDEBA

SUMMER ADDRESS

West Guilford ONT
K0M 2S0 **SUMMER PHONE** 1-800-461-6523

WINTER ADDRESS As above

ONT
WINTER PHONE

CONTACT PERSON Bruce Dunning
ACCREDITATION OCA
AFFILIATION Christian (nondenominational)
YEARS IN OPERATION 44
DATES OPEN July through early September
FEES $270 per one-week session.
SCHOLARSHIPS Available for needy families.
ACCOMODATION Cabins, washrooms with showers & toilets, main lodge.
SPECIALTY Traditional
OBJECTIVES To help youth develop self-esteem & grow into "whole" people.

ACTIVITIES Swimming, full range of water & boating skills, fishing, archery, riflery, hiking, team sports & games, arts & crafts, singing, Bible studies, nature studies, drama, campfire.

EVALUATIONS Yes; for some activities.
MEDICAL FACILITIES First aid station with nurse on site; hospital 10 minutes away.
VISITORS Allowed; calls on toll free number listed above.
SPECIAL NEEDS FACILITIES Yes
DESCRIPTION Located in the heart of the Haliburton Highlands on 78 acres of woodland with a large sandy beach waterfront.

NEAREST CITY/TOWN Toronto
AGE SPREAD 6 years & up
CAMPERS PER SESSION 86
STAFF PER SESSION 35-40
COUNSELLOR:CAMPER RATIO 1 to 5
BOYS OR GIRLS ☐ Boys only ☐ Girls only ☒ Co-ed
NOTES The camp has a co-operative program with Camp Horizons for developmentally disabled children.

CAMP MI-A-KON-DA

SUMMER ADDRESS	RR #2
	Dunchurch ONT
	P0A 1G0 **SUMMER PHONE**
WINTER ADDRESS	8 Catherwood Court
	Scarborough ONT
	M1W 1S1 **WINTER PHONE** 416-491-3894
CONTACT PERSON	Catherine Wells Ross
ACCREDITATION	OCA, CCA
AFFILIATION	None
YEARS IN OPERATION	39
DATES OPEN	July through August
FEES	$850 per 2-week session; $1550 per 4-week session.
SCHOLARSHIPS	Please enquire.
ACCOMODATION	Tents, wash-house, showers, main lodge with rec room.
SPECIALTY	Traditional
OBJECTIVES	To encourage independence & self-assurance as well as co-operative living in the out-of-doors. The camp is fun, but also offers learning experiences.
ACTIVITIES	Swimming, canoeing, sailing, kayaking, arts & crafts, drama, archery, hiking, exploring, ropes course, windsurfing, tripping, nature study.
EVALUATIONS	No
MEDICAL FACILITIES	Nurse on site; doctor on call.
VISITORS	Allowed
SPECIAL NEEDS FACILITIES	Unspecified
DESCRIPTION	Situated on its own 22-acre island in a sheltered corner of Lake Wah-Wash-Kesh, near Parry Sound. Includes a mile of shoreline with shallow sandy bays & deep water coves.
NEAREST CITY/TOWN	Parry Sound
AGE SPREAD	7 to 16 years
CAMPERS PER SESSION	Approximately 80
STAFF PER SESSION	19
COUNSELLOR:CAMPER RATIO	1 to 4
BOYS OR GIRLS	☐ Boys only ☒ Girls only ☐ Co-ed
NOTES	

CAMP MINWASSIN

SUMMER ADDRESS	RR #3		
	Eganville		ONT
	K0J 1T0	**SUMMER PHONE**	613-628-2403
WINTER ADDRESS	c/o Boys' & Girls' Club of Ottawa-Carleton		
	412 Nepean Street		
	Ottawa		ONT
	K1R 5G7	**WINTER PHONE**	613-232-0925

CONTACT PERSON Rick Sawyer
ACCREDITATION OCA, CCA
AFFILIATION Boys' & Girls' Club of Ottawa-Carleton
YEARS IN OPERATION 72
DATES OPEN July through August
FEES $400 per 12-day session; $200 per 6-day session.
SCHOLARSHIPS Yes
ACCOMODATION Cabins, washrooms, showers, dining hall.
SPECIALTY Traditional
OBJECTIVES To integrate all children into a happy camp experience without regard to financial, physical or emotional limitations.

ACTIVITIES Swimming, sailing, canoeing, waterskiing, campcraft, leadership training, special events.

EVALUATIONS No
MEDICAL FACILITIES Nurse on staff.
VISITORS Allowed
SPECIAL NEEDS FACILITIES Yes
DESCRIPTION Please enquire for details.

NEAREST CITY/TOWN Ottawa
AGE SPREAD 8 to 16 years
CAMPERS PER SESSION 100
STAFF PER SESSION 40
COUNSELLOR:CAMPER RATIO 1 to 4
BOYS OR GIRLS ☐ Boys only ☐ Girls only ☒ Co-ed
NOTES

CAMP MISHEWAH

SUMMER ADDRESS RR #5
Killaloe ONT
K0J 2A0 **SUMMER PHONE** 613-757-2828

WINTER ADDRESS c/o The Missionary Church Canada East
130 Fergus Avenue
Kitchener ONT
N2A 2H2 **WINTER PHONE** 519-894-9801

CONTACT PERSON Suzanne Rosenberg
ACCREDITATION OCA, CCI
AFFILIATION Christian
YEARS IN OPERATION 20
DATES OPEN July through August
FEES $155 - $195 per 6-day session
SCHOLARSHIPS Please enquire.
ACCOMODATION Cabins, dining hall, recreation hall, chapel.
SPECIALTY Christian Development
OBJECTIVES To challenge people to experience & know Jesus Christ, with an emphasis on renewal & instruction in a recreational environment.
ACTIVITIES Swimming, canoeing, kayaking, windsurfing, orienteering, crafts, archery, drama, nature & Bible studies, sports, campfires.

EVALUATIONS No
MEDICAL FACILITIES Infirmary on site with camp doctor; 28 km to hospital.
VISITORS Allowed
SPECIAL NEEDS FACILITIES Unspecified
DESCRIPTION Please enquire for details.

NEAREST CITY/TOWN Barry's Bay
AGE SPREAD 8 to 20 years
CAMPERS PER SESSION 100
STAFF PER SESSION 45
COUNSELLOR:CAMPER RATIO 1 to 4
BOYS OR GIRLS ☐ Boys only ☐ Girls only ☒ Co-ed
NOTES Family camping is an option; please enquire.

CAMP NEW MOON

SUMMER ADDRESS			
	Baysville P0B 1A0	**SUMMER PHONE**	ONT 705-767-3381
WINTER ADDRESS	57 Elm Ridge Drive		
	Toronto M6B 1A2	**WINTER PHONE**	ONT 416-787-4461

CONTACT PERSON Al or Jack Goodman
ACCREDITATION OCA, CCA
AFFILIATION None
YEARS IN OPERATION 34
DATES OPEN Late June through early September
FEES $1725 for 3 weeks; $2600 for 4 weeks; $3600 for 7 weeks.
SCHOLARSHIPS No
ACCOMODATION Cabins with toilets & electricity.
SPECIALTY Traditional
OBJECTIVES To encourage complete & balanced development of physical & social skills.

ACTIVITIES Swimming, waterskiing, windsurfing, sailing, kayaking, canoeing, tripping, tennis, drama, arts & crafts, gymnastics, special theme days, intercamp activities.

EVALUATIONS No
MEDICAL FACILITIES Resident doctor & nurse.
VISITORS Allowed
SPECIAL NEEDS FACILITIES No
DESCRIPTION Please enquire for details.

NEAREST CITY/TOWN Bracebridge
AGE SPREAD 7 to 16 years
CAMPERS PER SESSION 200
STAFF PER SESSION 80
COUNSELLOR:CAMPER RATIO 1 to 4
BOYS OR GIRLS ☐ Boys only ☐ Girls only ☒ Co-ed
NOTES

CAMP PONACKA

SUMMER ADDRESS			
	Highland Grove		ONT
	K0L 2A0	**SUMMER PHONE**	613-332-4125
WINTER ADDRESS	RR #4		
	Peterborough		ONT
	K9J 6X5	**WINTER PHONE**	705-748-9470

CONTACT PERSON Don Bocking & Anne Morawetz
ACCREDITATION OCA
AFFILIATION Christian (nondenominational)
YEARS IN OPERATION 47
DATES OPEN July through August
FEES $1955 per 4-week session.
SCHOLARSHIPS Please enquire
ACCOMODATION Platform tents for older boys, cabins for younger, showers.
SPECIALTY Traditional
OBJECTIVES Aims to give each camper an "I count, I belong" experience, & teach skills which promote self-confidence.

ACTIVITIES Horseback riding, swimming, windsurfing, sailing, canoeing, kayaking, waterskiing, singing, woodwork, lapidary, crafts, games, archery, survival skills.

EVALUATIONS No
MEDICAL FACILITIES Doctor in residence.
VISITORS Allowed
SPECIAL NEEDS FACILITIES Unspecified
DESCRIPTION Located on a secluded bay of Lake Baptiste.

NEAREST CITY/TOWN Bancroft
AGE SPREAD 8 to 15 years
CAMPERS PER SESSION 144
STAFF PER SESSION 65
COUNSELLOR:CAMPER RATIO 1 to 4
BOYS OR GIRLS ☒ Boys only ☐ Girls only ☐ Co-ed
NOTES 2-week programs for 8 & 9-year-olds only are available for $1020 per session.

CAMP QUEEN ELIZABETH

SUMMER ADDRESS c/o Post Office
Honey Harbour ONT
P0E 1E0 **SUMMER PHONE** 705-756-8300

WINTER ADDRESS c/o YM-YWCA of London
RR #5, Clarke Side Road
London ONT
N6A 4B9 **WINTER PHONE** 519-455-2519

CONTACT PERSON Jim Janzen
ACCREDITATION OCA, CCA
AFFILIATION YM-YWCA
YEARS IN OPERATION 41
DATES OPEN May through September
FEES $685 per 2-week session.
SCHOLARSHIPS Camperships may be available through the Y.
ACCOMODATION Cabins, dining hall, recreation hall, showers.
SPECIALTY Traditional
OBJECTIVES To develop the mind, spirit, & body through a supportive, caring environment that fosters interpersonal & personal growth & a sense of self-worth & belonging.
ACTIVITIES Swimming, canoeing, kayaking, sea kayaking, sailing, windsurfing, campcraft, arts & crafts, campfires, kite-flying, drama, earth education, wilderness pursuits.

EVALUATIONS Camper development forms are kept on file.
MEDICAL FACILITIES Doctor or nurse on staff; hospital nearby.
VISITORS Allowed on scheduled Visitors Day.
SPECIAL NEEDS FACILITIES Unspecified
DESCRIPTION Please enquire for details

NEAREST CITY/TOWN Midland
AGE SPREAD 7 to 16 years
CAMPERS PER SESSION 176
STAFF PER SESSION 56
COUNSELLOR:CAMPER RATIO 1 to 5
BOYS OR GIRLS ☐ Boys only ☐ Girls only ☒ Co-ed
NOTES

CAMP SHALOM

SUMMER ADDRESS PO Box 1830

Gravenhurst ONT
P1P 1V8 **SUMMER PHONE** 705-687-4244

WINTER ADDRESS 788 Marlee Street

Toronto ONT
M6B 3K1 **WINTER PHONE** 416-783-6744

CONTACT PERSON Steve Gillick
ACCREDITATION OCA
AFFILIATION Jewish
YEARS IN OPERATION 45
DATES OPEN July through August
FEES $2000-$2200 per 4-week session; $3600 full summer.
SCHOLARSHIPS Please enquire.
ACCOMODATION Cabins with electricity, showers; kosher dining facilities.
SPECIALTY Jewish Development
OBJECTIVES To provide campers with a safe & fun-filled summer, while developing within an environment steeped in Jewish & Zionist education, culture, tradition, & values.
ACTIVITIES Arts & crafts, drama, Israeli song & dance, tripping, water sports, swimming, guitar, scoutcraft, modern dance, archery, newspaper, sports.

EVALUATIONS No
MEDICAL FACILITIES Full time doctor and nurse on duty.
VISITORS Allowed on Visitors Day (one per session).
SPECIAL NEEDS FACILITIES Unspecified
DESCRIPTION Located on Lake Muskoka.

NEAREST CITY/TOWN Bracebridge
AGE SPREAD 8 to 13 years
CAMPERS PER SESSION 215
STAFF PER SESSION 85
COUNSELLOR:CAMPER RATIO Included in figure above.
BOYS OR GIRLS ☐ Boys only ☐ Girls only ☒ Co-ed
NOTES The camp kitchen is kosher and Kashruth is observed.

CAMP SHOMRIA

SUMMER ADDRESS	RR #3 Otty Lake Perth K7H 3C5	**SUMMER PHONE**	ONT 613-267-4396
WINTER ADDRESS	1111 Finch Avenue W. Suite #154 Downsview M3J 2E5	**WINTER PHONE**	ONT 416-736-1339

CONTACT PERSON Tuvia Lieberman
ACCREDITATION OCA
AFFILIATION Jewish
YEARS IN OPERATION 56
DATES OPEN July to August
FEES $1875 per 5-week session.
SCHOLARSHIPS Please enquire.
ACCOMODATION Cabins, showers, main dining room.
SPECIALTY Jewish Development
OBJECTIVES To strengthen the Jewish identity with focus on Israel & the Kibbutz, encouraging teamwork & co-operation.

ACTIVITIES Swimming, canoeing, trips, sports, arts & crafts, photography, drama, Hebrew, Jewish identity, Israeli folk dance, singing.

EVALUATIONS Yes, on request.
MEDICAL FACILITIES Infirmary & nurse on site, hospital 6 km away.
VISITORS Allowed on Parents Day.
SPECIAL NEEDS FACILITIES No
DESCRIPTION Please enquire for details.

NEAREST CITY/TOWN Perth
AGE SPREAD 9 to 16 years
CAMPERS PER SESSION Approximately 100
STAFF PER SESSION 8
COUNSELLOR:CAMPER RATIO 1 to 5
BOYS OR GIRLS ☐ Boys only ☐ Girls only ☒ Co-ed
NOTES Discount available for early registration.

CAMP SIMPRESCA

SUMMER ADDRESS	RR #1
	Penetang ONT
SUMMER PHONE	705-526-6619
WINTER ADDRESS	397 Manly Street
	Midland ONT L4R 3E4
WINTER PHONE	705-526-7714
CONTACT PERSON	Gary Price
ACCREDITATION	OCA
AFFILIATION	United Church
YEARS IN OPERATION	45
DATES OPEN	July through August
FEES	Approximately $272 per one-week session.
SCHOLARSHIPS	No
ACCOMODATION	Cabins, showers, main dining hall.
SPECIALTY	Christian Development
OBJECTIVES	To offer activities in an atmosphere which invites campers to challenge themselves physically, mentally, socially and spiritually, & to cultivate an awareness of God's presence.
ACTIVITIES	Swimming, canoeing, campcraft, sports, archery, outtripping, arts & crafts, Chapel, worship.
EVALUATIONS	Campers can receive award & swimming certificates.
MEDICAL FACILITIES	Infirmary & nurse on site.
VISITORS	Not allowed
SPECIAL NEEDS FACILITIES	Yes
DESCRIPTION	Situated on the wooded shore of Georgian Bay, with over 80 acres of forest & meadow.
NEAREST CITY/TOWN	Toronto
AGE SPREAD	6 to 16 years
CAMPERS PER SESSION	100
STAFF PER SESSION	25
COUNSELLOR:CAMPER RATIO	1 to 7
BOYS OR GIRLS	☐ Boys only ☐ Girls only ☒ Co-ed
NOTES	Special needs campers are accommodated, but with limited facilities. The terrain is very hilly; please enquire.

CAMP TAMAKWA

SUMMER ADDRESS	Algonquin Park		
	Huntsville		ONT
	P0A 1K0	**SUMMER PHONE**	705-633-5561
WINTER ADDRESS	950 Yonge Street		
	Suite #600		
	Toronto		ONT
	M4W 2J4	**WINTER PHONE**	416-924-7433

CONTACT PERSON Vic Norris & David Bale
ACCREDITATION OCA, CCA
AFFILIATION None
YEARS IN OPERATION 58
DATES OPEN July through August
FEES $3950 for 8 weeks; $2500 for 4 weeks; $1500 for 2 weeks.
SCHOLARSHIPS No
ACCOMODATION Cabins with electricity, bathrooms with shower, dining area.
SPECIALTY Traditional
OBJECTIVES To promote social growth, skill development, & outdoor appreciation among campers.

ACTIVITIES Pottery, photography, fishing, radio station, drama, music, halfcourt tennis, ropes course, campcraft, hiking, canoeing, swimming, waterskiing, archery, land sports, tripping, arts & crafts.
EVALUATIONS No
MEDICAL FACILITIES Nurse & doctor on site.
VISITORS Allowed on Visitors Day (one per session).
SPECIAL NEEDS FACILITIES Unspecified
DESCRIPTION Please enquire for details.

NEAREST CITY/TOWN Huntsville
AGE SPREAD 7 to 16 years
CAMPERS PER SESSION 225
STAFF PER SESSION 100
COUNSELLOR:CAMPER RATIO 1 to 4
BOYS OR GIRLS ☐ Boys only ☐ Girls only ☒ Co-ed
NOTES

CAMP TAMARACK

SUMMER ADDRESS	RR #2		
	Bracebridge		ONT
	P1L 1W9	**SUMMER PHONE**	705-645-4881
WINTER ADDRESS	1352 Bathurst Street		
	Suite #301		
	Toronto		ONT
	M5R 3H7	**WINTER PHONE**	416-539-9229

CONTACT PERSON Howard Kates
ACCREDITATION OCA
AFFILIATION None
YEARS IN OPERATION 13
DATES OPEN July through mid-August
FEES $3200 for 7 weeks; $2400 for 4 weeks; $1550 for 3 weeks.
SCHOLARSHIPS No
ACCOMODATION Cabins with washrooms, central showers, main dining room.
SPECIALTY Traditional
OBJECTIVES Skills development in a social environment.

ACTIVITIES Video, photography, arts & crafts, ceramics, theatre, dance, team sports, self-defense, ropes course, tennis, gym & trampoline, swimming, kayaking, windsurfing, water skiing, sailing, canoeing.
EVALUATIONS Upon request.
MEDICAL FACILITIES 2 nurses & a doctor on site.
VISITORS Allowed on Visitors Day.
SPECIAL NEEDS FACILITIES Unspecified
DESCRIPTION Please enquire for details.

NEAREST CITY/TOWN Bracebridge
AGE SPREAD 6 to 16 years
CAMPERS PER SESSION 320
STAFF PER SESSION 135
COUNSELLOR:CAMPER RATIO 1 to 6
BOYS OR GIRLS ☐ Boys only ☐ Girls only ☒ Co-ed
NOTES

CAMP TAPAWINGO

SUMMER ADDRESS	General Delivery		
	Parry Sound		ONT
	P2A 2X1	**SUMMER PHONE**	705-746-5455
WINTER ADDRESS	Toronto YWCA Camping Services		
	276 Merton Street		
	Toronto		ONT
	M4S 1A9	**WINTER PHONE**	416-487-7151

CONTACT PERSON Liz Greenway
ACCREDITATION OCA
AFFILIATION YWCA
YEARS IN OPERATION 63
DATES OPEN July through August
FEES $840 per 2-week session; $1160 per 3-week session.
SCHOLARSHIPS No
ACCOMODATION Cabins, showers, dining & recreation halls, craft shop.
SPECIALTY Traditional
OBJECTIVES To offer campers an enjoyable, fun experience of learning new skills that help build self-esteem & confidence.

ACTIVITIES Swimming, canoeing, sailing, kayaking, paddlemaking, crafts, pottery, drama, archery, dance, nature studies.

EVALUATIONS No
MEDICAL FACILITIES Infirmary on site; hospital 5 minutes away.
VISITORS Allowed during Open House before camp begins.
SPECIAL NEEDS FACILITIES No
DESCRIPTION Located on Georgian Bay.

NEAREST CITY/TOWN Parry Sound
AGE SPREAD 7 to 15 years
CAMPERS PER SESSION Approximately 100
STAFF PER SESSION 35
COUNSELLOR:CAMPER RATIO 1 to 4
BOYS OR GIRLS ☐ Boys only ☒ Girls only ☐ Co-ed
NOTES A 1-week session for 6-10 year-olds is available; please enquire.

CAMP TOWHEE

SUMMER ADDRESS			
	Haliburton		ONT
	K0M 1SO	**SUMMER PHONE**	
WINTER ADDRESS	c/o Integra 25 Imperial Street Toronto		ONT
	M5P 1C1	**WINTER PHONE**	416-486-8055

CONTACT PERSON Sarah Oosterhuis
ACCREDITATION OCA
AFFILIATION Ontario Ministry of Community & Social Services
YEARS IN OPERATION 25
DATES OPEN July through mid-August
FEES None; funded by Ministry of Community & Social Services.
SCHOLARSHIPS See above.
ACCOMODATION Cabins with showers, main dining hall.
SPECIALTY Special Needs: Learning Disabilities
OBJECTIVES To provide a therapeutic milieu conducive to treatment of psychosocial problems of children with learning disabilities.

ACTIVITIES Swimming, canoeing, arts & crafts, adventure programming, tripping, nature study, sports.

EVALUATIONS Yes
MEDICAL FACILITIES Nurse on site, hospital 10 minutes away.
VISITORS Allowed
SPECIAL NEEDS FACILITIES Yes
DESCRIPTION Please enquire for details.

NEAREST CITY/TOWN Haliburton
AGE SPREAD 8 to 12 years
CAMPERS PER SESSION 60
STAFF PER SESSION 60
COUNSELLOR:CAMPER RATIO 1 to 2
BOYS OR GIRLS ☐ Boys only ☐ Girls only ☒ Co-ed
NOTES Special needs refers to children with learning disabilities & social problems. Available for Ontario residents only.

CAMP TRILLIUM

SUMMER ADDRESS	PO Box 359
	Bloomfield ONT
	K0K 1G0 **SUMMER PHONE** 613-393-2384
WINTER ADDRESS	As above
	WINTER PHONE
CONTACT PERSON	Pauline McKenna
ACCREDITATION	OCA
AFFILIATION	Ontario Cancer Society
YEARS IN OPERATION	10
DATES OPEN	June through Labour Day
FEES	None
SCHOLARSHIPS	
ACCOMODATION	Cabins, showers, dining facilities.
SPECIALTY	Special Needs: Cancer
OBJECTIVES	To provide recreation & support for children with cancer & their families.
ACTIVITIES	Sailing, swimming, backpacking, canoeing, kayaking, photography, nature studies, arts & crafts, drama, campfires.
EVALUATIONS	No
MEDICAL FACILITIES	3 oncology nurses on site.
VISITORS	Not allowed
SPECIAL NEEDS FACILITIES	Yes
DESCRIPTION	Please enquire for details.
NEAREST CITY/TOWN	Belleville
AGE SPREAD	All ages
CAMPERS PER SESSION	Approximately 100
STAFF PER SESSION	50
COUNSELLOR:CAMPER RATIO	1 to 2
BOYS OR GIRLS	☐ Boys only ☐ Girls only ☒ Co-ed
NOTES	Special needs refers to cancer patients & their siblings.

CAMP WABANA

SUMMER ADDRESS c/o Jackson's Point Conference Centre
PO Box 137
Jackson's Point ONT
L0E 1L0 **SUMMER PHONE** 905-722-3455

WINTER ADDRESS 1645 Warden Avenue
Suite #305
Scarborough ONT
M1R 5B3 **WINTER PHONE** 416-321-2654

CONTACT PERSON Calvin Bennett
ACCREDITATION OCA, CCI
AFFILIATION Salvation Army
YEARS IN OPERATION 77
DATES OPEN July through August
FEES Sliding scale based on income.
SCHOLARSHIPS Yes; camps are subsidized.
ACCOMODATION Cabins, showers, dining room.
SPECIALTY Disadvantaged Youth
OBJECTIVES To provide fellowship & fun, & meet the natural hunger for adventure. Also to emphasize the presence of God in day-to-day living.
ACTIVITIES Canoeing, swimming, nature lore, overnights, crafts, music, archery, campfires, special guests, & Good News Club (Bible).

EVALUATIONS No
MEDICAL FACILITIES On-site clinic with nursing staff.
VISITORS Not allowed
SPECIAL NEEDS FACILITIES Unspecified
DESCRIPTION Approximately 50 acres of land on Lake Simcoe with plenty of trees.

NEAREST CITY/TOWN Newmarket
AGE SPREAD 7 to 19 years
CAMPERS PER SESSION 110
STAFF PER SESSION 75+
COUNSELLOR:CAMPER RATIO 1 to 5
BOYS OR GIRLS ☐ Boys only ☐ Girls only ☒ Co-ed
NOTES

CAMP WABIKON

SUMMER ADDRESS Temagami Island

Temagami ONT
P0H 2H0 **SUMMER PHONE** 705-237-8940

WINTER ADDRESS 48 Delhi Avenue

Toronto ONT
M5M 3B7 **WINTER PHONE** 416-483-3172

CONTACT PERSON Mr & Mrs M. Bernardo
ACCREDITATION OCA, CCA
AFFILIATION None
YEARS IN OPERATION 51
DATES OPEN July through August
FEES $1495 per 3-week session; $975 per 2-week session.
SCHOLARSHIPS No
ACCOMODATION Cabins, showers & flush toilets, dining hall, rec buildings.
SPECIALTY Traditional
OBJECTIVES An international camp encouraging lasting friendships, an understanding & appreciation of many languages and cultures.

ACTIVITIES Waterpolo, swimming, canoeing, sailing, kayaking, windsurfing, snorkeling, tennis, archery, team sports, fishing, drama, trampoline, paddlemaking, hiking, cookouts, music, dances, arts & crafts.

EVALUATIONS No
MEDICAL FACILITIES Doctor or nurse always in residence.
VISITORS Allowed
SPECIAL NEEDS FACILITIES Unspecified
DESCRIPTION Located on Lake Temagami (the Indian word for "deep blue waters"), the camp offers a sandy beach & access to the area's many lakes & countless islands.
NEAREST CITY/TOWN Toronto
AGE SPREAD 6 to 17 years
CAMPERS PER SESSION 150
STAFF PER SESSION 60
COUNSELLOR:CAMPER RATIO 1 to 3
BOYS OR GIRLS ☐ Boys only ☐ Girls only ☒ Co-ed
NOTES Shorter & longer sessions are offered, as well as extended canoe trips; please enquire. Due to the international nature of the camp, understanding of other languages & cultures often results for campers.

CAMP WAHANOWIN

SUMMER ADDRESS	PO Box 850		
	Orillia		ONT
	L3V 6K8	**SUMMER PHONE**	705-325-2285
WINTER ADDRESS	227 Eglinton Avenue W.		
	Toronto		ONT
	M4R 1A9	**WINTER PHONE**	416-482-2600

CONTACT PERSON Bruce Nashman
ACCREDITATION OCA, CCA, American Camping Association
AFFILIATION None
YEARS IN OPERATION 40
DATES OPEN Late June through mid-August
FEES Vary from $895 for 10 days to $3700 for 7 weeks.
SCHOLARSHIPS No
ACCOMODATION Cabins with bathrooms, & some with showers.
SPECIALTY Traditional
OBJECTIVES To provide safe, fun, learning experiences & challenges for children.

ACTIVITIES Swimming, sailing, canoeing, horseback riding, theatre, arts & crafts, rock climbing, creative arts, tennis, gymnastics, ropes course.

EVALUATIONS No
MEDICAL FACILITIES Health centre with 4 nurses & a doctor on site.
VISITORS Allowed on scheduled Visitors Day.
SPECIAL NEEDS FACILITIES No
DESCRIPTION Please enquire for details.

NEAREST CITY/TOWN Orillia
AGE SPREAD 6 to 15 years
CAMPERS PER SESSION 450
STAFF PER SESSION 175
COUNSELLOR:CAMPER RATIO 1 to 5
BOYS OR GIRLS ☐ Boys only ☐ Girls only ☒ Co-ed
NOTES

CAMP WAPATECK

SUMMER ADDRESS	General Delivery		
	Keewatin		ONT
	P0X 1C0	**SUMMER PHONE**	807-548-4151
WINTER ADDRESS	935 Nesbitt Bay		
	Winnipeg		MAN
	R3T 1W6	**WINTER PHONE**	204-453-6130

CONTACT PERSON Pam Flower
ACCREDITATION MCA
AFFILIATION Anglican Church
YEARS IN OPERATION 42
DATES OPEN July through August
FEES Approx $280 per session.
SCHOLARSHIPS Camperships are available.
ACCOMODATION Cabins, central dining hall, central wash-house with showers.
SPECIALTY Christian Development
OBJECTIVES To encourage & maintain a Christian community so that all coming to the island can experience God, creation, & self.

ACTIVITIES Swimming, canoeing, outtripping, arts & crafts, sports, jungle golf, Bible study, orienteering.

EVALUATIONS No
MEDICAL FACILITIES Infirmary with nurse on site.
VISITORS Not allowed
SPECIAL NEEDS FACILITIES Unspecified
DESCRIPTION Located on Anglican Island on beautiful Lake of the Woods.

NEAREST CITY/TOWN Kenora
AGE SPREAD 8 to 14 years
CAMPERS PER SESSION 48
STAFF PER SESSION 25
COUNSELLOR:CAMPER RATIO 1 to 3
BOYS OR GIRLS ☐ Boys only ☐ Girls only ☒ Co-ed
NOTES

CANADIAN ADVENTURE CAMP

SUMMER ADDRESS	Adventure Island Temagami ONT P0H 2H0 **SUMMER PHONE** 705-237-8906
WINTER ADDRESS	31 Helen Avenue Thornhill ONT L4J 1J6 **WINTER PHONE** 416-226-2672
CONTACT PERSON	F.B. (Skip) Connett
ACCREDITATION	OCA, CCA
AFFILIATION	None
YEARS IN OPERATION	20
DATES OPEN	July through August
FEES	$995 per 2-week session; $1880 per 4-week session
SCHOLARSHIPS	No
ACCOMODATION	Cabins, hot showers, sauna, dining room.
SPECIALTY	Traditional
OBJECTIVES	To help young people grow into responsible, well-rounded citizens through a fun camp atmosphere.
ACTIVITIES	Modern gymnasium, giant water slides, trampoline, water skiing, windsurfing, theatre, music, swimming, sailing, canoeing, kayaking, crafts, art, overnight trip, campfires.
EVALUATIONS	No, but counsellors write progress letters to parents.
MEDICAL FACILITIES	Doctor in residence.
VISITORS	Special Visitors Day every second Saturday.
SPECIAL NEEDS FACILITIES	No
DESCRIPTION	Located on Adventure Island in Lake Temagami.
NEAREST CITY/TOWN	North Bay
AGE SPREAD	6 to 16 years
CAMPERS PER SESSION	130
STAFF PER SESSION	60
COUNSELLOR:CAMPER RATIO	1 to 7
BOYS OR GIRLS	☐ Boys only ☐ Girls only ☒ Co-ed
NOTES	Offers specialty programs in waterskiing, gymnastics, & trampoline; please enquire.

CANTERBURY HILLS

SUMMER ADDRESS	Fiddlers Green P.O. Box 81089 Ancaster L9G 4X1	**SUMMER PHONE**	ONT 905-648-6337
WINTER ADDRESS	67 Victoria Avenue S. Hamilton L8N 2S8	**WINTER PHONE**	ONT 905-527-1316

CONTACT PERSON Brian Lisson
ACCREDITATION OCA
AFFILIATION Anglican Church, Association for Experimental Education
YEARS IN OPERATION 33
DATES OPEN July through August
FEES Unspecified; please enquire.
SCHOLARSHIPS Yes
ACCOMODATION Cabins with washrooms & showers, family-style dining hall.
SPECIALTY Christian Development
OBJECTIVES To provide a loving Christian community in which campers can explore their relationship with themselves, each other, the earth & God.
ACTIVITIES Archery, ropes course, nature, swimming, cycle trips, backpacking, crafts, campout.

EVALUATIONS No
MEDICAL FACILITIES Health centre with nurse on site.
VISITORS Not allowed
SPECIAL NEEDS FACILITIES Unspecified
DESCRIPTION Please enquire for details.

NEAREST CITY/TOWN Hamilton
AGE SPREAD 5 to 16 years
CAMPERS PER SESSION 72
STAFF PER SESSION 30
COUNSELLOR:CAMPER RATIO 1 to 4
BOYS OR GIRLS ☐ Boys only ☐ Girls only ☒ Co-ed
NOTES

CAVE SPRINGS CAMP

SUMMER ADDRESS			
	Near Beamsville		ONT
		SUMMER PHONE	
WINTER ADDRESS	9 Linhaven Court		
	St. Catharines		ONT
	L2N 6V3	**WINTER PHONE**	905-937-2746

CONTACT PERSON Gary Krupa
ACCREDITATION OCA
AFFILIATION United Church
YEARS IN OPERATION 44
DATES OPEN July through August
FEES Unspecified; please enquire.
SCHOLARSHIPS
ACCOMODATION Cabins, showers, dining hall.
SPECIALTY Christian Development
OBJECTIVES To give campers opportunities to worship God in new ways in new settings, & to experience new relationships with each other & with the natural world.
ACTIVITIES Ropes course, swimming, crafts, camping, hiking, chapel, campfires, archery, drama, canoeing.

EVALUATIONS No
MEDICAL FACILITIES Infirmary with nurse.
VISITORS No
SPECIAL NEEDS FACILITIES No
DESCRIPTION Located in the shade of the Niagara Escarpment near the Bruce Trail.

NEAREST CITY/TOWN St. Catharines
AGE SPREAD 6 to 14 years
CAMPERS PER SESSION 72
STAFF PER SESSION 21
COUNSELLOR:CAMPER RATIO 1 to 6
BOYS OR GIRLS ☐ Boys only ☐ Girls only ☒ Co-ed
NOTES

CEDAR VALLEY RANCH

SUMMER ADDRESS RR #1

Cambridge ONT
N1R 5S2 **SUMMER PHONE** 519-740-1986

WINTER ADDRESS As above

WINTER PHONE

CONTACT PERSON John or Carol Renner
ACCREDITATION OCA
AFFILIATION None
YEARS IN OPERATION 24
DATES OPEN June through August
FEES $350 per one-week session.
SCHOLARSHIPS No
ACCOMODATION Cabins, showers, dining hall.
SPECIALTY Horseback Riding
OBJECTIVES To teach children to ride safely & to their full potential.

ACTIVITIES English & western horseback riding, games, swimming, sports.

EVALUATIONS No
MEDICAL FACILITIES Doctor on call; medical centre nearby.
VISITORS Not allowed
SPECIAL NEEDS FACILITIES Unspecified
DESCRIPTION Please enquire for details.

NEAREST CITY/TOWN Cambridge
AGE SPREAD 7 to 15 years
CAMPERS PER SESSION 50
STAFF PER SESSION 13
COUNSELLOR:CAMPER RATIO 1 to 5
BOYS OR GIRLS ☐ Boys only ☐ Girls only ☒ Co-ed
NOTES

CHRISTIE LAKE CAMP FOR BOYS & GIRLS

SUMMER ADDRESS	RR 1		
	Westport		ONT
	K0G 1X0	**SUMMER PHONE**	613-267-4998
WINTER ADDRESS	PO Box 6980, Station J		
	Ottawa		ONT
	K2A 3Z6	**WINTER PHONE**	613-225-1328

CONTACT PERSON Dan Offord
ACCREDITATION OCA, CCA
AFFILIATION None
YEARS IN OPERATION 75
DATES OPEN July through August
FEES Considered individually; please enquire.
SCHOLARSHIPS Yes
ACCOMODATION Cabins, dining hall.
SPECIALTY Disadvantaged Youth
OBJECTIVES To provide traditional camping opportunities & promote skill development for children from financially disadvantaged homes.
ACTIVITIES Archery, arts & crafts, campfires, canoeing, outtripping, nature studies, swimming, boating.

EVALUATIONS Badges are awarded.
MEDICAL FACILITIES Nurse in residence.
VISITORS Not allowed.
SPECIAL NEEDS FACILITIES Unspecified
DESCRIPTION Please enquire for details.

NEAREST CITY/TOWN Kingston
AGE SPREAD 9 to 14 years
CAMPERS PER SESSION 120
STAFF PER SESSION 70
COUNSELLOR:CAMPER RATIO 1 to 5
BOYS OR GIRLS ☐ Boys only ☐ Girls only ☒ Co-ed
NOTES

CIRCLE R RANCH

SUMMER ADDRESS	RR #1 Delaware ONT N0L 1E0
SUMMER PHONE	519-471-3799
WINTER ADDRESS	As above
WINTER PHONE	
CONTACT PERSON	Russell family
ACCREDITATION	OCA
AFFILIATION	None
YEARS IN OPERATION	30
DATES OPEN	July through August
FEES	$335 per 1-week session; $680 per 2-week session.
SCHOLARSHIPS	No
ACCOMODATION	Tents, showers, washrooms, dining lodge.
SPECIALTY	Horseback Riding
OBJECTIVES	To provide an exciting camp program in a natural setting & to help campers develop socially by living in close contact with their peers.
ACTIVITIES	Western riding with instructors, overnight camp-out, swimming, crafts, canoeing, kayaking, archery, environmental & nature program.
EVALUATIONS	No
MEDICAL FACILITIES	Registered first aid trained staff; clinic 5 minutes away.
VISITORS	Not allowed
SPECIAL NEEDS FACILITIES	Unspecified
DESCRIPTION	Situated on 220 acres of rolling, wooded terrain in Dingman Creek Valley.
NEAREST CITY/TOWN	London
AGE SPREAD	8 to 15 years
CAMPERS PER SESSION	70
STAFF PER SESSION	40
COUNSELLOR:CAMPER RATIO	1 to 3
BOYS OR GIRLS	☐ Boys only ☐ Girls only ☒ Co-ed
NOTES	

EDGEWOOD CAMP

SUMMER ADDRESS	49 Station Street
	Eden Mills ONT
	N0B 1P0 **SUMMER PHONE** 519-856-9622
WINTER ADDRESS	As above
	WINTER PHONE
CONTACT PERSON	Bruce Bartleman
ACCREDITATION	OCA
AFFILIATION	Lutheran Church
YEARS IN OPERATION	50
DATES OPEN	July through August
FEES	$160 per one-week session.
SCHOLARSHIPS	No
ACCOMODATION	Cabins, showers, lodge.
SPECIALTY	Christian Development
OBJECTIVES	To encourage growth in campers' sense of personal identity, worth, & responsibility in a Christian setting.
ACTIVITIES	Swimming, canoeing, crafts, nature study, Bible study, hiking, campfires, cookouts, overnights.
EVALUATIONS	No
MEDICAL FACILITIES	Nurse on site; doctor on call.
VISITORS	Not allowed
SPECIAL NEEDS FACILITIES	Yes
DESCRIPTION	56 acres in a large forested area offering trails, a creek, & many opportunities to observe wildlife.
NEAREST CITY/TOWN	Guelph
AGE SPREAD	7 to 15+ years
CAMPERS PER SESSION	600 annually
STAFF PER SESSION	29
COUNSELLOR:CAMPER RATIO	1 to 5
BOYS OR GIRLS	☐ Boys only ☐ Girls only ☒ Co-ed
NOTES	Special needs refers to full access for physical disabilities.

FRASER LAKE CAMP

SUMMER ADDRESS	RR #4		
	Bancroft		ONT
	K0L 1C0	**SUMMER PHONE**	
WINTER ADDRESS	PO Box 969		
	Stouffville		ONT
	L4A 8A1	**WINTER PHONE**	905-642-2964

CONTACT PERSON Allan Nelson
ACCREDITATION OCA
AFFILIATION Mennonite Brethren
YEARS IN OPERATION 40
DATES OPEN July through August
FEES $300 per 1-week session; $600 per 2-week session.
SCHOLARSHIPS Yes
ACCOMODATION Cabins, showers, toilets & outhouses, dining hall.
SPECIALTY Christian Development
OBJECTIVES Camping with a Christian perspective: programs encourage campers to be aware of their responsibility for the care of the world & for those around them.
ACTIVITIES Horseback riding (ponies), Bible study, swimming, campfires, games, archery, nature study, canoeing, sports.

EVALUATIONS No
MEDICAL FACILITIES Dispensary & doctor on call.
VISITORS Allowed
SPECIAL NEEDS FACILITIES Yes
DESCRIPTION A 275-acre site of farmland, forests, a clean lake, & rugged terrain.

NEAREST CITY/TOWN Peterborough
AGE SPREAD 7 to 15
CAMPERS PER SESSION 100-120
STAFF PER SESSION Approximately 40
COUNSELLOR:CAMPER RATIO 1 to 4
BOYS OR GIRLS ☐ Boys only ☐ Girls only ☒ Co-ed
NOTES Special needs facilities refers to counsellors specializing in learning & behaviour disabilities; please enquire.

GLEN BERNARD CAMP

SUMMER ADDRESS			
	Sundridge		ONT
	P0A 1Z0	**SUMMER PHONE**	705-384-7062
WINTER ADDRESS	206 Lord Seaton Road		
	Willowdale		ONT
	M2P 1K9	**WINTER PHONE**	416-225-4166

CONTACT PERSON Jocelyn Palm
ACCREDITATION OCA, CCA
AFFILIATION None
YEARS IN OPERATION 73
DATES OPEN July through August
FEES $925 per 2-week session; $1375 per 3-week session.
SCHOLARSHIPS No
ACCOMODATION Cabins
SPECIALTY Traditional
OBJECTIVES A caring atmosphere in which campers can develop self-confidence. A fun environment aimed at fostering both group belonging & independence.
ACTIVITIES Sailing, canoeing, kayaking, board sailing, swimming, tennis, archery, trampoline, riding, music, theatre, crafts, earth education, high ropes.

EVALUATIONS No
MEDICAL FACILITIES Doctor in residence.
VISITORS Allowed on Visitors Day.
SPECIAL NEEDS FACILITIES Not specified
DESCRIPTION Please enquire for details.

NEAREST CITY/TOWN Huntsville
AGE SPREAD 7 to 16 years
CAMPERS PER SESSION 190
STAFF PER SESSION Combination of 80 staff and counsellors
COUNSELLOR:CAMPER RATIO Not specified.
BOYS OR GIRLS ☐ Boys only ☒ Girls only ☐ Co-ed
NOTES

HOCKEY OPPORTUNITY CAMP

SUMMER ADDRESS	PO Box 448		
	Sundridge		ONT
	P0A 1Z0	**SUMMER PHONE**	705-386-7702
WINTER ADDRESS	As above		
			ONT
		WINTER PHONE	

CONTACT PERSON Lance Barrs
ACCREDITATION OCA
AFFILIATION None
YEARS IN OPERATION 30
DATES OPEN July through August
FEES $425 per one-week session.
SCHOLARSHIPS Please enquire.
ACCOMODATION Cabins, washrooms with showers, dining hall, recreation hall.
SPECIALTY Hockey
OBJECTIVES A fun experience for children where they can develop confidence & self-esteem on & off the ice.

ACTIVITIES Hockey, multiple watersports including swimming, water skiing, kayaking, snorkeling, mountain biking, volleyball.

EVALUATIONS Yes; of hockey skills and 2 chosen alternate activities.
MEDICAL FACILITIES Infirmary with nurse on site.
VISITORS Not allowed
SPECIAL NEEDS FACILITIES No
DESCRIPTION Please enquire for details.

NEAREST CITY/TOWN Huntsville
AGE SPREAD 6 to 16 years
CAMPERS PER SESSION 210
STAFF PER SESSION 75
COUNSELLOR:CAMPER RATIO 1 to 10
BOYS OR GIRLS ☐ Boys only ☐ Girls only ☒ Co-ed
NOTES Girls are welcome but very few attend; ratio approximately 2 girls per 100 boys.

HOLLOWS CAMP

SUMMER ADDRESS RR #3

Cookstown ONT
L0L 1L0 **SUMMER PHONE** 416-775-2694

WINTER ADDRESS As above

WINTER PHONE

CONTACT PERSON Stephen & Janet Fine
ACCREDITATION OCA, CCA
AFFILIATION None
YEARS IN OPERATION 14
DATES OPEN July through August
FEES $875 per 2-week session.
SCHOLARSHIPS No
ACCOMODATION Cabins, main lodge, dining hall.
SPECIALTY Horseback Riding
OBJECTIVES To give each camper a safe & happy camp experience, & to instill in campers a love of sports & the outdoors.

ACTIVITIES English horseback riding, kayaking, archery, theatre, crafts, outtripping.

EVALUATIONS No
MEDICAL FACILITIES Doctor on 24-hour call; staff trained in first aid.
VISITORS Not allowed
SPECIAL NEEDS FACILITIES Unspecified
DESCRIPTION 287 acres with woodlands, meadows, & ponds: the site is a prime wildlife habitat & ideal for outdoor educational resource pursuits.
NEAREST CITY/TOWN Cookstown
AGE SPREAD 7 to 15 years
CAMPERS PER SESSION 40
STAFF PER SESSION 10
COUNSELLOR:CAMPER RATIO 1 to 4
BOYS OR GIRLS ☐ Boys only ☐ Girls only ☒ Co-ed
NOTES

HORSE PEOPLE

SUMMER ADDRESS	RR #1
	Wendover ONT
	K0A 3K0 **SUMMER PHONE** 613-673-5905
WINTER ADDRESS	As above
	WINTER PHONE
CONTACT PERSON	Bev & Wolfe Schinke
ACCREDITATION	OCA, CCA
AFFILIATION	None
YEARS IN OPERATION	18
DATES OPEN	Late June through August
FEES	$1150 - $4200 per 2-8 week session
SCHOLARSHIPS	Yes; through registered charities.
ACCOMODATION	Cabins with bathroom & shower, dining & rec hall, pool.
SPECIALTY	Horseback Riding
OBJECTIVES	To offer equestrian skills in a safe, fun, multi-cultural environment.
ACTIVITIES	Complete horsemanship including dressage, jumping, cross-country; swimming, dances, campfires, games, movies, drama.
EVALUATIONS	Yes. informally.
MEDICAL FACILITIES	Medical centre nearby.
VISITORS	Allowed on visiting day.
SPECIAL NEEDS FACILITIES	Unspecified
DESCRIPTION	Located in the Ottawa Valley surrounded by the Larose Forest. The compound has 3 barns, indoor & outdoor arenas, hunter, jumper & dressage rings, cross-country courses.
NEAREST CITY/TOWN	Cornwall
AGE SPREAD	9 to 18 years
CAMPERS PER SESSION	60
STAFF PER SESSION	20-25
COUNSELLOR:CAMPER RATIO	1 to 3
BOYS OR GIRLS	☐ Boys only ☐ Girls only ☒ Co-ed
NOTES	

HURON HOCKEY SCHOOL

SUMMER ADDRESS PO Box 203
Cornwall
ONT
K6H 5S7 **SUMMER PHONE** 613-933-2582

WINTER ADDRESS As above

WINTER PHONE

CONTACT PERSON Paul O'Dacre
ACCREDITATION
AFFILIATION None
YEARS IN OPERATION 23
DATES OPEN July through August
FEES $650 - $750 per one-week session.
SCHOLARSHIPS Please enquire.
ACCOMODATION St. Lawrence College residence, games room, fitness centre.
SPECIALTY Hockey
OBJECTIVES To provide professional hockey instruction improving skill development, aiding students in learning to better enjoy the game of hockey & creating lasting friendships.
ACTIVITIES Individualized hockey instruction, video analysis & recreational activities such as ball hockey, baseball, tennis, volleyball, soccer & various indoor/outdoor activities.

EVALUATIONS Yes
MEDICAL FACILITIES Trainer on staff.
VISITORS Allowed
SPECIAL NEEDS FACILITIES No
DESCRIPTION Facilities include the Cornwall Civic Complex (Ed Lumley Arena) with large, spacious dressing rooms, air-conditioned classrooms, lecture areas & conditioning rooms.
NEAREST CITY/TOWN Cornwall
AGE SPREAD 7 to 18 years
CAMPERS PER SESSION Unspecified; please enquire.
STAFF PER SESSION Unspecified; please enquire.
COUNSELLOR:CAMPER RATIO Unspecified; please enquire.
BOYS OR GIRLS ☐ Boys only ☐ Girls only ☒ Co-ed
NOTES Day student rates range from $399 - $435 per week.

HURONDA

SUMMER ADDRESS	RR #1		
	Huntsville		ONT
	P0A 1K0	**SUMMER PHONE**	705-789-7153
WINTER ADDRESS	Canadian Diabetes Association 412 Weddel Court		
	Newmarket		ONT
	L3Y 7H1	**WINTER PHONE**	416-853-5693

CONTACT PERSON Heather Anderson
ACCREDITATION OCA, CCA
AFFILIATION Canadian Diabetes Association
YEARS IN OPERATION 25
DATES OPEN End of June through August
FEES $675 per 2-week session.
SCHOLARSHIPS Yes
ACCOMODATION Cabins, chalets, recreation hall, showers.
SPECIALTY Special Needs: Diabetes
OBJECTIVES To give children with diabetes a positive outdoor experience & to foster independence & general skills.

ACTIVITIES Swimming, tennis, tripping, kayaking, canoeing, crafts, sing-songs, basketball, art, backpacking, archery, sailing, hiking.

EVALUATIONS No
MEDICAL FACILITIES 2-3 doctors & 4-5 nurses on staff.
VISITORS Not encouraged
SPECIAL NEEDS FACILITIES Yes
DESCRIPTION A 110-acre site on the wooded shores of Lake Waseosa.

NEAREST CITY/TOWN Huntsville
AGE SPREAD 8 to 15 years
CAMPERS PER SESSION 84
STAFF PER SESSION 40
COUNSELLOR:CAMPER RATIO 1 to 5
BOYS OR GIRLS ☐ Boys only ☐ Girls only ☒ Co-ed
NOTES Special needs refers to a general camp specifically for children with diabetes.

JOHN ISLAND CAMP

SUMMER ADDRESS			
	Spanish		ONT
	P0P 2A0	**SUMMER PHONE**	705-848-2838
WINTER ADDRESS	c/o Sudbury Family YM-YWCA 185 Lloyd Street		
	Sudbury		ONT
	P3B 1N1	**WINTER PHONE**	705-674-8315

CONTACT PERSON Rick Wise
ACCREDITATION OCA, CCA
AFFILIATION YM-YWCA
YEARS IN OPERATION 40
DATES OPEN July through August
FEES $350 per 8-day sesssion; $515 per 13-day session.
SCHOLARSHIPS Yes
ACCOMODATION Cabins, central showers, dining hall, electricity.
SPECIALTY Traditional
OBJECTIVES To foster personal growth & leadership through direct experiences in the outdoors within the spirit & aims of the YMCA.
ACTIVITIES Swimming, canoeing, arts & crafts, sailing, windsurfing, kayaking, ropes courses, rock climbing, archery, games, environmental education.

EVALUATIONS No
MEDICAL FACILITIES Health centre with resident nurse.
VISITORS Not encouraged
SPECIAL NEEDS FACILITIES Yes
DESCRIPTION An island in the north channel of Lake Huron, John Island has forests, streams, marshes, trails & a spring-fed lake. The camp buildings are on the south-east shore.
NEAREST CITY/TOWN Sudbury
AGE SPREAD 6 to 16 years
CAMPERS PER SESSION 134
STAFF PER SESSION 56
COUNSELLOR:CAMPER RATIO 1 to 4
BOYS OR GIRLS ☐ Boys only ☐ Girls only ☒ Co-ed
NOTES Special needs refers to the offering of a special needs integration program; please enquire.

JOY BIBLE CAMP

SUMMER ADDRESS	Box 1480		
	Bancroft		ONT
	K0L 1C0	**SUMMER PHONE**	613-332-3696
WINTER ADDRESS	As above		
		WINTER PHONE	

CONTACT PERSON John Coles
ACCREDITATION OCA, CCI
AFFILIATION Christian (nondenominational)
YEARS IN OPERATION 49
DATES OPEN July through August
FEES $184 - $214 per one-week session; please enquire.
SCHOLARSHIPS Yes, on a need basis
ACCOMODATION Cabins, central showers & washroom, main dining room.
SPECIALTY Christian Development
OBJECTIVES To promote the physical, spiritual & emotional maturity of individual campers through the study of God's word & interaction with peers & counsellors.
ACTIVITIES Bible study, swimming, boating, canoeing, rock diving, archery, nature study, crafts, games.

EVALUATIONS No
MEDICAL FACILITIES Infirmary on site; hospital within 10 km.
VISITORS Allowed
SPECIAL NEEDS FACILITIES Yes
DESCRIPTION Please enquire for details.

NEAREST CITY/TOWN Peterborough
AGE SPREAD 8 to 21 years
CAMPERS PER SESSION 100
STAFF PER SESSION 40
COUNSELLOR:CAMPER RATIO 1 to 5
BOYS OR GIRLS ☒ Boys only ☒ Girls only ☒ Co-ed
NOTES Some special needs facilities; please enquire.

KANDALORE

SUMMER ADDRESS	RR #2		
	Minden		ONT
	K0M 2K0	**SUMMER PHONE**	705-489-2419
WINTER ADDRESS	14 Bruce Park Avenue Suite #201		
	Toronto		ONT
	M4P 2S3	**WINTER PHONE**	416-322-9735

CONTACT PERSON Michael Moore
ACCREDITATION OCA
AFFILIATION None
YEARS IN OPERATION 47
DATES OPEN June through August
FEES $895 per 2-week session; $1695 per 4-week session.
SCHOLARSHIPS No
ACCOMODATION Cabins, showers, toilets, dining & rec hall, activity buildings.
SPECIALTY Traditional
OBJECTIVES To develop in each camper an appreciation of nature, a healthy sense of self-esteem, an understanding of others, & the necessary skills to become an effective leader.
ACTIVITIES Archery, arts & crafts, canoeing, water skiing, sailing, kayaking, swimming, outtripping, games, campfires.

EVALUATIONS No
MEDICAL FACILITIES Small infirmary with doctor & nurse on site.
VISITORS Not allowed
SPECIAL NEEDS FACILITIES Not specified
DESCRIPTION Situated on approximately one mile of shoreline on Lake Kabakwa amidst 75 acres of well-treed forest. Facilities include access to Chapel Island.
NEAREST CITY/TOWN Haliburton
AGE SPREAD 6 to 16 years
CAMPERS PER SESSION 110
STAFF PER SESSION Combination of 40 staff & counsellors.
COUNSELLOR:CAMPER RATIO Not specified
BOYS OR GIRLS ☐ Boys only ☐ Girls only ☒ Co-ed
NOTES Limited 1-week sessions are available; please enquire.

KAWABI

SUMMER ADDRESS	RR #2		
	Minden		ONT
	K0M 2K0	**SUMMER PHONE**	705-489-2510
WINTER ADDRESS	6 William Andrew Avenue		
	RR #4		
	Stouffville		ONT
	L4A 7X5	**WINTER PHONE**	416-642-1942

CONTACT PERSON Mr. & Mrs. Bruce Harris
ACCREDITATION OCA
AFFILIATION None
YEARS IN OPERATION 30
DATES OPEN June through August
FEES $895 per 2-week session; $1695 per 4-week session.
SCHOLARSHIPS No
ACCOMODATION Cabins, platform tents, showers, dining & recreation hall.
SPECIALTY Traditional
OBJECTIVES To create a warm, personal family setting with a wide range of activities encouraging involvement & a positive self-image.

ACTIVITIES Swimming, waterskiing, skin diving, multiple boating sports, riflery, fencing, crafts, trampoline.

EVALUATIONS No
MEDICAL FACILITIES Infirmary with resident physician.
VISITORS Allowed during Visitors Day (one per session).
SPECIAL NEEDS FACILITIES Unspecified
DESCRIPTION Please enquire for details.

NEAREST CITY/TOWN Bracebridge
AGE SPREAD 7 to 15 years
CAMPERS PER SESSION 140
STAFF PER SESSION 45
COUNSELLOR:CAMPER RATIO 1 to 7
BOYS OR GIRLS ☐ Boys only ☐ Girls only ☒ Co-ed
NOTES

KEEWAYDIN CAMPS

SUMMER ADDRESS			
	Temagami		ONT
	P0H 2H0	**SUMMER PHONE**	
WINTER ADDRESS	59 Cherry Valley Road		
	Greenwich		CT
	06831	**WINTER PHONE**	203-661-1924

CONTACT PERSON Dan Carpenter
ACCREDITATION OCA, CCA
AFFILIATION None
YEARS IN OPERATION 101
DATES OPEN July through August
FEES $2300 per 6-week session.
SCHOLARSHIPS Yes
ACCOMODATION Cabins, platform tents, toilets, showers, dining room, lodge.
SPECIALTY Wilderness Training
OBJECTIVES To experience unspoiled nature, to learn wilderness skills, & to accept internal challenges.

ACTIVITIES Wilderness canoe tripping, along with all the skills necessary to live comfortably & safely in such an activity (eg; canoeing, camping, cooking).

EVALUATIONS Yes
MEDICAL FACILITIES Infirmary with resident doctor or EMT.
VISITORS Allowed; there is a family vacation lodge for visitors.
SPECIAL NEEDS FACILITIES Unspecified
DESCRIPTION The camp is located on Lake Temagami in Canada's unspoiled north, with access to Devil's Island.

NEAREST CITY/TOWN North Bay
AGE SPREAD 10 to 18 years
CAMPERS PER SESSION 120
STAFF PER SESSION 45-50.
COUNSELLOR:CAMPER RATIO 1 to 3
BOYS OR GIRLS ☒ Boys only ☐ Girls only ☐ Co-ed
NOTES 3-week sessions for boys aged 10-11 are available at a cost of $1300.

KEMUR CAMP

SUMMER ADDRESS RR #4

Cambridge ONT
N1R 5S5 **SUMMER PHONE** 519-621-2109

WINTER ADDRESS As above

WINTER PHONE

CONTACT PERSON Chris Murray
ACCREDITATION OCA
AFFILIATION None
YEARS IN OPERATION 26
DATES OPEN July through August
FEES $350 per one-week session.
SCHOLARSHIPS No
ACCOMODATION Dormitory-style sleeping facilities, modern washrooms.
SPECIALTY Horseback Riding
OBJECTIVES To provide a thorough introduction to horses for beginners, & to develop new skills for accomplished young equestrians.

ACTIVITIES English riding lessons (beginner to advanced), horsemanship lectures, horse shows, dressage, swimming, sports, campfires.

EVALUATIONS No, but ribbons are awarded at the horse shows.
MEDICAL FACILITIES 15 minutes from hospital.
VISITORS Not allowed
SPECIAL NEEDS FACILITIES Unspecified
DESCRIPTION The camp is situated on 500 scenic acres, offering cross country trails.

NEAREST CITY/TOWN Cambridge
AGE SPREAD 7 to 14 years
CAMPERS PER SESSION 55
STAFF PER SESSION 10
COUNSELLOR:CAMPER RATIO 1 to 6
BOYS OR GIRLS ☐ Boys only ☒ Girls only ☐ Co-ed
NOTES

KILCOO CAMP

SUMMER ADDRESS			
	Minden		ONT
	K0M 2K0	**SUMMER PHONE**	705-286-1091
WINTER ADDRESS	150 Eglinton Avenue E.		
	Suite #204		
	Toronto		ONT
	M4P 1E8	**WINTER PHONE**	416-486-5264

CONTACT PERSON David Latimer
ACCREDITATION OCA
AFFILIATION None
YEARS IN OPERATION 63
DATES OPEN Late June through August
FEES $2045 per month.
SCHOLARSHIPS No
ACCOMODATION Cabins, showers, dining hall.
SPECIALTY Traditional
OBJECTIVES To promote self-reliance & encourage the development of the individual.

ACTIVITIES Swimming, water sports, crafts, mountain biking, archery, tripping, woodcraft, outward challenge (includes tower climbing, aerial course, ropes course, & rock climbing).

EVALUATIONS Yes
MEDICAL FACILITIES Infirmary on site with doctor & nurse.
VISITORS Allowed during Visitors Day (one per month).
SPECIAL NEEDS FACILITIES Yes
DESCRIPTION Located in the Haliburton Highlands.

NEAREST CITY/TOWN Bracebridge
AGE SPREAD 8 to 16 years
CAMPERS PER SESSION 225
STAFF PER SESSION 75
COUNSELLOR:CAMPER RATIO 1 to 7
BOYS OR GIRLS ☒ Boys only ☐ Girls only ☐ Co-ed
NOTES

KNOX ADVENTURE CAMP

SUMMER ADDRESS see below

ONT

SUMMER PHONE

WINTER ADDRESS c/o Knox Presbyterian Church
630 Spadina Avenue
Toronto ONT
M5S 2H4 **WINTER PHONE** 416-921-8993

CONTACT PERSON John Scott

ACCREDITATION

AFFILIATION Presbyterian

YEARS IN OPERATION 18

DATES OPEN Mid to late August

FEES $200 per one-week session.

SCHOLARSHIPS No

ACCOMODATION Cabins with electricity, showers, dining hall.

SPECIALTY Christian Development

OBJECTIVES To challenge children with demanding activities; to confront children with Biblical values; to provide an environment for social interaction and learning more about the world.

ACTIVITIES Water sports, land sports, trampoline, photography, Bible study, drama, rocket building & launching.

EVALUATIONS No

MEDICAL FACILITIES Infirmary with nurse on site.

VISITORS Not allowed

SPECIAL NEEDS FACILITIES Decided on an individual basis.

DESCRIPTION Situated on 800 acres of land surrounding Duck Lake.

NEAREST CITY/TOWN Bracebridge

AGE SPREAD 6 to 16 years

CAMPERS PER SESSION Maximum 75

STAFF PER SESSION Up to 25

COUNSELLOR:CAMPER RATIO 1 to 4

BOYS OR GIRLS ☐ Boys only ☐ Girls only ☒ Co-ed

NOTES

LAKEFIELD CAMP INTERNATIONAL

SUMMER ADDRESS c/o Lakefield College School
Lakefield ONT
K0L 2H0 **SUMMER PHONE** 705-652-7675

WINTER ADDRESS 980 Yonge Street
Suite #200
Toronto ONT
M4W 2J4 **WINTER PHONE** 416-323-9090

CONTACT PERSON Alice Yu
ACCREDITATION OCA
AFFILIATION Canadian International Student Services
YEARS IN OPERATION 8
DATES OPEN July through August
FEES $1115 for 2 weeks; $1700 for 3 weeks; $2215 for 4 weeks.
SCHOLARSHIPS No
ACCOMODATION Residence facilities of Lakefield College School.
SPECIALTY Traditional
OBJECTIVES To promote international understanding. The Canadian children host children from abroad.

ACTIVITIES Team sports, swimming, windsurfing, sailing, canoeing, tennis, archery, drama, arts & crafts, martial arts, computers, piano, music.

EVALUATIONS Yes, on request
MEDICAL FACILITIES Nurse on site; doctor in town.
VISITORS Not encouraged
SPECIAL NEEDS FACILITIES Unspecified
DESCRIPTION Please enquire for details.

NEAREST CITY/TOWN Peterborough
AGE SPREAD 8 to 16 years
CAMPERS PER SESSION Approximately 150
STAFF PER SESSION Approximately 40
COUNSELLOR:CAMPER RATIO Included above
BOYS OR GIRLS ☐ Boys only ☐ Girls only ☒ Co-ed
NOTES Two hours of ESL are available for international campers only. Canadian campers partake of sports & arts activities for the full day.

LAKEWOOD CAMP

SUMMER ADDRESS	RR #2		
	Wainfleet		ONT
	L0S 1V0	**SUMMER PHONE**	416-899-3043
WINTER ADDRESS	Easter Seals Society 250 Ferrand Drive, Suite #200		
	Don Mills		ONT
	M3C 3P2	**WINTER PHONE**	416-421-8377

CONTACT PERSON Mark Sack
ACCREDITATION OCA, CCA
AFFILIATION Easter Seals Society
YEARS IN OPERATION 59
DATES OPEN July through August
FEES $925 per one-week session.
SCHOLARSHIPS Yes
ACCOMODATION Cabins with showers, dining hall, recreation hall.
SPECIALTY Special Needs: Physical Disabilities
OBJECTIVES To provide oportunities & challenges for campers to develop independence, build self-esteem & develop creative expression skills.
ACTIVITIES Astronomy, horseback riding, campcraft, music, drama, canoeing, sailing, swimming, computers, archery, fishing, sports.

EVALUATIONS Yes
MEDICAL FACILITIES 3 nurses on staff; hospital nearby.
VISITORS Not encouraged
SPECIAL NEEDS FACILITIES Yes
DESCRIPTION Waterfront location with wooded nature trails.

NEAREST CITY/TOWN St. Catharines
AGE SPREAD 7 to 19 years
CAMPERS PER SESSION 72
STAFF PER SESSION Maximum 50
COUNSELLOR:CAMPER RATIO 1 to 2
BOYS OR GIRLS ☐ Boys only ☐ Girls only ☒ Co-ed
NOTES One of 5 Ontario Easter Seal Camps dedicated to offering warm, accessible environments & camping fun to physically disabled young people. Family camping is an option; please enquire.

LONG BAY CAMP

SUMMER ADDRESS	RR #1 Westport K0G 1X0	**SUMMER PHONE**	ONT 613-273-5728
WINTER ADDRESS	PO Box 2364 Station D Ottawa K1P 5W5	**WINTER PHONE**	ONT 819-682-4855

CONTACT PERSON Quasem Mahmud
ACCREDITATION OCA
AFFILIATION Muslim
YEARS IN OPERATION 9
DATES OPEN July through August
FEES $195 per one-week session; $390 per 2-week session.
SCHOLARSHIPS No
ACCOMODATION Cabins, washrooms with showers & toilets, dining lodge.
SPECIALTY Islamic Development
OBJECTIVES To provide an opportunity for Muslim children to interact with one another, learn about & practice their religion.

ACTIVITIES Sports, hiking, canoeing, swimming, drama, nature & environmental studies, prayers, Islamic education.

EVALUATIONS No
MEDICAL FACILITIES First aid room with doctor on call; hospital 30 minutes away.
VISITORS Allowed
SPECIAL NEEDS FACILITIES Unspecified
DESCRIPTION Located on Long Bay, on spring-fed Bob's Lake. The camp's 350 acres of land are divided into wooded & open areas, including a farm & orchard, ponds & streams.
NEAREST CITY/TOWN Kingston
AGE SPREAD 7 to 15 years
CAMPERS PER SESSION 60
STAFF PER SESSION 10
COUNSELLOR:CAMPER RATIO 1 to 6
BOYS OR GIRLS ☐ Boys only ☐ Girls only ☒ Co-ed
NOTES

MANITOBA PIONEER CAMP

SUMMER ADDRESS	Kejick Post Office
	Kenora ONT
	P0X 1E0 **SUMMER PHONE** 807-543-4040
WINTER ADDRESS	202 - 159 Henderson Hwy
	Winnipeg MAN
	R2L 1L4 **WINTER PHONE** 204-663-1481
CONTACT PERSON	Hildy Leverton
ACCREDITATION	MCA
AFFILIATION	Christian (nondenominational)
YEARS IN OPERATION	52
DATES OPEN	July through August
FEES	$195 for 7 days; $270 for 10 days; $370 for 14 days.
SCHOLARSHIPS	Yes
ACCOMODATION	Cabins, central washrooms with showers.
SPECIALTY	Christian Development
OBJECTIVES	To use the environment as a means to teach children skills with which to enjoy life & be safe in God's creation. Committed to campers having fun, growing & learning.
ACTIVITIES	Swimming, canoeing, sailing, archery, first aid, crafts, outtripping, fishing, Bible studies, kayaking, campfires.
EVALUATIONS	Letters are sent to parents at the start & finish of each camp.
MEDICAL FACILITIES	Nurse on site.
VISITORS	Allowed on Visitors Day.
SPECIAL NEEDS FACILITIES	Yes
DESCRIPTION	Located on two natural islands on Lake of the Woods, in a Canadian Shield setting of rugged beauty.
NEAREST CITY/TOWN	Kenora
AGE SPREAD	8 to 17 years
CAMPERS PER SESSION	Approximately 80
STAFF PER SESSION	25
COUNSELLOR:CAMPER RATIO	1 to 4
BOYS OR GIRLS	☒ Boys only ☒ Girls only ☒ Co-ed
NOTES	Camperships are available. Family camping is also an option; please enquire. Special needs refers to ability to accommodate many physically or mentally disabled campers. Each case is considered individually.

MARYGROVE CAMP

SUMMER ADDRESS RR #2

Penetanguishene ONT
L0K 1P0 **SUMMER PHONE** 705-549-8951

WINTER ADDRESS c/o Society of St. Vincent de Paul
240 Church Street
Toronto ONT
M5B 1Z2 **WINTER PHONE** 416-364-5577

CONTACT PERSON Louise Coutu
ACCREDITATION OCA
AFFILIATION Society of St. Vincent de Paul
YEARS IN OPERATION 50
DATES OPEN June to August
FEES None; all children are sponsored for 8-day session.
SCHOLARSHIPS See above
ACCOMODATION Cabins, showers, sports & rec hall, dining hall, chapel.
SPECIALTY Disadvantaged Youth
OBJECTIVES To allow campers to explore personal interests in a wide range of activities. Emphasis is on harmonious community living & an appreciation of personal identity, worth & dignity.
ACTIVITIES Swimming, canoeing, crafts, drama, sports, cookouts, hiking, tenting, co-operative games.

EVALUATIONS No
MEDICAL FACILITIES Infirmary with a doctor on call.
VISITORS Not allowed
SPECIAL NEEDS FACILITIES Yes
DESCRIPTION Located on Georgian Bay, Marygrove.

NEAREST CITY/TOWN Midland
AGE SPREAD 5 to 13 years
CAMPERS PER SESSION 130
STAFF PER SESSION 24
COUNSELLOR:CAMPER RATIO 1 to 5
BOYS OR GIRLS ☐ Boys only ☒ Girls only ☐ Co-ed
NOTES Special needs refers to learning impaired children, or those with behavioural problems.

MERRYWOOD CAMP

SUMMER ADDRESS	RR #5		
	Perth		ONT
	K7H 3C7	**SUMMER PHONE**	613-267-1244
WINTER ADDRESS	Easter Seals Society 250 Ferrand Drive, Suite #200		
	Don Mills		ONT
	M3C 3P2	**WINTER PHONE**	416-421-8377

CONTACT PERSON Mark Sack
ACCREDITATION OCA, CCA
AFFILIATION Easter Seals Society
YEARS IN OPERATION 59
DATES OPEN July through August
FEES $925 per one-week session.
SCHOLARSHIPS Yes
ACCOMODATION Cabins with showers, dining hall, recreation hall.
SPECIALTY Special Needs: Physical Disabilities
OBJECTIVES To provide oportunities & challenges for campers to develop independence, build self-esteem & develop creative expression skills.
ACTIVITIES Astronomy, horseback riding, campcraft, music, drama, canoeing, sailing, swimming, computers, archery, fishing, sports.

EVALUATIONS Yes
MEDICAL FACILITIES 3 nurses on staff; hospital nearby.
VISITORS Not encouraged
SPECIAL NEEDS FACILITIES Yes
DESCRIPTION Waterfront location with wooded nature trails.

NEAREST CITY/TOWN Ottawa
AGE SPREAD 7 to 19 years
CAMPERS PER SESSION 72
STAFF PER SESSION Maximum 50
COUNSELLOR:CAMPER RATIO 1 to 2
BOYS OR GIRLS ☐ Boys only ☐ Girls only ☒ Co-ed
NOTES One of 5 Ontario Easter Seal camps dedicated to offering warm, accessible environments & camping fun to physically disabled young people. Family camping is also an option; please enquire.

MISSANABIE WOODS ACADEMY

SUMMER ADDRESS	Dog Lake		
	Missanabie		ONT
	P0M 2H0	**SUMMER PHONE**	1-800-333-4009
WINTER ADDRESS	c/o New Horizons Youth Ministries 1002 South at 350 East		
	Marion		IN
	46953-9562	**WINTER PHONE**	317-668-4010

CONTACT PERSON Steve Green
ACCREDITATION OCA, CCA, CCI, Association for Experimental Education
AFFILIATION Christian (nondenominational)
YEARS IN OPERATION 17
DATES OPEN Mid-June through mid-August
FEES Approximately $2000 per month.
SCHOLARSHIPS Yes
ACCOMODATION Cabins, main dining hall, one shower facility.
SPECIALTY Christian Development
OBJECTIVES To develop high achievement & self-esteem through physical, social, mental, moral & spiritual accomplishments. To learn of God by understanding & experiencing creation.
ACTIVITIES Group and individual counselling, character leadership development, first aid, swimming, canoeing, fishing, work projects, ropes course, survival training.

EVALUATIONS Yes; monthly & bi-weekly reports are sent to parents.
MEDICAL FACILITIES Infirmary run by nurse or EMT.
VISITORS Allowed during Visitors Days.
SPECIAL NEEDS FACILITIES No
DESCRIPTION Located in the unspoiled wilderness of the Canadian north woods. The camp is only accessible by boat, & there is no electricity.
NEAREST CITY/TOWN Wawa
AGE SPREAD 12 to 17 years
CAMPERS PER SESSION 50
STAFF PER SESSION 35
COUNSELLOR:CAMPER RATIO 1 to 3
BOYS OR GIRLS ☐ Boys only ☐ Girls only ☒ Co-ed
NOTES

NEW FRENDA YOUTH CAMP

SUMMER ADDRESS National Camps for the Blind
Route #2
Port Carling ONT
P0B 1J0 **SUMMER PHONE** 705-765-5597

WINTER ADDRESS As above

WINTER PHONE 519-369-6692

CONTACT PERSON Chris Risk
ACCREDITATION CCA, CCI
AFFILIATION Christian (nondenominational)
YEARS IN OPERATION 20
DATES OPEN One week in August
FEES Free to all legally blind persons aged 9 & up.
SCHOLARSHIPS See above.
ACCOMODATION Cabins, showers, dining hall.
SPECIALTY Special Needs: Blind / Visually Impaired
OBJECTIVES To allow the blind participant to discover undeveloped potential, increase self-confidence, improve physical vigour, & develop an appreciation for God's love & care.
ACTIVITIES Archery, boating, camp council, canoeing, crafts, hiking, horseback riding, rock climbing, sailing, swimming, rappelling, water skiing.

EVALUATIONS No
MEDICAL FACILITIES Infirmary with medical staff on duty 24 hours.
VISITORS Allowed on talent night.
SPECIAL NEEDS FACILITIES Yes
DESCRIPTION Please enquire for details.

NEAREST CITY/TOWN Bracebridge
AGE SPREAD 9 years & up.
CAMPERS PER SESSION 40
STAFF PER SESSION Varies
COUNSELLOR:CAMPER RATIO 1 to 2
BOYS OR GIRLS ☐ Boys only ☐ Girls only ☒ Co-ed
NOTES Special needs refers to blind or visually impaired campers. This program is designed to place emphasis on ability rather than the disability of the visually impaired individual.

NORTHWAY-WENDIGO

SUMMER ADDRESS Cache Lake

Algonquin Park ONT
P0A 1K0 **SUMMER PHONE** 705-633-5595

WINTER ADDRESS 294 Regent Street
PO Box 1184
Niagara-on-the-Lake ONT
L0S 1J0 **WINTER PHONE** 905-468-4455

CONTACT PERSON Brookes Prewitt
ACCREDITATION OCA, CCA
AFFILIATION None
YEARS IN OPERATION 88
DATES OPEN July through August
FEES $2000 per 7 weeks; $1250 per 3.5 weeks; $780 per 2 weeks.
SCHOLARSHIPS No
ACCOMODATION Platform tents, main log cabin for meals & gatherings.
SPECIALTY Traditional
OBJECTIVES To provide a true wilderness experience for campers, & to teach them outdoor & survival skills.

ACTIVITIES Canoe trips, canoeing, swimming, sailing, crafts, archery, hiking, drama, nature studies, windsurfing, team sports.

EVALUATIONS No
MEDICAL FACILITIES Nurse on site & doctor on call.
VISITORS Allowed on scheduled Visitors Day.
SPECIAL NEEDS FACILITIES Unspecified
DESCRIPTION The base camp is situated in the wilderness of Algonquin Park.

NEAREST CITY/TOWN Huntsville
AGE SPREAD Girls 8-16 years; Boys 10-16 years
CAMPERS PER SESSION Girls - 50; Boys - 15.
STAFF PER SESSION 40
COUNSELLOR:CAMPER RATIO 1 to 3
BOYS OR GIRLS ☒ Boys only ☒ Girls only ☐ Co-ed
NOTES Northway is a girls-only camp; Wendigo is the boys-only camp. The two camps share some activites.

NORTHWOOD CAMP

SUMMER ADDRESS Site 3, Box B-8

Sesekinika ONT
P0K 1S0 **SUMMER PHONE** 705-642-3414

WINTER ADDRESS Easter Seals Society
250 Ferrand Drive, Suite #200
Don Mills ONT
M3C 3P2 **WINTER PHONE** 416-421-8377

CONTACT PERSON Mark Sack
ACCREDITATION OCA, CCA
AFFILIATION Easter Seals Society
YEARS IN OPERATION 59
DATES OPEN July through August
FEES $925 per one-week session.
SCHOLARSHIPS Yes; assistance available on request.
ACCOMODATION Cabins with showers, dining hall, recreation hall.
SPECIALTY Special Needs: Physical Disabilities
OBJECTIVES To provide oportunities & challenges for campers to develop independence, build self-esteem & develop creative expression skills.
ACTIVITIES Astronomy, horseback riding, campcraft, music, drama, canoeing, sailing, swimming, computers, archery, fishing, sports.

EVALUATIONS Yes
MEDICAL FACILITIES 3 nurses on staff; hospital nearby.
VISITORS Not encouraged
SPECIAL NEEDS FACILITIES Yes
DESCRIPTION Waterfront location with wooded nature trails.

NEAREST CITY/TOWN Matheson
AGE SPREAD 7 to 19 years
CAMPERS PER SESSION 72
STAFF PER SESSION Maximum 50
COUNSELLOR:CAMPER RATIO 1 to 2
BOYS OR GIRLS ☐ Boys only ☐ Girls only ☒ Co-ed
NOTES One of 5 Ontario Easter Seal camps dedicated to offering warm, accessible environments & camping fun to physically disabled young people. Family camping is an option; please enquire.

OLYMPIA SPORTS CAMP

SUMMER ADDRESS	RR #4		
	Huntsville		ONT
	P0A 1K0	**SUMMER PHONE**	705-635-2491
WINTER ADDRESS	485 Lawrence Avenue W.		
	Toronto		ONT
	M5M 1C6	**WINTER PHONE**	416-789-2967

CONTACT PERSON Dave Grace

ACCREDITATION OCA

AFFILIATION None

YEARS IN OPERATION 20

DATES OPEN July through early September

FEES $415 per one-week session.

SCHOLARSHIPS Unspecified

ACCOMODATION Dorm-style heated cabins, washroom facilities with showers.

SPECIALTY Sports

OBJECTIVES To provide an intensive training program in the chosen sport/activity, the skills and attitudes to achieve one's best, and the traditional camp experience.

ACTIVITIES 22 specialized camps to chose from, including wrestling, windsurfing, volleyball, tennis, tae kwon do, swimming, soccer, sailing, rugby, karate, football, dance, cheerleading, boxing, basketball, aqua sports, basketball, and triathlons.

EVALUATIONS Player evaluations are issued; certificates are presented.

MEDICAL FACILITIES Heath centre with 1 doctor, 3 RNs & 3 athletic therapists.

VISITORS Allowed

SPECIAL NEEDS FACILITIES Unspecified

DESCRIPTION Facilities include indoor courts, fieldhouse & gym, outdoor courts, playing fields, lake pool, indoor lap pool, training studios, fitness centre, indoor running track & aerobic floor.

NEAREST CITY/TOWN Huntsville

AGE SPREAD 8 to 19 years

CAMPERS PER SESSION 356

STAFF PER SESSION 120

COUNSELLOR:CAMPER RATIO 1 to 9

BOYS OR GIRLS ☒ Boys only ☒ Girls only ☒ Co-ed

NOTES A fee discount is offered for early registration.

ONTARIO PIONEER CAMP

SUMMER ADDRESS	c/o Inter Varsity Christian Fellowship RR #1 Port Sydney ONT P0B 1L0
SUMMER PHONE	1-800-361-CAMP
WINTER ADDRESS	As above
WINTER PHONE	
CONTACT PERSON	Peter Bloom
ACCREDITATION	OCA, CCI
AFFILIATION	Christian (nondenominational)
YEARS IN OPERATION	64
DATES OPEN	July through August
FEES	$295 per 6-day session; $570 per 13-day session
SCHOLARSHIPS	Please enquire
ACCOMODATION	Chalets (cabin/tent hybrids), flush toilets, showers.
SPECIALTY	Christian Development
OBJECTIVES	To encourage campers to grow personally & experience God in His creation.
ACTIVITIES	Swimming, sailing, kayaking, canoeing, crafts, archery, windsurfing, Bible study, drama, puppetry.
EVALUATIONS	Certification in RLSS, ORCA or Red Cross can be achieved.
MEDICAL FACILITIES	Infirmary, doctors & nurses on site; hospital 30 mins away.
VISITORS	Allowed
SPECIAL NEEDS FACILITIES	Yes
DESCRIPTION	Located on Lake Clearwater in the quiet natural beauty of Muskoka.
NEAREST CITY/TOWN	Toronto
AGE SPREAD	5 to 19 years
CAMPERS PER SESSION	Maximum 160
STAFF PER SESSION	45
COUNSELLOR:CAMPER RATIO	1 to 5
BOYS OR GIRLS	☐ Boys only ☐ Girls only ☒ Co-ed
NOTES	Family & music camps are available. Integrated special needs program is also available; please enquire.

OUTWARD BOUND WILDERNESS SCHOOL

SUMMER ADDRESS	150 Laird Drive Suite #302 Toronto M4G 3V7	**SUMMER PHONE**	ONT 1-800-268-7329
WINTER ADDRESS	As above	**WINTER PHONE**	ONT

CONTACT PERSON Philip Blackford
ACCREDITATION OCA, CCA
AFFILIATION None
YEARS IN OPERATION 18
DATES OPEN June through August
FEES $1995 per 21-day session.
SCHOLARSHIPS Yes
ACCOMODATION Tents provided for outtrips; full facilities at base camp.
SPECIALTY Wilderness Training
OBJECTIVES To promote self-reliance, care & respect for others, responsibility to the community & concern for the environment.

ACTIVITIES Canoe tripping, rock climbing, kayaking, map & compass reading, group skills development, campcraft, hiking. Each trip includes an expedition by canoe.

EVALUATIONS Yes; senior high school credit may be earned.
MEDICAL FACILITIES Unspecified
VISITORS Allowed, but impractical given nature of outtrips.
SPECIAL NEEDS FACILITIES Yes
DESCRIPTION The base camp is situated on Black Sturgeon Lake, a boreal forest terrain. Outtrips are in Pukasdwa National Park, Algonquin Park & Baffin Island.
NEAREST CITY/TOWN Thunder Bay
AGE SPREAD 15 years & up
CAMPERS PER SESSION 450 annually
STAFF PER SESSION 70 annually
COUNSELLOR:CAMPER RATIO Not specified
BOYS OR GIRLS ☐ Boys only ☐ Girls only ☒ Co-ed
NOTES Special needs campers can be integrated into the various programs; please enquire. See also *Outward Bound BC.*

PROJECT C.A.N.O.E.

SUMMER ADDRESS	PO Box 720 Station P Toronto M5S 2Y4	**SUMMER PHONE**	ONT 416-222-2203
WINTER ADDRESS	As above	**WINTER PHONE**	

CONTACT PERSON Cameron Wong
ACCREDITATION OCA
AFFILIATION None
YEARS IN OPERATION 17
DATES OPEN July through August
FEES Approximately $200 per one-week session.
SCHOLARSHIPS Yes
ACCOMODATION Tents
SPECIALTY Disadvantaged Youth
OBJECTIVES To provide underpriviledged adolescents with wilderness excursions in N. Ontario. To help them acquire self-esteem & self-awareness, & encourage positive group dynamics.
ACTIVITIES 10-day wilderness canoe trips, hiking trips, nature programs.

EVALUATIONS Yes
MEDICAL FACILITIES None
VISITORS Not allowed
SPECIAL NEEDS FACILITIES No
DESCRIPTION Please enquire for details.

NEAREST CITY/TOWN Varies according to program.
AGE SPREAD 12 to 17 years
CAMPERS PER SESSION 16
STAFF PER SESSION 8
COUNSELLOR:CAMPER RATIO 1 to 3
BOYS OR GIRLS ☐ Boys only ☐ Girls only ☒ Co-ed
NOTES Fees are charged according to ability to pay. C.A.N.O.E. stands for Creative and Natural Outdoor Experience.

RIDEAU HILL CAMP

SUMMER ADDRESS RR #3

Manotick ONT
K4M 1B4 **SUMMER PHONE** 613-826-2046

WINTER ADDRESS RR #2

Mountain ONT
K0E 1S0 **WINTER PHONE** 613-989-5295

CONTACT PERSON George Suffel
ACCREDITATION OCA
AFFILIATION United Church
YEARS IN OPERATION 45
DATES OPEN July through August
FEES Unspecified; please enquire.
SCHOLARSHIPS Some fee asistance may be available.
ACCOMODATION Cabins, main dining room, recreation hall, swimming pool.
SPECIALTY Christian Development
OBJECTIVES To provide character enrichment through living, sharing & developing within a Christian environment.

ACTIVITIES Swimming, arts & crafts, archery, canoeing, dance, drama, nature studies, Bible studies.

EVALUATIONS No
MEDICAL FACILITIES Nurse on duty.
VISITORS Not allowed
SPECIAL NEEDS FACILITIES Unspecified
DESCRIPTION Located by the Rideau River on an 18-acre site including wooded areas, grassy fields & river frontage.

NEAREST CITY/TOWN Ottawa
AGE SPREAD 6 to 15 years
CAMPERS PER SESSION Up to 80
STAFF PER SESSION 20
COUNSELLOR:CAMPER RATIO 1 to 8
BOYS OR GIRLS ☐ Boys only ☐ Girls only ☒ Co-ed
NOTES

RKY CAMP

SUMMER ADDRESS	RR #1 Parham ONT K0H 2K0 **SUMMER PHONE** 613-375-6295
WINTER ADDRESS	c/o Kingston Family YMCA 100 Wright Crescent Kingston ONT K7L 4T9 **WINTER PHONE** 613-546-2647
CONTACT PERSON	Eric Bogstad
ACCREDITATION	OCA, CCA
AFFILIATION	YM-YWCA
YEARS IN OPERATION	61
DATES OPEN	July through August
FEES	$449 per 2-week session.
SCHOLARSHIPS	Subsidy applications are available.
ACCOMODATION	Cabins, (tents for offsite trips), showers, toilets, dining hall.
SPECIALTY	Traditional
OBJECTIVES	To encourage the growth of young people in spirit, mind, & body, & in a sense of responsibility to each other & to the human community.
ACTIVITIES	Swimming, canoeing, kayaking, sailing, crafts, archery, sports, nature study, outtripping.
EVALUATIONS	No
MEDICAL FACILITIES	Infirmary with trained health care staff.
VISITORS	Allowed during Open House in advance of camp sessions.
SPECIAL NEEDS FACILITIES	Yes
DESCRIPTION	Located on the southern arm of Eagle Lake, on 15 acres of secluded property amid the forest of the Canadian Shield.
NEAREST CITY/TOWN	Kingston
AGE SPREAD	7 to 16 years
CAMPERS PER SESSION	95
STAFF PER SESSION	40-45
COUNSELLOR:CAMPER RATIO	1 to 4
BOYS OR GIRLS	☐ Boys only ☐ Girls only ☒ Co-ed
NOTES	Inclusive program for special needs campers, but poor accessibility. Family camping is also an option; please enquire.

SHADOW LAKE CENTRE

SUMMER ADDRESS RR #2

Stouffville ONT
L4A 7X3 **SUMMER PHONE** 905-640-6432

WINTER ADDRESS As above

WINTER PHONE

CONTACT PERSON Gary R. Ouellette
ACCREDITATION OCA
AFFILIATION Metro Toronto Association for Community Living
YEARS IN OPERATION 29
DATES OPEN June through August
FEES Unspecified; please enquire.
SCHOLARSHIPS
ACCOMODATION Cottages, dining hall, crafts & rec centre, workshop, gym.
SPECIALTY Special Needs: Mental Disabilities
OBJECTIVES To provide individual & small group camping & recreation programs.

ACTIVITIES Swimming, boating, fishing, crafts, sports, tenting, hiking.

EVALUATIONS Yes
MEDICAL FACILITIES Fully equipped infirmary & 2 health care staff.
VISITORS Allowed
SPECIAL NEEDS FACILITIES Yes
DESCRIPTION Located 56 km from downtown Toronto on over 300 acres of rolling terrain, with a sand-bottom lake, open fields, woodland areas, & an abundance of wildlife.
NEAREST CITY/TOWN Toronto
AGE SPREAD 7 years & up
CAMPERS PER SESSION 98
STAFF PER SESSION 50
COUNSELLOR:CAMPER RATIO 1 to 3
BOYS OR GIRLS ☐ Boys only ☐ Girls only ☒ Co-ed
NOTES Special needs camp for those who are developmentally handicapped.

SILVER LAKE UNITED CHURCH CAMP

SUMMER ADDRESS RR #4

Kincardine ONT
N2Z 2X5 **SUMMER PHONE** 519-395-2450

WINTER ADDRESS #401 - 3063 Kingsway Drive

Kitchener ONT
N2C 1A9 **WINTER PHONE** 519-894-1579

CONTACT PERSON Ken Christner
ACCREDITATION OCA
AFFILIATION United Church
YEARS IN OPERATION 30
DATES OPEN July through August
FEES $75 - $215 per session; please enquire.
SCHOLARSHIPS Some assistance available.
ACCOMODATION Cabins, dining hall.
SPECIALTY Christian Development
OBJECTIVES To tell youth about God.

ACTIVITIES Swimming, canoeing, sports, cookouts, overnights, Bible study.

EVALUATIONS No
MEDICAL FACILITIES Unspecified; please enquire.
VISITORS Not allowed
SPECIAL NEEDS FACILITIES Unspecified
DESCRIPTION Located on a wooded 225 acre site overlooking Silver Lake.

NEAREST CITY/TOWN Kincardine
AGE SPREAD 6 to 19 years
CAMPERS PER SESSION 66
STAFF PER SESSION 20
COUNSELLOR:CAMPER RATIO 1 to 5
BOYS OR GIRLS ☐ Boys only ☐ Girls only ☒ Co-ed
NOTES

SMUSHKIN'S HOCKEY CAMP

SUMMER ADDRESS 131 - 901 Torresdale Avenue

Willowdale ONT
M2R 3T1 **SUMMER PHONE** 416-663-1052

WINTER ADDRESS As above

WINTER PHONE

CONTACT PERSON Dr. Yasha Smushkin
ACCREDITATION
AFFILIATION None
YEARS IN OPERATION 13
DATES OPEN July through August
FEES $580 per 4-day session plus billeting, see Notes below.
SCHOLARSHIPS No
ACCOMODATION Billeting is available.
SPECIALTY Hockey
OBJECTIVES To provide body conditioning & individual skills development for hockey players of all levels & ages.

ACTIVITIES Aerobics, skating development, balance development, turning techniques, puck control, puck control, body contact skills, passing/receiving techniques, shooting skills, figure skating, endurance development, game performance.
EVALUATIONS No
MEDICAL FACILITIES Hospital 10 minutes away.
VISITORS Allowed
SPECIAL NEEDS FACILITIES No
DESCRIPTION Please enquire for details.

NEAREST CITY/TOWN Toronto
AGE SPREAD 5 years to adult
CAMPERS PER SESSION Unspecified
STAFF PER SESSION Unspecified
COUNSELLOR:CAMPER RATIO Unspecified
BOYS OR GIRLS ☐ Boys only ☐ Girls only ☒ Co-ed
NOTES This is not a residential camp; billeting can be arranged for an additional $225 per person per session.

SWALLOWDALE

SUMMER ADDRESS	RR #4		
	Huntsville		ONT
	P0A 1K0	**SUMMER PHONE**	705-789-9761
WINTER ADDRESS	As above		
		WINTER PHONE	1-800-461-2201

CONTACT PERSON Ron & Margaret Walbank
ACCREDITATION OCA
AFFILIATION Christian (nondenominational)
YEARS IN OPERATION 50
DATES OPEN July through August
FEES Please enquire for session fees.
SCHOLARSHIPS No
ACCOMODATION Cabins, showers, dining hall.
SPECIALTY Traditional
OBJECTIVES To balance structure with non-structure, promoting camper individuality. To allow choices in activities, enabling skills development & the achievement of realistic goals.
ACTIVITIES Tennis, archery, cycling, gym-fit, canoeing, swimming, sailing, windsurfing, team sports, ATVs, power boating, arts & crafts.

EVALUATIONS Yes, on request.
MEDICAL FACILITIES Infirmary & dispensary; nurse on duty, doctor on call.
VISITORS Allowed for campers staying longer than 2 weeks.
SPECIAL NEEDS FACILITIES Unspecified
DESCRIPTION Located on a half mile of sandy beach waterfront along the south shore of Fairy Lake in Muskoka, with 95 acres of forested hills & open playing fields.
NEAREST CITY/TOWN Huntsville
AGE SPREAD 5 to 14 years
CAMPERS PER SESSION 125
STAFF PER SESSION 40
COUNSELLOR:CAMPER RATIO 1 to 4
BOYS OR GIRLS ☐ Boys only ☐ Girls only ☒ Co-ed
NOTES

TANAMAKOON

SUMMER ADDRESS			
	Algonquin Park		ONT
	P0A 1K0	**SUMMER PHONE**	705-633-5541
WINTER ADDRESS	235 Church Street Suite #3 Oakville		ONT
	L6J 1N4	**WINTER PHONE**	905-338-9464

CONTACT PERSON Mr & Mrs Kim Smith & Patti Thom
ACCREDITATION OCA, CCA
AFFILIATION None
YEARS IN OPERATION 68
DATES OPEN July through August
FEES $1000 for 2 weeks; $1855 for 4 weeks; $3710 for 8 weeks.
SCHOLARSHIPS No
ACCOMODATION Cabins, tents, showers, main lodge.
SPECIALTY Traditional
OBJECTIVES Programs which allow campers to excel in their areas of interest at their own pace. To develop an appreciation for the outdoors & to encourage fun & friendships.
ACTIVITIES Swimming, canoeing, sailing, kayaking, windsurfing, campcraft, lapidary, arts & crafts, drama, tennis, pottery, sketching, tripping, miniature horse care.

EVALUATIONS Yes
MEDICAL FACILITIES Doctor & nurse always on duty.
VISITORS Allowed
SPECIAL NEEDS FACILITIES Yes
DESCRIPTION Located on its own lake in Algonquin Park.

NEAREST CITY/TOWN Toronto
AGE SPREAD 7 to 16 years
CAMPERS PER SESSION 160
STAFF PER SESSION 60
COUNSELLOR:CAMPER RATIO 1 to 4
BOYS OR GIRLS ☐ Boys only ☒ Girls only ☐ Co-ed
NOTES

TORONTO BRIGANTINE

SUMMER ADDRESS	283 Queen's Quay West		
	Toronto		ONT
	M5V 1A2	**SUMMER PHONE**	416-364-9949
WINTER ADDRESS	As above		
		WINTER PHONE	

CONTACT PERSON Capt. Richard Birchall
ACCREDITATION OCA, Ontario Sailing Association
AFFILIATION None
YEARS IN OPERATION 31
DATES OPEN Late June through August
FEES Approximately $50 per day.
SCHOLARSHIPS Please enquire.
ACCOMODATION Tents, ships, galley.
SPECIALTY Sailing
OBJECTIVES Motto: "To build character through adventure."

ACTIVITIES General seamanship skills (such as docking and anchoring), safety practices, sailing tactics, manoeuvring procedures, shipboard terminology.

EVALUATIONS Evaluations are kept on file.
MEDICAL FACILITIES Trained staff & good first aid kit; use local hospitals.
VISITORS Allowed at dock, at open ships, & at presentation sessions.
SPECIAL NEEDS FACILITIES Yes, limited.
DESCRIPTION Courses are conducted on Lake Ontario; various ports are visitied.

NEAREST CITY/TOWN Toronto
AGE SPREAD 12 to 18 years (& up)
CAMPERS PER SESSION Varies according to course & ship.
STAFF PER SESSION Varies according to course & ship.
COUNSELLOR:CAMPER RATIO Varies according to course & ship.
BOYS OR GIRLS ☐ Boys only ☐ Girls only ☒ Co-ed
NOTES Also an accredited member of CSTA & ASTA.
Learning disabled children are successful on courses.
Year-round programs are offered. Please enquire for detailed breakdown of ages, courses & costs.

WATERBROOK FARM CAMP

SUMMER ADDRESS	PO Box 10		
	Hagersville		ONT
	N0A 1H0	**SUMMER PHONE**	905-768-1486
WINTER ADDRESS	As above		
		WINTER PHONE	

CONTACT PERSON Charlie & Jannette Matheson
ACCREDITATION OCA
AFFILIATION Christian
YEARS IN OPERATION 30
DATES OPEN July through August
FEES $132 per one-week session
SCHOLARSHIPS No
ACCOMODATION Cabins, main dining room.
SPECIALTY Christian Development
OBJECTIVES To glorify God & give children a hands-on experience of farm life. In doing so, the camp aims to make the children more spiritually aware, physically fit, & mentally stimulated.
ACTIVITIES Bible studies, riding lessons, horse shows, hayrides, crafts, photography, swimming, campfires, care of farm animals.

EVALUATIONS No
MEDICAL FACILITIES 8 km from hospital.
VISITORS Not allowed
SPECIAL NEEDS FACILITIES Unspecified
DESCRIPTION This camp is a farm, situated on 100 acres of land.

NEAREST CITY/TOWN Hamilton
AGE SPREAD 7 to 14 years
CAMPERS PER SESSION 40
STAFF PER SESSION 10 + volunteers.
COUNSELLOR:CAMPER RATIO 1 to 5
BOYS OR GIRLS ☐ Boys only ☐ Girls only ☒ Co-ed
NOTES

WESTCOAST CONNECTION TRAVEL CAMP

SUMMER ADDRESS	87 Stillwater Crescent Willowdale		
			ONT
	M2R 3S3	**SUMMER PHONE**	416-667-1288
WINTER ADDRESS	217 Wolseley N		
	Montreal West		QUE
	H4X 1W1	**WINTER PHONE**	514-488-8920

CONTACT PERSON Fran Grundman , Stan Browman
ACCREDITATION OCA
AFFILIATION None
YEARS IN OPERATION 12
DATES OPEN June through August
FEES Vary according to trip; please enquire.
SCHOLARSHIPS No
ACCOMODATION Varies according to trip; from hotels to log cabins to dorms.
SPECIALTY Travel
OBJECTIVES To provide young people with the opportunity to travel with others in a safe & well-planned program.

ACTIVITIES Range from skiing in Whistler to hiking in the Grand Canyon to bicycle touring in Europe.

EVALUATIONS No
MEDICAL FACILITIES Unspecified
VISITORS Allowed
SPECIAL NEEDS FACILITIES No
DESCRIPTION A travel camp encompassing the Western U.S., Canada, & Europe.

NEAREST CITY/TOWN Varies with program.
AGE SPREAD 14 to 17 years
CAMPERS PER SESSION 40
STAFF PER SESSION 6
COUNSELLOR:CAMPER RATIO 1 to 7
BOYS OR GIRLS ☐ Boys only ☐ Girls only ☒ Co-ed
NOTES Fees include all meals, accommodation, recreation & entertainment, taxes & gratuities.

WHITE PINE

SUMMER ADDRESS

Haliburton ONT
K0M 1S0 **SUMMER PHONE** 705-457-2131

WINTER ADDRESS 40 Lawrence Avenue W.

Toronto ONT
M5M 1A4 **WINTER PHONE** 416-322-6250

CONTACT PERSON Joseph or Adam Kronick
ACCREDITATION OCA, CCA, American Camping Association
AFFILIATION None
YEARS IN OPERATION 38
DATES OPEN July through August
FEES $3995 for full season; $2600 for July; $2300 for August.
SCHOLARSHIPS Yes
ACCOMODATION Cabins with electricity, wash & shower houses, dining lodge.
SPECIALTY Traditional
OBJECTIVES To provide a unique camp experience in a small group setting, emphasizing social growth & development.

ACTIVITIES Aquatics, waterskiing, sailing, canoe tripping, mountain biking, tennis, creative arts, drama, windsurfing, gymnastics.

EVALUATIONS Yes
MEDICAL FACILITIES Infirmary with 2 nurses & 1 doctor.
VISITORS Allowed only on scheduled Visitors Day.
SPECIAL NEEDS FACILITIES Yes
DESCRIPTION Please enquire for details.

NEAREST CITY/TOWN Haliburton
AGE SPREAD 7 to 16 years
CAMPERS PER SESSION 400
STAFF PER SESSION 190
COUNSELLOR:CAMPER RATIO 1 to 3
BOYS OR GIRLS ☐ Boys only ☐ Girls only ☒ Co-ed
NOTES Can accommodate learning disabled children. There are 2 psychologists & 3 social workers on site. Some financial assistance may be available; please enquire.

WINNEBAGOE

SUMMER ADDRESS	RR #1		
	Huntsville		ONT
	P0A 1K0	**SUMMER PHONE**	705-789-5892
WINTER ADDRESS	4 Silverwood Avenue		
	Toronto		ONT
	M5P 1W4	**WINTER PHONE**	416-486-1110

CONTACT PERSON Ben Lustig
ACCREDITATION OCA
AFFILIATION None
YEARS IN OPERATION 60
DATES OPEN July through August
FEES $3850 per 8-week session; $2600 for July; $2400 for August.
SCHOLARSHIPS No
ACCOMODATION Cabins, separate shower houses, dining lodge.
SPECIALTY Traditional
OBJECTIVES To offer fun through learning in a safe, healthy environment.

ACTIVITIES Horseback riding, riflery, tennis, land sports, arts & crafts, ceramics, drama, music, swimming, waterskiing, sailing, canoeing, kayaking, windsurfing, canoe tripping.

EVALUATIONS No
MEDICAL FACILITIES Doctor & nurse always on site.
VISITORS Allowed on scheduled Visitors Day.
SPECIAL NEEDS FACILITIES Unspecified
DESCRIPTION Please enquire for details.

NEAREST CITY/TOWN Huntsville
AGE SPREAD 8 to 16 years
CAMPERS PER SESSION 250
STAFF PER SESSION 130
COUNSELLOR:CAMPER RATIO 1 to 5
BOYS OR GIRLS ☐ Boys only ☐ Girls only ☒ Co-ed
NOTES

WOODEDEN CAMP

SUMMER ADDRESS	RR #3		
	London		ONT
	N6A 4B7	**SUMMER PHONE**	519-471-6640
WINTER ADDRESS	Easter Seals Society 250 Ferrand Drive, Suite #200		
	Don Mills		ONT
	M3C 3P2	**WINTER PHONE**	416-421-8377

CONTACT PERSON Mark Sack
ACCREDITATION OCA, CCA
AFFILIATION Easter Seals Society
YEARS IN OPERATION 59
DATES OPEN July through August
FEES $925 per one-week session.
SCHOLARSHIPS Yes
ACCOMODATION Cabins with showers, dining hall, recreation hall.
SPECIALTY Special Needs: Physical Disabilities
OBJECTIVES To provide oportunities & challenges for campers to develop independence, build self-esteem & develop creative expression skills.
ACTIVITIES Astronomy, horseback riding, campcraft, music, drama, canoeing, sailing, swimming, computers, archery, fishing, sports.

EVALUATIONS Yes
MEDICAL FACILITIES 3 nurses on staff; hospital nearby.
VISITORS Not encouraged
SPECIAL NEEDS FACILITIES Yes
DESCRIPTION Waterfront location with wooded nature trails.

NEAREST CITY/TOWN London
AGE SPREAD 7 to 19 years
CAMPERS PER SESSION 72
STAFF PER SESSION Maximum 50
COUNSELLOR:CAMPER RATIO 1 to 2
BOYS OR GIRLS ☐ Boys only ☐ Girls only ☒ Co-ed
NOTES One of 5 Ontario-based Easter Seal Camps dedicated to offering warm, accessible environments & camping fun to physically disabled young people. Family camping is an option.

PRINCE EDWARD ISLAND

ANDREW'S HOCKEY GROWTH PROGRAMS

SUMMER ADDRESS	P.O. Box 99		
	Slemon Park		PEI
	C0B 2A0	**SUMMER PHONE**	902-436-6699
WINTER ADDRESS	As above		
		WINTER PHONE	

CONTACT PERSON	Dave Dunn
ACCREDITATION	
AFFILIATION	None
YEARS IN OPERATION	15
DATES OPEN	June to August
FEES	Approximately $475 per week; varies with program.
SCHOLARSHIPS	Yes, please enquire.
ACCOMODATION	Campus dorms—double rooms with shared washroom.
SPECIALTY	Sports: Hockey
OBJECTIVES	To increase the confidence and skill level of each player. This is an intensive, strenuous program.
ACTIVITIES	Skating, puck skills, on-ice workouts, dryland training, daily scrimmages, classroom sessions, video analysis, goalie program.
EVALUATIONS	Yes
MEDICAL FACILITIES	First aid facilities; hospital nearby.
VISITORS	Yes
SPECIAL NEEDS FACILITIES	No
DESCRIPTION	Campus and gym, arena, fitness centre, pool, cafeteria, playing fields.
NEAREST CITY/TOWN	Summerside
AGE SPREAD	7 to 20 years
CAMPERS PER SESSION	36
STAFF PER SESSION	25
COUNSELLOR:CAMPER RATIO	N/A
BOYS OR GIRLS	☐ Boys only ☐ Girls only ☒ Co-ed
NOTES	Also offers camps for basketball and soccer; please enquire.

CAMP BUCHAN

SUMMER ADDRESS P.O. Box 533

Charlottetown PEI
C1A 7O1 **SUMMER PHONE** 902-566-9153

WINTER ADDRESS As above

WINTER PHONE

CONTACT PERSON Joan Willis
ACCREDITATION
AFFILIATION Boy Scouts of Canada
YEARS IN OPERATION 53
DATES OPEN June through August
FEES Beavers $16.50 per day; Cubs $65 per 5-day session.
SCHOLARSHIPS No
ACCOMODATION Cabins, tents, main dining hall.
SPECIALTY Traditional
OBJECTIVES To give every Cub and Boy Scout the opportunity to attend summer camp.

ACTIVITIES Swimming, nature crafts, camp-wide games, sports, campfires.

EVALUATIONS No, but may work on badges.
MEDICAL FACILITIES First aid room; 30 minutes to hospital.
VISITORS Yes
SPECIAL NEEDS FACILITIES Yes
DESCRIPTION 60 acres of pine groves and open fields on the south shore.

NEAREST CITY/TOWN Charlottetown
AGE SPREAD 5 to 18 years
CAMPERS PER SESSION 100
STAFF PER SESSION 20
COUNSELLOR:CAMPER RATIO Averages 1 to 5 (varies with age group).
BOYS OR GIRLS ☒ Boys only ☐ Girls only ☐ Co-ed
NOTES

CAMP FAIRHAVEN

SUMMER ADDRESS Girl Guides of Canada — PEI Council
100 Upper Prince St.
Charlottetown PEI
C1A 4S3 **SUMMER PHONE** 902-894-4936

WINTER ADDRESS As above

WINTER PHONE

CONTACT PERSON Camp Committee

ACCREDITATION

AFFILIATION Girl Guides of Canada

YEARS IN OPERATION 24

DATES OPEN June to August

FEES $16.50 per day

SCHOLARSHIPS Please enquire

ACCOMODATION Dormitory with washrooms and showers.

SPECIALTY Traditional

OBJECTIVES To help girls develop as individuals through the rewarding experience of outdoor living.

ACTIVITIES Hiking, river swimming, campfires, arts & crafts.

EVALUATIONS No

MEDICAL FACILITIES Staff trained in first aid; 20 minutes to hospital.

VISITORS Yes

SPECIAL NEEDS FACILITIES No

DESCRIPTION 90 acres of old-growth forest with a sandy beach on the salt water Murray River.

NEAREST CITY/TOWN Montague

AGE SPREAD 6 years to adult

CAMPERS PER SESSION 24

STAFF PER SESSION 8

COUNSELLOR:CAMPER RATIO 1 to 6

BOYS OR GIRLS ☐ Boys only ☒ Girls only ☐ Co-ed

NOTES

CAMP GENCHEFF

SUMMER ADDRESS P.O. Box 412

Charlottetown PEI
C1A 7K7 **SUMMER PHONE** 902-569-2669

WINTER ADDRESS As above

WINTER PHONE 902-569-5747

CONTACT PERSON Marlene Wood
ACCREDITATION
AFFILIATION Canadian Foundation for Poliomyelatis
YEARS IN OPERATION 41
DATES OPEN July through August
FEES $20 per one-week session.
SCHOLARSHIPS Yes, please enquire.
ACCOMODATION Cabins, central dining hall, central washrooms.
SPECIALTY Special Needs
OBJECTIVES To encourage children to become more independent, have fun and make new friends by focussing on their abilities rather than their disabilities.
ACTIVITIES Crafts, swimming, canoeing, horseback riding, talent shows, sports, campfires, drama.

EVALUATIONS Yes
MEDICAL FACILITIES Trained staff; nurse & doctor on call; 10 minutes to hospital.
VISITORS Not encouraged.
SPECIAL NEEDS FACILITIES Yes
DESCRIPTION 23 acres on the south shore at Bellevue Cove with a sports field, sandy beach and nature trails through the woods.

NEAREST CITY/TOWN Charlottetown
AGE SPREAD 7 to 20 years
CAMPERS PER SESSION 25
STAFF PER SESSION 11
COUNSELLOR:CAMPER RATIO 1 to 4
BOYS OR GIRLS ☐ Boys only ☐ Girls only ☒ Co-ed
NOTES

CAMP KEIR

SUMMER ADDRESS	P.O. Box 1009		
	Cornwall		PEI
	C0A 1H0	**SUMMER PHONE**	
WINTER ADDRESS	RR#2		
	North Wiltshire		PEI
	C0A 1Y0	**WINTER PHONE**	902-675-3734

CONTACT PERSON Reverend Mark Buell
ACCREDITATION
AFFILIATION Presbyterian Church
YEARS IN OPERATION 50
DATES OPEN July through August
FEES $45 for 4 days; $80 for 6 days; $200 maximum per family.
SCHOLARSHIPS Camperships are available; please enquire.
ACCOMODATION Dormitories with central dining hall, recreation hall.
SPECIALTY Christian Development
OBJECTIVES To provide children with a Christian camping experience.

ACTIVITIES Swimming, arts & crafts, chapel, sing-songs, campfires, games.

EVALUATIONS No
MEDICAL FACILITIES Nurse on call; 10 minutes to hospital.
VISITORS Not encouraged.
SPECIAL NEEDS FACILITIES No
DESCRIPTION Surrounded by trees with open playing fields at the edge of the ocean.

NEAREST CITY/TOWN Charlottetown
AGE SPREAD 7 to 14 years
CAMPERS PER SESSION 38
STAFF PER SESSION 7
COUNSELLOR:CAMPER RATIO 1 to 7
BOYS OR GIRLS ☐ Boys only ☐ Girls only ☒ Co-ed
NOTES

CANOE COVE CHRISTIAN CAMP

SUMMER ADDRESS c/o Maritime Christian College
503 University Ave.
Charlottetown PEI
C1A 7Z4 **SUMMER PHONE** 902-628-8887

WINTER ADDRESS As above

WINTER PHONE

CONTACT PERSON Jim Dewar
ACCREDITATION
AFFILIATION Church of Christ
YEARS IN OPERATION 42
DATES OPEN July
FEES $70 per one-week session.
SCHOLARSHIPS Yes, please enquire
ACCOMODATION Dormitories, central dining hall, activity hall, chapel.
SPECIALTY Christian Development
OBJECTIVES To introduce children to Christ's teachings in a fun and natural environment.

ACTIVITIES Swimming, crafts, drama, Bible study, sing-songs, hiking, volleyball, daytrips, chapel, campfires.

EVALUATIONS No
MEDICAL FACILITIES Nurse on site.
VISITORS Phone first.
SPECIAL NEEDS FACILITIES No
DESCRIPTION Wooded site with playing fields, on the south shore.

NEAREST CITY/TOWN Charlottetown
AGE SPREAD 8 to 17 years
CAMPERS PER SESSION 60
STAFF PER SESSION 15
COUNSELLOR:CAMPER RATIO 1 to 5
BOYS OR GIRLS ☐ Boys only ☐ Girls only ☒ Co-ed
NOTES

EMMANUEL BIBLE CAMP

SUMMER ADDRESS	RR#3		
	St. Peters		PEI
	C0A 2A0	**SUMMER PHONE**	902-583-2805
WINTER ADDRESS	As above		
		WINTER PHONE	902-569-3307

CONTACT PERSON Clifford Campbell
ACCREDITATION
AFFILIATION Christian (nondenominational)
YEARS IN OPERATION 43
DATES OPEN July through August
FEES $75 per one-week session.
SCHOLARSHIPS Yes, please enquire
ACCOMODATION Cabins, central dining hall, central washrooms with showers.
SPECIALTY Christian Development
OBJECTIVES To help campers develop a Christian character in an atmosphere of fun and recreation in the outdoors.

ACTIVITIES Swimming, biking, canoeing, archery, riflery, arts & crafts, singing, chapel, baseball, campfires, Bible study, basketball, paddle boating.

EVALUATIONS No
MEDICAL FACILITIES Staff trained in first aid; 15 minutes to hospital.
VISITORS Yes
SPECIAL NEEDS FACILITIES No
DESCRIPTION Located on 80 wooded acres on an inland freshwater lake, with playing fields, a mountain bike course and basketball court.
NEAREST CITY/TOWN Montague
AGE SPREAD 8 to 18 years
CAMPERS PER SESSION 78
STAFF PER SESSION 8
COUNSELLOR:CAMPER RATIO 1 to 8
BOYS OR GIRLS ☐ Boys only ☐ Girls only ☒ Co-ed
NOTES

YMCA VOYAGEURS

SUMMER ADDRESS	YM-YWCA of Charlottetown 252 Prince St. Charlottetown C1A 4S1	**SUMMER PHONE**	PEI 902-566-3966
WINTER ADDRESS	As above	**WINTER PHONE**	

CONTACT PERSON Lou Gannon

ACCREDITATION

AFFILIATION YM-YWCA

YEARS IN OPERATION 2

DATES OPEN July to August

FEES $135 per one-week session.

SCHOLARSHIPS Yes, please enquire.

ACCOMODATION Tents

SPECIALTY Traditional

OBJECTIVES To provide opportunities for personal development through adventure programs and environmental and cultural education.

ACTIVITIES Outtrips by canoe, bicycle or foot. Activities may include crafts, games, swimming, star-gazing, foraging, beach-combing, fishing, campfires, pow-wows, guest presentations, orienteering, reflective time.

EVALUATIONS No

MEDICAL FACILITIES Staff trained in first aid and CPR.

VISITORS No

SPECIAL NEEDS FACILITIES Each case considered individually

DESCRIPTION Camp in various locations on Crown or private land; varies depending on program. Every effort is made to practice "no-trace" camping.

NEAREST CITY/TOWN Varies

AGE SPREAD 12 to 15 years.

CAMPERS PER SESSION 10

STAFF PER SESSION 3

COUNSELLOR:CAMPER RATIO 1 to 5

BOYS OR GIRLS ☐ Boys only ☐ Girls only ☒ Co-ed

NOTES Fee includes transportation and all equipment.

QUEBEC

AUBERGE DU LAC DES ÎLES

SUMMER ADDRESS Route Principale

St-Roch-de-Mékinac QUE
G0X 2E0 **SUMMER PHONE** 819-646-5600

WINTER ADDRESS 97, rue Dessureault

Cap-de-la-Madeleine QUE
G8T 2L3 **WINTER PHONE**

CONTACT PERSON Gilles Sinotte
ACCREDITATION ACQ
AFFILIATION None
YEARS IN OPERATION 12
DATES OPEN June to August
FEES $126 for 1/2 week; $180 for 1 week; $360 for 2 weeks.
SCHOLARSHIPS Please enquire.
ACCOMODATION Dorms, cabins, washrooms with showers.
SPECIALTY Traditional
OBJECTIVES To guarantee that each camper will have a safe, enjoyable & well-rounded summer camp experience.

ACTIVITIES Canoe camping, swimming, water slides, fishing, campfires, archery, mini-golf, sport activities & fairs.

EVALUATIONS No
MEDICAL FACILITIES Infirmary; health centre nearby.
VISITORS Allowed
SPECIAL NEEDS FACILITIES No
DESCRIPTION An exceptional setting for a summer camp, located on the shores of a lake surrounded by mountains.

NEAREST CITY/TOWN Quebec City
AGE SPREAD 5 to 17 years
CAMPERS PER SESSION 110
STAFF PER SESSION 20
COUNSELLOR:CAMPER RATIO 1 to 9
BOYS OR GIRLS ☐ Boys only ☐ Girls only ☒ Co-ed
NOTES This is a French-speaking camp.

BASE DE PLEIN AIR ST-JOVITE

SUMMER ADDRESS	PO Box 515 St-Jovite QUE J0T 2H0
SUMMER PHONE	819-425-2461
WINTER ADDRESS	As above
WINTER PHONE	
CONTACT PERSON	Jean-Pierre l'Heureux
ACCREDITATION	ACQ
AFFILIATION	None
YEARS IN OPERATION	23
DATES OPEN	June to August
FEES	\$250-\$290 per 1-week session; \$500-\$580 per 2-week session.
SCHOLARSHIPS	No
ACCOMODATION	Cabins, showers, dining hall.
SPECIALTY	Sports
OBJECTIVES	To establish a harmonious relationship with the natural environment. To offer an outdoor education fostering the physical, intellectual & moral development of each child.
ACTIVITIES	Sailing, sailboarding, canoeing, swimming, rock climbing, archery, camping, orienteering, ecology, volleyball, kayaking, arts & crafts, theatre, tennis, horseback riding.
EVALUATIONS	No
MEDICAL FACILITIES	Unspecified; please enquire.
VISITORS	Yes
SPECIAL NEEDS FACILITIES	No
DESCRIPTION	A beautiful lakefront site with plenty of trees.
NEAREST CITY/TOWN	Montreal
AGE SPREAD	6 to 15 years
CAMPERS PER SESSION	140
STAFF PER SESSION	40
COUNSELLOR:CAMPER RATIO	1 to 7
BOYS OR GIRLS	☐ Boys only ☐ Girls only ☒ Co-ed
NOTES	This is a bilingual camp. Winter sessions are also offered.

BEAUVALLON VACANCES INTERNATIONAL

SUMMER ADDRESS	Rang du Bord de l'eau Intersection 43ème Avenue Sabrevois J0J 2G0	**SUMMER PHONE**	QUE 514-346-4046
WINTER ADDRESS	286, Rang de l'Église Henryville J0J 1E0	**WINTER PHONE**	QUE 514-299-2506

CONTACT PERSON Serge A. Piquette
ACCREDITATION ACQ, CCA
AFFILIATION None
YEARS IN OPERATION 7
DATES OPEN Late June through August
FEES $890 per two-week session.
SCHOLARSHIPS Please enquire
ACCOMODATION Dormitories, washrooms, dining hall.
SPECIALTY Cultural Development
OBJECTIVES The camp operates with the belief that only as children get a better understanding of cultural and geographic differences can they build a better world.
ACTIVITIES Guided tours of the main tourist & cultural sites of Quebec, horseback riding, archery, canoeing, ecology, sports & games, golf, swimming, obstacle courses, mountain biking, windsurfing, and arts.
EVALUATIONS No
MEDICAL FACILITIES First aid on site, doctor on call, clinic & hospital nearby.
VISITORS Not allowed
SPECIAL NEEDS FACILITIES Unspecified
DESCRIPTION Situated in the countryside of the beautiful Richelieu Valley.

NEAREST CITY/TOWN Montreal
AGE SPREAD 11 to 16 years.
CAMPERS PER SESSION 96
STAFF PER SESSION 5
COUNSELLOR:CAMPER RATIO 1 to 5
BOYS OR GIRLS ☐ Boys only ☐ Girls only ☒ Co-ed
NOTES All-French, all-English, or bilingual community camps are available for all programs.

CAMP AMY MOLSON

SUMMER ADDRESS	245 Scotch Road		
	Grenville J0V 1J0	**SUMMER PHONE**	QUE 819-242-6083
WINTER ADDRESS	8530 Jean Brillon, Suite #100		
	Lasalle H8N 2J9	**WINTER PHONE**	QUE
CONTACT PERSON	Cathy Mann		
ACCREDITATION	CCA		
AFFILIATION	United Way		
YEARS IN OPERATION	48		
DATES OPEN	Late June to August		
FEES	Based on a sliding scale; please enquire.		
SCHOLARSHIPS			
ACCOMODATION	Cabins, showers, dining hall.		
SPECIALTY	Traditional		
OBJECTIVES	To promote co-operation & to foster a positive self-image in campers.		
ACTIVITIES	Swimming, boating, arts & crafts, reading, nature lore, pottery, live arts, special events, co-operative games & sports.		
EVALUATIONS	Behaviour reports are kept on each camper.		
MEDICAL FACILITIES	Infirmary with first aid technician & a visiting doctor.		
VISITORS	Not allowed		
SPECIAL NEEDS FACILITIES	Yes		
DESCRIPTION	Please enquire for details.		
NEAREST CITY/TOWN	Montreal		
AGE SPREAD	5 to 9 years		
CAMPERS PER SESSION	Maximum 144		
STAFF PER SESSION	45		
COUNSELLOR:CAMPER RATIO	1 to 6		
BOYS OR GIRLS	☐ Boys only ☐ Girls only ☒ Co-ed		
NOTES	Special needs refers to integration programs for various disabilities, considered on an individual basis; please enquire. This is a bilingual camp.		

CAMP ANGLOFUN

SUMMER ADDRESS 600, chemin de la Diligence

Stukely-Sud QUE
J0E 2J0 **SUMMER PHONE** 514-297-3717

WINTER ADDRESS As above

WINTER PHONE

CONTACT PERSON Sandra Lebeau
ACCREDITATION ACQ
AFFILIATION None
YEARS IN OPERATION 7
DATES OPEN Late June to August
FEES $375 per 1-week session; $835 per 2-week session
SCHOLARSHIPS Please enquire
ACCOMODATION Tents, showers, cafeteria, classroom.
SPECIALTY English Immersion
OBJECTIVES To enable youngsters to learn English in a farm-like environment.

ACTIVITIES Swimming, volleyball, badminton, walking & hiking, archery, campfires, drama, English instruction, cultural activities.

EVALUATIONS Yes
MEDICAL FACILITIES Small infirmary on site; hospital 10 minutes away.
VISITORS Not allowed
SPECIAL NEEDS FACILITIES No
DESCRIPTION Situated on a farm.

NEAREST CITY/TOWN Montreal
AGE SPREAD 7 to 17 years
CAMPERS PER SESSION 125
STAFF PER SESSION 60
COUNSELLOR:CAMPER RATIO 1 to 4
BOYS OR GIRLS ☐ Boys only ☐ Girls only ☒ Co-ed
NOTES Various sessions for different age groups are offered throughout the season; please enquire.
This is an English-speaking camp.

CAMP CAROWANIS INC.

SUMMER ADDRESS	785 Plymouth Avenue Suite 210 Mont-Royal QUE H4P 1B3
SUMMER PHONE	514-731-2683
WINTER ADDRESS	As above
WINTER PHONE	
CONTACT PERSON	Flora Rondina
ACCREDITATION	ACQ
AFFILIATION	None
YEARS IN OPERATION	36
DATES OPEN	July through August
FEES	Approximately $275 per week. Fees differ for non-residents.
SCHOLARSHIPS	Yes
ACCOMODATION	Tents, showers, dining hall.
SPECIALTY	Special Needs: Diabetes
OBJECTIVES	To provide clinical & practical teaching of diabetes mellitus, & to improve the treatment & care dispensed to diabetic campers while providing them with a camping experience.
ACTIVITIES	Swimming, boating, kayaking, tennis, archery, volleyball, baseball, mountain biking, excursions, canoe trips, Indian games, films, dances, rowing, table tennis, drama, choir, picnics, field trips, nature study, campfires.
EVALUATIONS	Awards given at the end of each session.
MEDICAL FACILITIES	Infirmary with doctor, 2 residents, 4 nurses & 1 lab tech.
VISITORS	Not allowed
SPECIAL NEEDS FACILITIES	Yes
DESCRIPTION	The campsite spreads over 150 acres of wooded land on the shores of Lake Didi near Ste-Agathe-des-Monts in the Laurentians.
NEAREST CITY/TOWN	Montreal
AGE SPREAD	8 to 15 years
CAMPERS PER SESSION	110
STAFF PER SESSION	60
COUNSELLOR:CAMPER RATIO	1 to 4
BOYS OR GIRLS	☐ Boys only ☐ Girls only ☒ Co-ed
NOTES	Special needs refers to insulin-dependent diabetic campers. Insulin injections under supervision; teaching & educational programs about diabetes are regular parts of the day. "No diabetic child is ever refused admission for financial reasons." This is a bilingual camp.

CAMP D'ÉCOLOGIE SAINT-VIATEUR INC.

SUMMER ADDRESS 450, avenue Querbes

Outremont QUE
H2V 3W5 **SUMMER PHONE** 514-274-3624

WINTER ADDRESS As above

WINTER PHONE

CONTACT PERSON Jean-Baptiste Genest
ACCREDITATION ACQ
AFFILIATION None
YEARS IN OPERATION 34
DATES OPEN Late June through July
FEES Unspecified; please enquire.
SCHOLARSHIPS
ACCOMODATION Tents, showers, dining hall.
SPECIALTY Science: Natural Science
OBJECTIVES To teach children biology & natural science.

ACTIVITIES Labs, excursions, chapel, ecological studies, games, nature & science studies, sports, campfires.

EVALUATIONS No
MEDICAL FACILITIES Doctor 15 km away; hospital 20 km away.
VISITORS Allowed
SPECIAL NEEDS FACILITIES No
DESCRIPTION Please enquire for details.

NEAREST CITY/TOWN Quebec City
AGE SPREAD 12 to 16 years
CAMPERS PER SESSION Maximum 60
STAFF PER SESSION 15
COUNSELLOR:CAMPER RATIO 1 to 6
BOYS OR GIRLS ☐ Boys only ☐ Girls only ☒ Co-ed
NOTES This is a French-speaking camp.

CAMP DE CRÉATIVITÉ SCIENTIFIQUE

SUMMER ADDRESS Bureau 1036, Pavillon Alexandre-Vachon
Université Laval
Québec QUE
G1K 7P4 **SUMMER PHONE** 418-656-3515

WINTER ADDRESS As above

WINTER PHONE

CONTACT PERSON Nathalie Gagné
ACCREDITATION
AFFILIATION Laval University
YEARS IN OPERATION 4
DATES OPEN Late June through August
FEES $125 per 1-week session.
SCHOLARSHIPS No
ACCOMODATION Residences of Laval University.
SPECIALTY Science
OBJECTIVES To initiate adolescents to the fields of science & technology; to encourage girls to pursue a career in science.

ACTIVITIES Science projects, visiting laboratories, sports.

EVALUATIONS No
MEDICAL FACILITIES Unspecified; please enquire.
VISITORS Allowed on Friday afternoons.
SPECIAL NEEDS FACILITIES The university is accessible to the handicapped.
DESCRIPTION Located on the Laval University campus.

NEAREST CITY/TOWN Quebec City
AGE SPREAD 10 to 14 years
CAMPERS PER SESSION 75
STAFF PER SESSION 13
COUNSELLOR:CAMPER RATIO 1 to 6
BOYS OR GIRLS ☐ Boys only ☐ Girls only ☒ Co-ed
NOTES While residence is provided, activities are planned between 9:00 am and 4:00 pm only.
This is a French-speaking camp.

CAMP ÉCOLE KÉNO

SUMMER ADDRESS 2315, chemin Saint-Louis

Sillery QUE
G1T 1R5 **SUMMER PHONE** 418-658-4198

WINTER ADDRESS As above

WINTER PHONE

CONTACT PERSON Hélène Côté-Auger
ACCREDITATION ACQ
AFFILIATION Catholic Church
YEARS IN OPERATION 27
DATES OPEN June to August
FEES $250 per 7-9 day session; $740 per 26-27 day session.
SCHOLARSHIPS Please enquire
ACCOMODATION Cabins, cafeteria.
SPECIALTY Christian Development
OBJECTIVES To develop self-reliance, autonomy, sociability; foster humanitarian/Christian values & discover the natural environment.
ACTIVITIES Boating, archery, kayak, sailing, swimming, arts & crafts, rock climbing, natural sciences.

EVALUATIONS No
MEDICAL FACILITIES Doctor or nurse on site.
VISITORS Not permitted
SPECIAL NEEDS FACILITIES No
DESCRIPTION Located on Lac Long and surrounded by mountains, the camp boasts many natural and wildlife attractions.

NEAREST CITY/TOWN Quebec City
AGE SPREAD 7 to 17 years
CAMPERS PER SESSION 180
STAFF PER SESSION 61
COUNSELLOR:CAMPER RATIO 1 to 5
BOYS OR GIRLS ☐ Boys only ☐ Girls only ☒ Co-ed
NOTES This is a French-speaking camp.

CAMP EDPHY INTERNATIONAL

SUMMER ADDRESS	14th Avenue Val-Morin		
	Québec		QUE
	J0T 2R0	**SUMMER PHONE**	1-800-36-EDPHY
WINTER ADDRESS	As above		
		WINTER PHONE	

CONTACT PERSON Luc Dubois
ACCREDITATION ACQ, American Camping Association
AFFILIATION None
YEARS IN OPERATION 28
DATES OPEN Late June through August
FEES Unspecified; please enquire.
SCHOLARSHIPS Unspecified; please enquire.
ACCOMODATION Lodge with 8 campers per room, washrooms, dining hall.
SPECIALTY Traditional
OBJECTIVES The camp focuses on education & the autonomy & integral development of children, plus the acquisition of basics in many sports.
ACTIVITIES Circus, horseback riding, sailing, windsurfing, canoeing, archery, language lessons, golf, judo, tennis, swimming, gymnastics, cycling, hiking, sports.

EVALUATIONS Yes
MEDICAL FACILITIES Infirmary with 2 staff; hospital 9 km away.
VISITORS Allowed if campers are registered for more than 3 weeks.
SPECIAL NEEDS FACILITIES Unspecified
DESCRIPTION Nestled at the foot of the Laurentians, amidst 590 acres of evergreen woodland, 3 lakes, & the Rivière du Nord.

NEAREST CITY/TOWN Montreal
AGE SPREAD 4 to 16 years
CAMPERS PER SESSION Maximum 300
STAFF PER SESSION 150
COUNSELLOR:CAMPER RATIO 1 to 3
BOYS OR GIRLS ☐ Boys only ☐ Girls only ☒ Co-ed
NOTES This is a bilingual camp.

CAMP GARAGONA

SUMMER ADDRESS 23 Chemin Garagona

Freligshburg QUE
J0J 1C0 **SUMMER PHONE** 514-298-5159

WINTER ADDRESS As above

WINTER PHONE

CONTACT PERSON André LaRochelle
ACCREDITATION ACQ
AFFILIATION Association Garagona Inc.
YEARS IN OPERATION 23
DATES OPEN Mid-May through August
FEES Unspecified; please enquire.
SCHOLARSHIPS Unspecified; please enquire.
ACCOMODATION Cabins, recreation hall, dining hall, and tents.
SPECIALTY Special Needs: Mental Disabilities
OBJECTIVES To offer each camper an enriching camp experience which responds to their particular needs.

ACTIVITIES Nature lore, camping, sports, arts & crafts, music, thematic days.

EVALUATIONS Yes
MEDICAL FACILITIES Infirmary with nurse on staff.
VISITORS Allowed
SPECIAL NEEDS FACILITIES No
DESCRIPTION Surrounded by mountains & woods near the town of Freligshburg.

NEAREST CITY/TOWN Cowansville
AGE SPREAD 8 years & up
CAMPERS PER SESSION 62
STAFF PER SESSION 30
COUNSELLOR:CAMPER RATIO 1 to 3
BOYS OR GIRLS ☐ Boys only ☐ Girls only ☒ Co-ed
NOTES This is a bilingual camp.

CAMP GATINEAU INC.

SUMMER ADDRESS 7, rue Dumas

Hull QUE
J8Y 2M4 **SUMMER PHONE** 819-777-6164

WINTER ADDRESS As above

WINTER PHONE

CONTACT PERSON Edith Martel
ACCREDITATION ACQ
AFFILIATION None
YEARS IN OPERATION 21
DATES OPEN Late June through August
FEES $456 per 12-day session.
SCHOLARSHIPS Please enquire
ACCOMODATION Cabins, showers, dining hall.
SPECIALTY Special Needs: Mental Disabilities
OBJECTIVES To provide leisure & outdoor recreation for people with mental disabilities.

ACTIVITIES Canoeing, camping, paddle boating, co-operative games.

EVALUATIONS No
MEDICAL FACILITIES Infirmary with a nurse & assistant.
VISITORS Not allowed
SPECIAL NEEDS FACILITIES Yes
DESCRIPTION Situated on Lac Leblanc near Masham.

NEAREST CITY/TOWN Hull
AGE SPREAD 7 years & up
CAMPERS PER SESSION 125
STAFF PER SESSION 65
COUNSELLOR:CAMPER RATIO 1 to 3
BOYS OR GIRLS ☐ Boys only ☐ Girls only ☒ Co-ed
NOTES Special needs refers to mentally handicapped campers. This is a bilingual camp.

CAMP GYMN-EAU LAVAL

SUMMER ADDRESS 4901, St. Joseph Street
Suite 307
Laval QUE
H7C 1H6 **SUMMER PHONE** 514-664-4316

WINTER ADDRESS As above

WINTER PHONE

CONTACT PERSON Francine Larivière
ACCREDITATION ACQ
AFFILIATION None
YEARS IN OPERATION 4
DATES OPEN July through August
FEES $300 per one-week session.
SCHOLARSHIPS Please enquire.
ACCOMODATION Cottage with cafeteria.
SPECIALTY Special Needs: Learning Disabilities
OBJECTIVES To offer recreational & outdoor activities to children with learning disabilities; to offer a safe group environment & to develop learning skills.
ACTIVITIES Canoeing, rowing, co-operatave games, treasure hunts, arts, natural sciences, exercises (Activities are planned by an occupational therapist).

EVALUATIONS No
MEDICAL FACILITIES Unspecified; please enquire.
VISITORS Allowed
SPECIAL NEEDS FACILITIES Yes
DESCRIPTION On the shore of Lac l'Achigan

NEAREST CITY/TOWN Montreal
AGE SPREAD 5 to 10 years.
CAMPERS PER SESSION 30
STAFF PER SESSION 7
COUNSELLOR:CAMPER RATIO 1 to 4
BOYS OR GIRLS ☐ Boys only ☐ Girls only ☒ Co-ed
NOTES Special needs refers to campers with learning disabilities. This is a French-speaking camp.

CAMP INTERNATIONAL ALTITUDE 2001

SUMMER ADDRESS 386, rang 3

Ste-Hélène-de-Chester QUE
G0P 1H0 **SUMMER PHONE**

WINTER ADDRESS As above

QUE
WINTER PHONE

CONTACT PERSON Richard Caisse
ACCREDITATION ACQ
AFFILIATION None
YEARS IN OPERATION 6
DATES OPEN July through August
FEES Unspecified; please enquire.
SCHOLARSHIPS Unspecified; please enquire.
ACCOMODATION Tipis, dining hall.
SPECIALTY French & English Immersion
OBJECTIVES To allow exchanges with other countries, such as France, England, Spain, USA & Mexico.

ACTIVITIES Tourist sightseeing, biking, canoeing, climbing, films, sports & games, farm activities.

EVALUATIONS No
MEDICAL FACILITIES 2 hospitals 30 minutes away.
VISITORS Allowed
SPECIAL NEEDS FACILITIES Yes
DESCRIPTION Situated on 400 acres of forest & farm land with sheep, horses, cows & chickens.

NEAREST CITY/TOWN Quebec City
AGE SPREAD 6 to 18 years
CAMPERS PER SESSION 50 - 200
STAFF PER SESSION 10 - 50
COUNSELLOR:CAMPER RATIO 1to 7
BOYS OR GIRLS ☐ Boys only ☐ Girls only ☒ Co-ed
NOTES This is a bilingual camp.

CAMP KINKORA

SUMMER ADDRESS	265 chemin Lac Beauchamp St. Adolphe d'Howard Ste-Agathe-des-Monts QUE J0T 2B0 **SUMMER PHONE** 819-327-2255
WINTER ADDRESS	Catholic Community Services Inc. 1857 de Maisonneuve Blvd W Montreal QUE H3H 1J9 **WINTER PHONE** 514-937-5351
CONTACT PERSON	Arleen Boyer-Fontaine
ACCREDITATION	ACQ
AFFILIATION	Catholic Church
YEARS IN OPERATION	68
DATES OPEN	Late June through August
FEES	Based on a sliding scale according to income.
SCHOLARSHIPS	Yes
ACCOMODATION	Cabins, toilet & shower facilities, dining hall.
SPECIALTY	Traditional
OBJECTIVES	To provide an enjoyable, safe, well-rounded stay for campers in an open & accepting environment.
ACTIVITIES	Water regattas, canoeing, boating, bonfires, sports, swimming, hiking, baseball, music, campfires.
EVALUATIONS	No
MEDICAL FACILITIES	Infirmary with medical officer on site.
VISITORS	Allowed
SPECIAL NEEDS FACILITIES	Yes
DESCRIPTION	Ideal setting for outdoor activities; private lake with supervised beach.
NEAREST CITY/TOWN	Montreal
AGE SPREAD	All ages
CAMPERS PER SESSION	110-176
STAFF PER SESSION	20
COUNSELLOR:CAMPER RATIO	1 to 7
BOYS OR GIRLS	☐ Boys only ☐ Girls only ☒ Co-ed
NOTES	This is a rental facility available for use by groups only. Special needs refers to limited wheelchair accessibility. This is a bilingual camp.

CAMP KINNERET BILUIM

SUMMER ADDRESS	Lac Mercier Rue Harrison Mont Tremblant J0T 1Z0	**SUMMER PHONE**	QUE 819-425-3332
WINTER ADDRESS	4950, Queen Mary Road Suite 411 Montreal H3W 1X3	**WINTER PHONE**	QUE 514-735-3167

CONTACT PERSON Gadi Anavi
ACCREDITATION ACQ
AFFILIATION Hadassah-Wizo Organization of Canada
YEARS IN OPERATION 11
DATES OPEN July through August
FEES Unspecified; please enquire.
SCHOLARSHIPS Yes
ACCOMODATION Cabins for ages 7-5, tents for ages 16-17, communal showers.
SPECIALTY Jewish Development
OBJECTIVES Jewish & Zionist Education.

ACTIVITIES Sports, trips, games, swimming, canoeing, singing, thematic programs.

EVALUATIONS Yes
MEDICAL FACILITIES Infirmary with nurse on duty.
VISITORS Allowed on Visitors Day.
SPECIAL NEEDS FACILITIES No
DESCRIPTION Set in the Laurentian mountains by Mercier Lake.

NEAREST CITY/TOWN Montreal
AGE SPREAD 7 to 17 years
CAMPERS PER SESSION 180
STAFF PER SESSION 45
COUNSELLOR:CAMPER RATIO 1 to 7
BOYS OR GIRLS ☐ Boys only ☐ Girls only ☒ Co-ed
NOTES This is an English-speaking camp.

CAMP LE MANOIR

SUMMER ADDRESS	Les Frères du Sacre-Coeur CP 67 les Eboulements Charlevoix QUE G0A 2M0 **SUMMER PHONE** 418-635-2666
WINTER ADDRESS	1400, route de l'Aéroport Ancienne Lorette QUE G2G 1G6 **WINTER PHONE**
CONTACT PERSON	Guy Sheedy
ACCREDITATION	ACQ
AFFILIATION	Les Frères du Sacré-Coeur
YEARS IN OPERATION	28
DATES OPEN	July to August
FEES	$285 per one-week session.
SCHOLARSHIPS	Please enquire.
ACCOMODATION	Cabins, showers, dining hall.
SPECIALTY	Traditional
OBJECTIVES	Fosters holistic personal development from a Christian perspective.
ACTIVITIES	Arts & crafts, volunteering, excursions, sports & games, swimming, spiritual activities, natural sciences, archery & riflery.
EVALUATIONS	Yes
MEDICAL FACILITIES	Infirmary
VISITORS	Not permitted.
SPECIAL NEEDS FACILITIES	No
DESCRIPTION	The camp is located on the site of a French seigneury.
NEAREST CITY/TOWN	Quebec City
AGE SPREAD	9 to 13 years
CAMPERS PER SESSION	64
STAFF PER SESSION	45
COUNSELLOR:CAMPER RATIO	1 to 12
BOYS OR GIRLS	☒ Boys only ☐ Girls only ☐ Co-ed
NOTES	This is a French-speaking camp.

CAMP MARISTE

SUMMER ADDRESS 8082, chemin Morgan

Rawdon QUE
J0K 1S0 **SUMMER PHONE** 514-834-6383

WINTER ADDRESS As above

WINTER PHONE

CONTACT PERSON Gérard Bachand
ACCREDITATION ACQ
AFFILIATION Les Frères Maristes
YEARS IN OPERATION 36
DATES OPEN End of June to mid-August
FEES $370 per 1-day session
SCHOLARSHIPS Yes
ACCOMODATION Dormitories
SPECIALTY Traditional
OBJECTIVES To foster holistic personal development from a Christian perspective.

ACTIVITIES Aquatics, camping, boating, rock climbing, archery, volleyball, soccer, ecology, arts & crafts, spiritual activities.

EVALUATIONS Yes
MEDICAL FACILITIES Nurse on site; hospital nearby.
VISITORS Yes
SPECIAL NEEDS FACILITIES Accessible to the handicapped.
DESCRIPTION Lakefront with 1200 acres of diverse ecological habitats and panoramic views.

NEAREST CITY/TOWN Montreal
AGE SPREAD 6 to 16 years
CAMPERS PER SESSION 220
STAFF PER SESSION 72
COUNSELLOR:CAMPER RATIO 1 to 5
BOYS OR GIRLS ☐ Boys only ☐ Girls only ☒ Co-ed
NOTES This is a French-speaking camp.

CAMP MAROMAC

SUMMER ADDRESS 231, chemin Lac Quenouille
Val des Lacs QUE
J0T 2P0 **SUMMER PHONE** 819-326-4488

WINTER ADDRESS 4999, rue Ste-Catherine Ouest
Suite 325
Westmount QUE
H3Z 1T3 **WINTER PHONE** 514-485-1135

CONTACT PERSON Esther, Syd, or Joseph Marovitch
ACCREDITATION ACQ, CCA
AFFILIATION None
YEARS IN OPERATION 27
DATES OPEN July to mid-August
FEES $1750 - $1850 per 3.5 week session; $3300 per 7 week session.
SCHOLARSHIPS No
ACCOMODATION Cabins, bathrooms, main dining & recreation halls.
SPECIALTY Traditional
OBJECTIVES To provide campers with an enjoyable & creative camp experience.

ACTIVITIES Tennis, sailboarding, sailing, swimming, aerobics, physical education, arts & crafts, drama, sports.

EVALUATIONS No
MEDICAL FACILITIES Modern equipped clinic with doctor, RN & nursing assistant.
VISITORS Allowed on visiting day.
SPECIAL NEEDS FACILITIES No
DESCRIPTION Located on beautiful Lac Quenouille in the heart of the Laurentian Mountains.

NEAREST CITY/TOWN Montreal
AGE SPREAD 7 to 16 years
CAMPERS PER SESSION 180
STAFF PER SESSION 90
COUNSELLOR:CAMPER RATIO 1 to 9
BOYS OR GIRLS ☐ Boys only ☐ Girls only ☒ Co-ed
NOTES This is an English-speaking camp.

CAMP MASQU'ARCAD INC

SUMMER ADDRESS	1964, rang 7 CP 52 St-Théodore d'Acton QUE J0H 1Z0
SUMMER PHONE	514-546-7076
WINTER ADDRESS	As above
WINTER PHONE	514-546-4947
CONTACT PERSON	Marie Villineuve Lavigueur
ACCREDITATION	ACQ
AFFILIATION	None
YEARS IN OPERATION	6
DATES OPEN	June through August
FEES	$475-$825 per 8-13 day session.
SCHOLARSHIPS	Please enquire.
ACCOMODATION	Rooms, washrooms with showers, kitchen and work station.
SPECIALTY	Arts: Theatre
OBJECTIVES	Holistic personal development by means of apprenticeship in the theatrical arts.
ACTIVITIES	Drama, improvisation, comedy, creative writing, circus-type activities, sculpture, singing, painting.
EVALUATIONS	Yes, certificate of participation is awarded.
MEDICAL FACILITIES	Medical clinic 5 km away; hospital 25 km away.
VISITORS	Yes
SPECIAL NEEDS FACILITIES	Yes
DESCRIPTION	Situated in the countryside near St. Theodore d'Acton.
NEAREST CITY/TOWN	Iberville
AGE SPREAD	7 to 17 years
CAMPERS PER SESSION	36
STAFF PER SESSION	10
COUNSELLOR:CAMPER RATIO	1 to 6
BOYS OR GIRLS	☐ Boys only ☐ Girls only ☒ Co-ed
NOTES	This is a French-speaking camp.

CAMP MINOGAMI

SUMMER ADDRESS	Lac Minogami RR #2 Shawinigan G9N 6T6	**SUMMER PHONE**	QUE 819-539-4544
WINTER ADDRESS	11, rue Crémazie Est Québec G1R 1Y1	**WINTER PHONE**	QUE 418-529-5323

CONTACT PERSON Pierre Bigaouette
ACCREDITATION ACQ
AFFILIATION None
YEARS IN OPERATION 31
DATES OPEN Late June to mid-August
FEES From $145 per 4-day session to $1060 per 26-day session.
SCHOLARSHIPS No
ACCOMODATION Cabins, showers, cafeteria.
SPECIALTY Traditional
OBJECTIVES To initiate the camper to outdoor life; to encourage the development of a sense of responsibility, self-esteem and spiritual values.
ACTIVITIES Canoeing, natural science, mountain biking, photography, archery, swimming, campfires.

EVALUATIONS Yes
MEDICAL FACILITIES Infirmary with 2 nurses on duty 24 hours.
VISITORS Not allowed
SPECIAL NEEDS FACILITIES No
DESCRIPTION Situated on a wooded, waterfront property.

NEAREST CITY/TOWN Shawinigan
AGE SPREAD 7 to 17 years
CAMPERS PER SESSION 280
STAFF PER SESSION 110
COUNSELLOR:CAMPER RATIO 1 to 5
BOYS OR GIRLS ☐ Boys only ☐ Girls only ☒ Co-ed
NOTES This is primarily a French-speaking camp.

CAMP MUSICAL ACCORD PARFAIT

SUMMER ADDRESS	CP 47029
	Sillery QUE
	G1S 4X1 **SUMMER PHONE** 418-624-1636
WINTER ADDRESS	CP 147
	Sillery QUE
	G1T 2P7 **WINTER PHONE** 418-624-1636
CONTACT PERSON	André Desrosiers
ACCREDITATION	ACQ
AFFILIATION	None
YEARS IN OPERATION	30
DATES OPEN	July to August
FEES	$225 for one week; $395 for 2 weeks; $525 for 3 weeks.
SCHOLARSHIPS	Please enquire
ACCOMODATION	Dorms, showers, cafeteria
SPECIALTY	Arts: Music
OBJECTIVES	To initiate, develop and improve musical skills and abilities in a relaxed environment.
ACTIVITIES	Choir, orchestra, jazz ensembles, accompaniment, music reading & composition. Concert performance at end of camp session. Also: arts, dance, theatre, aquatic & sporting activities.
EVALUATIONS	Yes
MEDICAL FACILITIES	Nurse on premises; hospital 15 minutes away.
VISITORS	Not permitted.
SPECIAL NEEDS FACILITIES	No
DESCRIPTION	On the shore of Simon Lake.
NEAREST CITY/TOWN	Quebec City
AGE SPREAD	7 to 17 years
CAMPERS PER SESSION	80
STAFF PER SESSION	30
COUNSELLOR:CAMPER RATIO	1 to 16
BOYS OR GIRLS	☐ Boys only ☐ Girls only ☒ Co-ed
NOTES	This is a French-speaking camp.

CAMP MUSICAL ST-ALEXANDRE INC

SUMMER ADDRESS 267, 5e Rang Est

St-Alexandre QUE
G0L 2G0 **SUMMER PHONE** 418-495-2898

WINTER ADDRESS As above

WINTER PHONE

CONTACT PERSON Michel Lebel
ACCREDITATION ACQ
AFFILIATION Catholic Church
YEARS IN OPERATION 23
DATES OPEN June to August
FEES $380 per 13-day session; $480 per 16-day session.
SCHOLARSHIPS Please enquire.
ACCOMODATION Dorms, main lodge.
SPECIALTY Arts: Music
OBJECTIVES To teach musical skills & mastery with a principal musical instrument, and proficiency with a second instrument.

ACTIVITIES Choir, dramatic & fine arts, dance, rhythm & ensembles. Instruments offered: piano, violin, guitar, flute, recorder, trumpet, saxophone, clarinet & percussion instruments.

EVALUATIONS Yes
MEDICAL FACILITIES Not specified
VISITORS Not allowed
SPECIAL NEEDS FACILITIES No
DESCRIPTION Please enquire for details.

NEAREST CITY/TOWN Rivière-du-Loup
AGE SPREAD 8 to 15 years
CAMPERS PER SESSION 80
STAFF PER SESSION 20
COUNSELLOR:CAMPER RATIO 1 to 4
BOYS OR GIRLS ☐ Boys only ☐ Girls only ☒ Co-ed
NOTES This is a French-speaking camp.

CAMP NOMININGUE

SUMMER ADDRESS	1889 Chemin des Mésanges Lac Nominingue QUE J0W 1R0 **SUMMER PHONE** 819-278-3383
WINTER ADDRESS	119 Cragmore Road Pointe Claire QUE H9R 3K7 **WINTER PHONE** 514-694-4020
CONTACT PERSON	Peter or Shannon Van Wagner
ACCREDITATION	ACQ, CCA
AFFILIATION	None
YEARS IN OPERATION	69
DATES OPEN	June through August
FEES	$1000 per 2-week session; $2500 per 36-day session.
SCHOLARSHIPS	No
ACCOMODATION	Tents on raised platforms, showers, lodge with dining hall.
SPECIALTY	Traditional
OBJECTIVES	To teach campers to feel comfortable in a group living experience & in the wilderness.
ACTIVITIES	Swimming, windsurfing, sailing, canoeing, tennis, riflery, archery, nature lore, canoeing, drama, athletics, campcraft, cooking, woodworking, lifesaving, first aid, golf, orienteering.
EVALUATIONS	No
MEDICAL FACILITIES	Infirmary with doctor, nurse, & nurse's assistant on site.
VISITORS	Allowed on Visitors Day.
SPECIAL NEEDS FACILITIES	Unspecified
DESCRIPTION	Situated on Petit lac Nominingue, with one mile of shoreline, natural woods, open fields, & a large tree farm making up the camp's 400 acres of property.
NEAREST CITY/TOWN	Montreal
AGE SPREAD	7 to 15 years
CAMPERS PER SESSION	220
STAFF PER SESSION	20
COUNSELLOR:CAMPER RATIO	1 to 3
BOYS OR GIRLS	☒ Boys only ☐ Girls only ☐ Co-ed
NOTES	3-day canoe trips are offered during each session. An English-as-a-second-language program is also offered. The camp is run in English, but most staff are bilingual.

CAMP NOTRE-DAME

SUMMER ADDRESS 881, rang Camp Notre-Dame
St-Ligouri
Cté Montcalm QUE
J0K 2X0 **SUMMER PHONE** 514-834-2852

WINTER ADDRESS As above
QUE
WINTER PHONE

CONTACT PERSON Monique Boisvert
ACCREDITATION ACQ
AFFILIATION None
YEARS IN OPERATION 53
DATES OPEN Year round
FEES $25 per day.
SCHOLARSHIPS Please enquire
ACCOMODATION Cabins, showers, cafeteria
SPECIALTY Traditional
OBJECTIVES To provide campers with an enriching experience in a natural setting.

ACTIVITIES Boating, archery, aquatic games, orienteering, cycling, swimming, fishing, excursions away from camp.

EVALUATIONS No
MEDICAL FACILITIES Medical facilities nearby.
VISITORS Yes
SPECIAL NEEDS FACILITIES No
DESCRIPTION Situated on the Ouareau river.

NEAREST CITY/TOWN Joliette
AGE SPREAD 5 to 16 years
CAMPERS PER SESSION 300
STAFF PER SESSION 70
COUNSELLOR:CAMPER RATIO 1 to 30
BOYS OR GIRLS ☐ Boys only ☐ Girls only ☒ Co-ed
NOTES This is a French-speaking camp.

CAMP OUAREAU

SUMMER ADDRESS 2494 Rte 125 Sud

St. Donat QUE
J0T 2C0 **SUMMER PHONE** 819-424-2662

WINTER ADDRESS 29 Summer Street

Lennoxville QUE
J1M 1G4 **WINTER PHONE** 819-562-9641

CONTACT PERSON Madelene Allen
ACCREDITATION ACQ, OCA
AFFILIATION None
YEARS IN OPERATION 73
DATES OPEN June through August
FEES $860 per 2-week session; $3000 per 8-week session.
SCHOLARSHIPS Please enquire
ACCOMODATION Cabins, tents, showers, main dining hall.
SPECIALTY Traditional
OBJECTIVES To provide a unique experience for English & French children to dispel the myth of "two solitudes" by bringing them together to exchange ideas & get to know one another.
ACTIVITIES Swimming, sailing, canoeing, kayaking, drama, tennis, arts & crafts, windsurfing, ropes course.

EVALUATIONS No
MEDICAL FACILITIES Health centre with RN or nurse's assistant & doctor on call.
VISITORS Allowed on Visitors Day.
SPECIAL NEEDS FACILITIES No
DESCRIPTION Located in the Laurentian Mountains.

NEAREST CITY/TOWN St. Agathe
AGE SPREAD 8 to 15 years
CAMPERS PER SESSION 106 (53 English & 53 French)
STAFF PER SESSION 33
COUNSELLOR:CAMPER RATIO 1 to 3
BOYS OR GIRLS ☐ Boys only ☒ Girls only ☐ Co-ed
NOTES The camp is bilingual; English is the working language for 2 days, then French for 2 days, & so on throughout the session.

CAMP PETIT POISSON BLANC

SUMMER ADDRESS	RR #1		
	Gracefield		QUE
	J0X 1W0	**SUMMER PHONE**	819-463-2367
WINTER ADDRESS	1943 Marquis Avenue		
	Gloucester		ONT
	K1J 8J1	**WINTER PHONE**	613-748-1142

CONTACT PERSON Akbar Manoussi
ACCREDITATION ACQ
AFFILIATION None
YEARS IN OPERATION 37
DATES OPEN May through August
FEES $250 per 1-week session; $900 per 4-week session.
SCHOLARSHIPS No
ACCOMODATION Cabins with washroom facilities, main lodge.
SPECIALTY English & French Immersion
OBJECTIVES To offer a location for environmental studies & outdoor education.

ACTIVITIES Sailing, swimming, climbing, fishing, hiking.

EVALUATIONS Yes
MEDICAL FACILITIES Staff is trained in first aid.
VISITORS Allowed
SPECIAL NEEDS FACILITIES No
DESCRIPTION Situated on a point jutting out into Lac Heney, near Gracefield in the Gatineau valley.

NEAREST CITY/TOWN Hull
AGE SPREAD 5 to 17 years
CAMPERS PER SESSION 120
STAFF PER SESSION 14
COUNSELLOR:CAMPER RATIO 1 to 8
BOYS OR GIRLS ☐ Boys only ☐ Girls only ☒ Co-ed
NOTES This is a bilingual camp.

CAMP QUATRE-SAISONS

SUMMER ADDRESS	1192, chemin du Lac Caché CP 9 Labelle J0T 1H0	**SUMMER PHONE**	QUE 819-686-2123
WINTER ADDRESS	20, rue St-Charles CP 303 Ste-Thérèse J7E 4J4	**WINTER PHONE**	QUE 514-435-5341

CONTACT PERSON Alain Roy
ACCREDITATION ACQ
AFFILIATION None
YEARS IN OPERATION 30
DATES OPEN June to August
FEES $410 per 13-day session.
SCHOLARSHIPS Please enquire.
ACCOMODATION Tents, washrooms with showers, cafeteria.
SPECIALTY Traditional
OBJECTIVES Outdoor education in a natural environment.

ACTIVITIES Canoeing, kayaking, swimming, rock climbing, hiking, orienteering, archery, camping, ecology, astronomy.

EVALUATIONS No
MEDICAL FACILITIES First aid services on site; hospital nearby.
VISITORS Yes
SPECIAL NEEDS FACILITIES No
DESCRIPTION 21 hectares located on the shores of Lac Cache. Mont Gorille extends its 40 km of trails for hiking.

NEAREST CITY/TOWN Labelle
AGE SPREAD 9 to 16 years
CAMPERS PER SESSION 60
STAFF PER SESSION 25
COUNSELLOR:CAMPER RATIO 1 to 3
BOYS OR GIRLS ☐ Boys only ☐ Girls only ☒ Co-ed
NOTES This is a French-speaking camp.

CAMP SABLE CHAUD

SUMMER ADDRESS	530 St-Phillippe CP 2018 Amqui QUE G0J 1B0
SUMMER PHONE	418-629-3747
WINTER ADDRESS	As above
WINTER PHONE	
CONTACT PERSON	Francine Michaud
ACCREDITATION	ACQ
AFFILIATION	None
YEARS IN OPERATION	19
DATES OPEN	June through August
FEES	$110 per 6-day session; $220 per 12-day session.
SCHOLARSHIPS	Please enquire.
ACCOMODATION	Tents, dormitories, showers, cafeteria.
SPECIALTY	Traditional
OBJECTIVES	To provide campers with an enjoyable outdoor experience in a natural environment.
ACTIVITIES	Sailing, canoeing, kayaking, snorkeling, archery, cycling, camping, campfires, nature study.
EVALUATIONS	Yes
MEDICAL FACILITIES	Infirmary with nurse on site.
VISITORS	Allowed
SPECIAL NEEDS FACILITIES	Yes
DESCRIPTION	Located on the shores of Lac Matapedia in the St. Lawrence valley.
NEAREST CITY/TOWN	Rimouski
AGE SPREAD	6 to 17 years
CAMPERS PER SESSION	100
STAFF PER SESSION	18
COUNSELLOR:CAMPER RATIO	1 to 5
BOYS OR GIRLS	☐ Boys only ☐ Girls only ☒ Co-ed
NOTES	This is a French-speaking camp.

CAMP ST-DONAT

SUMMER ADDRESS	60, chemin Baie de l'Ours Nord
	St-Donat de Montcalm QUE
	J0T 2C0 **SUMMER PHONE** 819-424-2525
WINTER ADDRESS	CP 328
	Repentigny QUE
	J6A 7C6 **WINTER PHONE** 514-582-0553
CONTACT PERSON	Gilles or Carole Ledoux
ACCREDITATION	ACQ
AFFILIATION	United Way
YEARS IN OPERATION	27
DATES OPEN	June through August
FEES	Based on family income; please enquire.
SCHOLARSHIPS	Please enquire.
ACCOMODATION	Tents, cabins.
SPECIALTY	Traditional
OBJECTIVES	To initiate campers to the outdoors, & help build self-esteem, respect for others & for the natural environment.
ACTIVITIES	Sailing, canoeing, kayaking, swimming, archery, obstacle courses, arts & crafts, ecology, sports, scientific games, campfires, treasure hunts, drama, shows.
EVALUATIONS	Yes
MEDICAL FACILITIES	Infirmary with student nurses on site.
VISITORS	Allowed during Open House.
SPECIAL NEEDS FACILITIES	Yes
DESCRIPTION	On 150 acres of mountains, lakes & forests.
NEAREST CITY/TOWN	Montreal
AGE SPREAD	6 to 16 years
CAMPERS PER SESSION	Maximum 350
STAFF PER SESSION	115-140
COUNSELLOR:CAMPER RATIO	1 to 5
BOYS OR GIRLS	☐ Boys only ☐ Girls only ☒ Co-ed
NOTES	Special needs refers to facilities for the learning impaired only; the site is not appropriate for wheelchairs. This is a French-speaking camp.

CAMP ST-FRANCOIS L'ÎLE D'ORLÉANS

SUMMER ADDRESS 383 Lemelin Road

St-François Île d'Orléans QUE
G0A 3S0 **SUMMER PHONE** 418-829-2453

WINTER ADDRESS 6035, 10avenue est

Charlesbourg QUE
G1H 4B7 **WINTER PHONE** 418-626-1016

CONTACT PERSON Pierre Shaienks
ACCREDITATION ACQ
AFFILIATION None
YEARS IN OPERATION 45
DATES OPEN July to August
FEES $233 for 6 days; $299 for 8 days; $431 for 12 days.
SCHOLARSHIPS Please enquire.
ACCOMODATION Rooms in main building, showers, cafeteria.
SPECIALTY Traditional
OBJECTIVES To provide campers with a varied and exciting program of activities.

ACTIVITIES Archery, swimming, sports, animation, natural science, theatre.

EVALUATIONS Yes
MEDICAL FACILITIES Nurse on site.
VISITORS Not allowed
SPECIAL NEEDS FACILITIES No
DESCRIPTION Situated on the lovely shores of the St. Lawrence river.

NEAREST CITY/TOWN Quebec City
AGE SPREAD 6 to 12 years
CAMPERS PER SESSION Maximum 96
STAFF PER SESSION 24
COUNSELLOR:CAMPER RATIO 1 to 10
BOYS OR GIRLS ☐ Boys only ☐ Girls only ☒ Co-ed
NOTES This is a French-speaking camp.

CAMP TROIS SAUMONS

SUMMER ADDRESS Lac Trois-Saumons
RR #1
Saint-Aubert QUE
G0R 2R0 **SUMMER PHONE** 418-598-6410

WINTER ADDRESS 11, rue Crémazie Est

Québec QUE
G1R 1Y1 **WINTER PHONE** 418-529-5323

CONTACT PERSON Pierre Bigaouette
ACCREDITATION ACQ
AFFILIATION None
YEARS IN OPERATION 48
DATES OPEN Late June to mid-August
FEES From $145 per 4-day session to $845 per 20-day session.
SCHOLARSHIPS Please enquire.
ACCOMODATION Cabins, showers, cafeteria.
SPECIALTY Traditional
OBJECTIVES To encourage self-reliance & build self-esteem.

ACTIVITIES Windsurfing, archery, handicrafts, drama, sports, canoeing, swimming, hiking.

EVALUATIONS Yes
MEDICAL FACILITIES Infirmary with 2 nurses on duty 24 hours.
VISITORS Not allowed
SPECIAL NEEDS FACILITIES No
DESCRIPTION A lovely wooded, waterfront site.

NEAREST CITY/TOWN Quebec City
AGE SPREAD 5 to 16 years
CAMPERS PER SESSION 300 (per season)
STAFF PER SESSION 120
COUNSELLOR:CAMPER RATIO 1 to 5
BOYS OR GIRLS ☐ Boys only ☐ Girls only ☒ Co-ed
NOTES This is a French-speaking camp.

CENTRE DE PLEIN AIR DU LAC FLAVRIAN

SUMMER ADDRESS CP 1055

Rouyn-Noranda QUE
J9X 5C8

SUMMER PHONE 819-762-6592

WINTER ADDRESS As above

WINTER PHONE

CONTACT PERSON Fernand Tremblay
ACCREDITATION ACQ
AFFILIATION None
YEARS IN OPERATION 12
DATES OPEN Mid-June through mid-August
FEES $200 per one-week session.
SCHOLARSHIPS Please enquire.
ACCOMODATION Dorms with showers, cafeteria.
SPECIALTY Special Needs
OBJECTIVES Autonomy & integration for all campers.

ACTIVITIES Outdoor games, boating, arts & crafts, music, aquatics, shows.

EVALUATIONS Yes
MEDICAL FACILITIES Two nurses on site.
VISITORS Allowed
SPECIAL NEEDS FACILITIES Yes
DESCRIPTION Nestled in the heart of a beautiful forest on the shores of Lac Flavrian.

NEAREST CITY/TOWN Rouyn-Noranda
AGE SPREAD 5 years & up
CAMPERS PER SESSION Maximum 65
STAFF PER SESSION 25
COUNSELLOR:CAMPER RATIO 1 to 4
BOYS OR GIRLS ☐ Boys only ☐ Girls only ☒ Co-ed
NOTES Special Needs refers to all sorts of camp opportunities for the disabled; the site is specially adapted for all types of disabilities.
This is a French-speaking camp.

CENTRE DE PLEIN AIR L'ESTACADE

SUMMER ADDRESS 64, 13e Avenue

St-Paul-Ile-Aux-Noix QUE
J0J 1G0 **SUMMER PHONE** 514-246-3554

WINTER ADDRESS As above

WINTER PHONE

CONTACT PERSON Jean-Pierre Cyr
ACCREDITATION ACQ
AFFILIATION None
YEARS IN OPERATION 16
DATES OPEN June through August
FEES $225 - $275 per session.
SCHOLARSHIPS No
ACCOMODATION Cabins, showers, cafeteria.
SPECIALTY Traditional
OBJECTIVES Education of & through sports; teaching campers teamwork.

ACTIVITIES Swimming, canoeing, sailing, fishing, archery, cycling, bird-watching, nature study, environmental studies, campfires.

EVALUATIONS Yes
MEDICAL FACILITIES First aid on site; doctor 1 km away, hospital 25 km away.
VISITORS Not allowed
SPECIAL NEEDS FACILITIES No
DESCRIPTION Located on the shore of the Richelieu river.

NEAREST CITY/TOWN St-Jean-sur-Richelieu
AGE SPREAD 6 to 15 years
CAMPERS PER SESSION 108
STAFF PER SESSION 20
COUNSELLOR:CAMPER RATIO 1 to 5
BOYS OR GIRLS ☐ Boys only ☐ Girls only ☒ Co-ed
NOTES This is a French-speaking camp.

CENTRE DE PLEIN AIR LE SAISONNIER

SUMMER ADDRESS	78 chemin du Brûlé
	Lac-Beauport QUE
	G0A 2C0 **SUMMER PHONE** 418-849-2821
WINTER ADDRESS	As above
	WINTER PHONE
CONTACT PERSON	Yves Roy
ACCREDITATION	ACQ
AFFILIATION	Catholic Church
YEARS IN OPERATION	52
DATES OPEN	June to August
FEES	$215 per one-week session.
SCHOLARSHIPS	Please enquire.
ACCOMODATION	Cabins with washrooms, cafeteria.
SPECIALTY	Traditional
OBJECTIVES	To assist campers to develop to their fullest potential on the cognitive, emotional & psycho-motor levels.
ACTIVITIES	Rock climbing, canoeing, aquatics, archery, sports & games, natural sciences.
EVALUATIONS	No
MEDICAL FACILITIES	Medical clinic nearby.
VISITORS	Not permitted
SPECIAL NEEDS FACILITIES	Accessible to the handicapped.
DESCRIPTION	Please enquire for details.
NEAREST CITY/TOWN	Quebec City
AGE SPREAD	7 to 13 years
CAMPERS PER SESSION	72
STAFF PER SESSION	50
COUNSELLOR:CAMPER RATIO	1 to 5
BOYS OR GIRLS	☐ Boys only ☐ Girls only ☒ Co-ed
NOTES	This is a French-speaking camp.

CENTRE DE PLEIN AIR LES FORESTIERS

SUMMER ADDRESS 1677, chemin St-Dominique

Les Cèdres QUE
J0P 1L0 **SUMMER PHONE** 514-455-6771

WINTER ADDRESS As above

WINTER PHONE

CONTACT PERSON Alexandre Maclean
ACCREDITATION ACQ
AFFILIATION None
YEARS IN OPERATION 14
DATES OPEN July to mid-August
FEES Average $240 per one-week session.
SCHOLARSHIPS Please enquire.
ACCOMODATION Cabins, main lodge, cafeteria.
SPECIALTY Traditional
OBJECTIVES To educate by means of social & recreational activities in the natural environment.

ACTIVITIES Mountain climbing, hiking, canoeing, archery, arts & crafts, swimming, nature discovery, camping, trampoline, orienteering, co-operative games.

EVALUATIONS Yes
MEDICAL FACILITIES Hospital 10 km away.
VISITORS Allowed for 3-week campers only.
SPECIAL NEEDS FACILITIES Yes
DESCRIPTION Please enquire for details.

NEAREST CITY/TOWN Valleyfield
AGE SPREAD 5 to 14 years
CAMPERS PER SESSION 116
STAFF PER SESSION 40
COUNSELLOR:CAMPER RATIO 1 to 4
BOYS OR GIRLS ☐ Boys only ☐ Girls only ☒ Co-ed
NOTES This is a French-speaking camp.

CENTRE DE PLEIN AIR MARIE-PAULE

SUMMER ADDRESS 316, chemin Tour du Lac

Sainte-Veronique QUE
J0W 1X0 **SUMMER PHONE** 819-275-3522

WINTER ADDRESS 2515, rue Delisle
local 200
Montréal QUE
H3J 1K8 **WINTER PHONE** 514-937-7131

CONTACT PERSON Raymond Brun
ACCREDITATION ACQ
AFFILIATION None
YEARS IN OPERATION 24
DATES OPEN July through August
FEES Unspecified; please enquire.
SCHOLARSHIPS Unspecified; please enquire.
ACCOMODATION Dormitories, cafeteria.
SPECIALTY Disadvantaged Youth
OBJECTIVES To offer an adequate environment for personal & social growth.

ACTIVITIES Swimming, archery, cycling, sailing, canoeing, sports.

EVALUATIONS No
MEDICAL FACILITIES First aid; hospital 10 km away.
VISITORS Not allowed.
SPECIAL NEEDS FACILITIES Yes
DESCRIPTION Situated on the side of a mountain by a lake.

NEAREST CITY/TOWN St-Jovite
AGE SPREAD 4 years & up
CAMPERS PER SESSION 110
STAFF PER SESSION 6
COUNSELLOR:CAMPER RATIO 1 to 7
BOYS OR GIRLS ☐ Boys only ☐ Girls only ☒ Co-ed
NOTES The camp gives priority to low income familes & individuals. This is a French-speaking camp.

CENTRE DE PLEIN-AIR FERME BEAUVALLON

SUMMER ADDRESS	Rang du Bord de l'eau Intersection 43e Avenue Sabrevois J0J 2G0	**SUMMER PHONE**	QUE 514-346-4046
WINTER ADDRESS	286, rang de l'Église Henryville J0J 1E0	**WINTER PHONE**	QUE 514-299-2506

CONTACT PERSON Serge A. Piquette
ACCREDITATION ACQ, CCA
AFFILIATION None
YEARS IN OPERATION 17
DATES OPEN Late June through August
FEES $335 per one-week session; $575 per 13-day session.
SCHOLARSHIPS No
ACCOMODATION Cabins with toilet & shower, dining hall.
SPECIALTY Traditional
OBJECTIVES The camp operates with the belief that respect for others begins with respect for animals. Offers a realistic experience of farm life.
ACTIVITIES Farm activities, horseback riding, archery, canoeing, ecology, sports & games, swimming, obstacle courses, mountain biking, windsurfing.

EVALUATIONS No
MEDICAL FACILITIES First aid on site; medical clinic and hospital within 10 km.
VISITORS Not allowed
SPECIAL NEEDS FACILITIES No
DESCRIPTION Situated on the Richelieu River, the site offers a real farm experience with roosters, cows & other farm animals, as well as a pool.
NEAREST CITY/TOWN Montreal
AGE SPREAD 6 to 14 years
CAMPERS PER SESSION 130
STAFF PER SESSION 5
COUNSELLOR:CAMPER RATIO 1 to 4
BOYS OR GIRLS ☐ Boys only ☐ Girls only ☒ Co-ed
NOTES This is a French-speaking camp.

CENTRE PLEIN AIR L'ÉTINCELLE

SUMMER ADDRESS 300 Lac Long Sud

St-Alphonse Rodriguez QUE
J0K 1W0 **SUMMER PHONE** 514-883-5376

WINTER ADDRESS As above

WINTER PHONE

CONTACT PERSON Dyane Filiatrault
ACCREDITATION ACQ
AFFILIATION None
YEARS IN OPERATION 27
DATES OPEN Year round
FEES $65-75 per 3-day session; $100-$110 per one-week session.
SCHOLARSHIPS Please enquire.
ACCOMODATION Rooms in main building, showers, dining hall.
SPECIALTY Traditional
OBJECTIVES To provide a fun and active camping experience.

ACTIVITIES Archery, swimming, sports, camping, astronomy, sports, ecology, canoeing, nature study.

EVALUATIONS No
MEDICAL FACILITIES Employees are trained in first aid; hospital nearby.
VISITORS Allowed
SPECIAL NEEDS FACILITIES Yes
DESCRIPTION Located on the south end of Long Lake.

NEAREST CITY/TOWN Montreal
AGE SPREAD All ages
CAMPERS PER SESSION 70
STAFF PER SESSION 10
COUNSELLOR:CAMPER RATIO 1 to 12
BOYS OR GIRLS ☐ Boys only ☐ Girls only ☒ Co-ed
NOTES This is a French-speaking camp.

CITÉ JOIE

SUMMER ADDRESS	28 chemin des Cascades
	Lac Beauport QUE
	G0A 2C0 **SUMMER PHONE** 418-849-7183
WINTER ADDRESS	As above
	WINTER PHONE
CONTACT PERSON	Denis Savard
ACCREDITATION	ACQ
AFFILIATION	None
YEARS IN OPERATION	32
DATES OPEN	June to August
FEES	Unspecified; please enquire.
SCHOLARSHIPS	
ACCOMODATION	Lodges, campground
SPECIALTY	Special Needs: Physical Disabilities
OBJECTIVES	To enrich campers by providing them with opportunities to experience the natural environment. To provide support services to the families / caregivers of the disabled.
ACTIVITIES	Swimming, canoeing, bicycling, fishing, arts & crafts, co-operative games, archery, hiking, scientific experiments, treasure hunts, obstacle courses, campfires.
EVALUATIONS	No
MEDICAL FACILITIES	Unspecified; please enquire.
VISITORS	Allowed
SPECIAL NEEDS FACILITIES	Yes
DESCRIPTION	Beautiful, scenic location surrounded by mountains near Lac Beauport.
NEAREST CITY/TOWN	Quebec City
AGE SPREAD	5 years & up
CAMPERS PER SESSION	90
STAFF PER SESSION	15-65
COUNSELLOR:CAMPER RATIO	1 to 18
BOYS OR GIRLS	☐ Boys only ☐ Girls only ☒ Co-ed
NOTES	This is a French-speaking camp.

COLONIE STE-JEANNE D'ARC

SUMMER ADDRESS 9951, Marie-Victorin est

Contrecoeur QUE
J0L 1C0 **SUMMER PHONE** 800-363-0098

WINTER ADDRESS As above

WINTER PHONE 514-743-8265

CONTACT PERSON Yves Legault
ACCREDITATION ACQ
AFFILIATION Kiwanis Club
YEARS IN OPERATION 64
DATES OPEN Late June to August
FEES Based on family income; please enquire
SCHOLARSHIPS Unspecified; please enquire.
ACCOMODATION Cabins, showers, dining hall.
SPECIALTY Traditional
OBJECTIVES To encourage young girls to discover their strengths, values and feelings; to develop their self-esteem.

ACTIVITIES Boating, arts & crafts, archery, swimming, campfires, hiking, horseback riding, camping.

EVALUATIONS Yes
MEDICAL FACILITIES Infirmary on site; hospital 5 km away.
VISITORS Not allowed
SPECIAL NEEDS FACILITIES No
DESCRIPTION Located on a large wooded site on the St. Lawrence river.

NEAREST CITY/TOWN Montreal
AGE SPREAD 4 to 14 years.
CAMPERS PER SESSION 140
STAFF PER SESSION 50
COUNSELLOR:CAMPER RATIO 1 to 4
BOYS OR GIRLS ☐ Boys only ☒ Girls only ☐ Co-ed
NOTES This is a French-speaking camp.

DOMAINE DE L'AMITIÉ

SUMMER ADDRESS 6939, boulevard Talbot
CP 53
Laterrière QUE
G0V 1K0 **SUMMER PHONE** 418-678-2455

WINTER ADDRESS As above

WINTER PHONE

CONTACT PERSON Emmanuel Colomb
ACCREDITATION ACQ
AFFILIATION None
YEARS IN OPERATION 24
DATES OPEN Mid-June through July
FEES Unspecified; please enquire.
SCHOLARSHIPS No
ACCOMODATION Tents, cabins, showers, cafeteria.
SPECIALTY Traditional
OBJECTIVES To teach campers the values of team spirit, sharing, self discovery, self-respect, respect for others and for the environment.
ACTIVITIES Swimming, sports, canoeing, mountain biking, farm activities, campfires, games.

EVALUATIONS No
MEDICAL FACILITIES Infirmary with nurse on site.
VISITORS Not allowed
SPECIAL NEEDS FACILITIES Yes
DESCRIPTION A small farm and lakefront property.

NEAREST CITY/TOWN Chicoutimi
AGE SPREAD 7 to 15 years
CAMPERS PER SESSION 84
STAFF PER SESSION 34
COUNSELLOR:CAMPER RATIO 1 to 4
BOYS OR GIRLS ☐ Boys only ☐ Girls only ☒ Co-ed
NOTES Special needs refers to ability to accommodate autonomous, mildly disabled campers. Boys are accepted only until age 12. This is a French-speaking camp.

I.F.A.C.E.F./ CAMP COEUR JOIE

SUMMER ADDRESS	C.P. 285 Cheneville Cté. Papineau J0V 1E0	**SUMMER PHONE**	QUE 819-428-4298
WINTER ADDRESS	10295, avenue de l'Esplanade Montréal H3L 2X9	**WINTER PHONE**	QUE 514-388-7216

CONTACT PERSON François Oligny
ACCREDITATION ACQ
AFFILIATION None
YEARS IN OPERATION 11
DATES OPEN June to September
FEES $400 per 2-week session.
SCHOLARSHIPS Please enquire.
ACCOMODATION Tents, dorms, cabins, rooms, washrooms, showers, cafeteria.
SPECIALTY Traditional
OBJECTIVES Emphasis on outdoor education & activities.

ACTIVITIES Archery, rock climbing, bicycle camping, mountain biking, horseback riding, boating, swimming, ecology, theatre, outdoor games.

EVALUATIONS No
MEDICAL FACILITIES Nearby
VISITORS Yes
SPECIAL NEEDS FACILITIES Yes
DESCRIPTION On the shores of Lake Dumouchel in the heart of the Vinoy mountains.

NEAREST CITY/TOWN Hull
AGE SPREAD 6 to 16 years
CAMPERS PER SESSION 215
STAFF PER SESSION 50
COUNSELLOR:CAMPER RATIO 1 to 6
BOYS OR GIRLS ☐ Boys only ☐ Girls only ☒ Co-ed
NOTES Special Needs refers to the camp's ability to integrate campers with mental disabilities.
This is a French-speaking camp.

LA VILLA NOTRE-DAME DE FATIMA

SUMMER ADDRESS 21000, route Transcanadienne

Vaudreuil QUE
J7V 8P3 **SUMMER PHONE**

WINTER ADDRESS As above

WINTER PHONE

CONTACT PERSON Benoit Lorrain
ACCREDITATION ACQ
AFFILIATION None
YEARS IN OPERATION 47
DATES OPEN Mid-June to late August
FEES Based on ability to pay.
SCHOLARSHIPS Unspecified; please enquire.
ACCOMODATION Dormitories, showers, cafeteria.
SPECIALTY Special Needs: Deaf/Hearing Impaired
OBJECTIVES To provide a facility for deaf children, with or without other handicaps.

ACTIVITIES Swimming, canoeing, arts & crafts, cycling, archery.

EVALUATIONS Yes
MEDICAL FACILITIES Infirmary with full-time nurse on duty.
VISITORS Not allowed
SPECIAL NEEDS FACILITIES Yes
DESCRIPTION Please enquire for details.

NEAREST CITY/TOWN Vaudreuil
AGE SPREAD 5 to 17 years
CAMPERS PER SESSION 30-45
STAFF PER SESSION 7
COUNSELLOR:CAMPER RATIO 1 to 3
BOYS OR GIRLS ☐ Boys only ☐ Girls only ☒ Co-ed
NOTES Special needs refers to deaf campers; all staff & counsellors are trained in sign language.
This is a French-speaking camp.

MCGILL REDMEN HOCKEY SCHOOL

SUMMER ADDRESS 475 Pine Avenue West

Montreal QUE
H2W 1S4 **SUMMER PHONE**

WINTER ADDRESS As above

WINTER PHONE

CONTACT PERSON Geoffrey Phillips
ACCREDITATION
AFFILIATION None
YEARS IN OPERATION 4
DATES OPEN August
FEES $460 per week for resident campers; $325 for day campers.
SCHOLARSHIPS No
ACCOMODATION University residence, 3 meals per day for resident campers.
SPECIALTY Hockey
OBJECTIVES To stress the concepts of teamwork, sportsmanship, fair play, skill development, & having fun.

ACTIVITIES Hockey, softball, flag football, swimming, basketball & a variety of other outdoor pursuits.

EVALUATIONS Yes
MEDICAL FACILITIES First aid room & hospital nearby.
VISITORS Allowed
SPECIAL NEEDS FACILITIES No
DESCRIPTION Please enquire for details.

NEAREST CITY/TOWN Montreal
AGE SPREAD 8 to 16 years
CAMPERS PER SESSION 100
STAFF PER SESSION 20
COUNSELLOR:CAMPER RATIO 15
BOYS OR GIRLS ☐ Boys only ☐ Girls only ☒ Co-ed
NOTES The camp is affiliated with McGill University.
This is a bilingual camp.

SPACE CAMP CANADA

SUMMER ADDRESS 2150 Autoroute Space des Laurentides

Laval QUE
H7T 2T8 **SUMMER PHONE** 1-800-565-2267

WINTER ADDRESS As above

WINTER PHONE

CONTACT PERSON Sonya Sachdeva
ACCREDITATION ACQ
AFFILIATION None
YEARS IN OPERATION 1
DATES OPEN Year round
FEES $320 per 3-day session; $680 per 5-day session.
SCHOLARSHIPS No
ACCOMODATION One building with lodging modules, cafeteria, rec areas.
SPECIALTY Science: Space
OBJECTIVES To initiate young people to the application of sciences in the study of space.

ACTIVITIES Study rocket propulsion, practice on simulators, walk in a low-gravity environment, execute a simulated space mission aboard a full-scale model of the Shuttle Endeavour.

EVALUATIONS Certificate of achievement.
MEDICAL FACILITIES Nurse on site.
VISITORS No
SPECIAL NEEDS FACILITIES Yes
DESCRIPTION The camp is located in the Cosmodome which includes the Space Science Centre.

NEAREST CITY/TOWN Montreal
AGE SPREAD 9 to 14 years
CAMPERS PER SESSION 270
STAFF PER SESSION 50
COUNSELLOR:CAMPER RATIO 1 to 12
BOYS OR GIRLS ☐ Boys only ☐ Girls only ☒ Co-ed
NOTES This is a bilingual camp.

TRAIL'S END CAMP

SUMMER ADDRESS Catholic Community Services
1857 de Maisonneuve West
Montreal QUE
H3H 1J9 **SUMMER PHONE** 514-937-5351 ext 49

WINTER ADDRESS As above

WINTER PHONE

CONTACT PERSON Arleen Boyer-Fontaine
ACCREDITATION ACQ
AFFILIATION Catholic Church
YEARS IN OPERATION 45
DATES OPEN Late June to mid-August
FEES Sliding scale according to family income.
SCHOLARSHIPS Unspecified; please enquire.
ACCOMODATION Cabins, showers, dining hall.
SPECIALTY Traditional
OBJECTIVES To provide a safe, fun camping experience encouraging fellowship & personal growth.

ACTIVITIES Arts & crafts, games, sports, swimming, canoeing, nature studies, & traditional outdoor activities.

EVALUATIONS Yes, upon request only.
MEDICAL FACILITIES Medical officer on site.
VISITORS Not encouraged.
SPECIAL NEEDS FACILITIES No
DESCRIPTION Located in Ste-Beatrix along the Assomption River with vast, rolling terrain.

NEAREST CITY/TOWN Joliette
AGE SPREAD 7 to 14 years
CAMPERS PER SESSION 160
STAFF PER SESSION 55
COUNSELLOR:CAMPER RATIO 1 to 6
BOYS OR GIRLS ☐ Boys only ☐ Girls only ☒ Co-ed
NOTES Catholic Community Services also operates Camp Kinkora nestled among the hills on private Lac de la Borne, near Ste-Agathe des Monts.
This is a bilingual camp.

WILVAKEN

SUMMER ADDRESS	241, chemin Willis RR #1 Magog J1X 3W2	**SUMMER PHONE**	QUE 819-843-5353
WINTER ADDRESS	PO Box 141 Hudson Heights J0P 1J0	**WINTER PHONE**	QUE 514-458-5051

CONTACT PERSON David & Maya Willis
ACCREDITATION ACQ
AFFILIATION None
YEARS IN OPERATION 36
DATES OPEN Late June to late August
FEES From $820 for 2 weeks to $3020 for 8 weeks.
SCHOLARSHIPS No
ACCOMODATION Cabins, showers, dining hall.
SPECIALTY Traditional
OBJECTIVES To provide a considerable degree of freedom of choice, as campers are on holiday & should not be subject to a highly regimented routine outside of the school year.
ACTIVITIES Sailing, horseback riding, swimming, boating, canoeing, boardsailing, kayaking, arts & crafts, archery, riflery, camping, canoe & hiking outtrips, tennis, waterskiing.

EVALUATIONS No
MEDICAL FACILITIES Resident first aid attendant (RN or graduate nurse).
VISITORS Allowed
SPECIAL NEEDS FACILITIES No
DESCRIPTION A lovely forested waterfront site.

NEAREST CITY/TOWN Magog
AGE SPREAD 8 to 15 years
CAMPERS PER SESSION 100
STAFF PER SESSION 38
COUNSELLOR:CAMPER RATIO 1 to 4
BOYS OR GIRLS ☐ Boys only ☐ Girls only ☒ Co-ed
NOTES The camp is bilingual. The camp offers an English-style riding program at additional cost to the regular camp; please enquire.

Y COUNTRY CAMP

SUMMER ADDRESS			
	Huberdeau		QUE
	J0T 1G0	**SUMMER PHONE**	819-687-3271
WINTER ADDRESS	5500 Westbury Avenue		
	Montreal		QUE
	H3W 2W8	**WINTER PHONE**	514-737-6551

CONTACT PERSON Rob Dainow
ACCREDITATION ACQ, CCA
AFFILIATION Jewish
YEARS IN OPERATION 32
DATES OPEN Late June to mid-August
FEES $2195 per 4-week session; $3195 per 7.5-week session.
SCHOLARSHIPS Please enquire.
ACCOMODATION Cabins, tents, showers, dining hall.
SPECIALTY Jewish Development
OBJECTIVES To provide a fun, safe, supervised environment that provides opportunity for learning & personal development, while reinforcing Jewish values & sound ethical standards.
ACTIVITIES Tennis, swimming, sailing, windsurfing, kayaking, canoeing, pedal boating, sports, archery, aerobics, dance, fitness, arts & crafts, theatre, music, campfires, hayrides, Oneg Shabbat & creative cultural programming.
EVALUATIONS Yes; issued for swimming & sports.
MEDICAL FACILITIES Infirmary with doctor & nurse.
VISITORS Allowed
SPECIAL NEEDS FACILITIES Yes
DESCRIPTION Set on 600 acres of countryside in the Laurentian mountains with 3 private lakes.

NEAREST CITY/TOWN St-Jovite
AGE SPREAD 8 to 16 years
CAMPERS PER SESSION 500 (per season)
STAFF PER SESSION 200
COUNSELLOR:CAMPER RATIO 1 to 3
BOYS OR GIRLS ☐ Boys only ☐ Girls only ☒ Co-ed
NOTES Specialty camps are offered in the areas of fine arts, water sports, tennis, & baseball. Family camping is also an option; please enquire. This is a bilingual camp.

SASKATCHEWAN

BEAVER CREEK CAMP

SUMMER ADDRESS Site 509, Box 19, RR #5

Saskatoon SASK
S7K 3J8 **SUMMER PHONE**

WINTER ADDRESS 2040 McIntyre Street

Regina SASK
S4P 2R6 **WINTER PHONE** 306-543-1809

CONTACT PERSON
ACCREDITATION SCA, CCI
AFFILIATION Salvation Army
YEARS IN OPERATION 76
DATES OPEN July through August
FEES None
SCHOLARSHIPS Fully funded by community Salvation Army.
ACCOMODATION Cabins, full washrooms & showers, main dining hall.
SPECIALTY Disadvantaged Youth
OBJECTIVES To teach environmental awareness & communicate Christian messages & values. To provide an enjoyable camp experience to children who may not be able to afford other camps.
ACTIVITIES Swimming, Bible studies, crafts, recreation, campfires.

EVALUATIONS Certificates are issued.
MEDICAL FACILITIES Camp clinic on site.
VISITORS Not allowed
SPECIAL NEEDS FACILITIES Unspecified
DESCRIPTION Please enquire for details.

NEAREST CITY/TOWN Saskatoon
AGE SPREAD All ages
CAMPERS PER SESSION 80
STAFF PER SESSION 12
COUNSELLOR:CAMPER RATIO 1 to 8
BOYS OR GIRLS ☐ Boys only ☐ Girls only ☒ Co-ed
NOTES

CAMP CAPERNAUM

SUMMER ADDRESS Box 56

Moose Jaw SASK
S6H 4N7 **SUMMER PHONE** 306-638-4452

WINTER ADDRESS As above

WINTER PHONE

CONTACT PERSON Jeanne Large
ACCREDITATION
AFFILIATION United Church
YEARS IN OPERATION 28
DATES OPEN June through August
FEES $100 per one-week session.
SCHOLARSHIPS Some sponsorships available.
ACCOMODATION Cabins, main dining lodge, church.
SPECIALTY Christian Development
OBJECTIVES To provide campers with an enjoyable week of Bible study & fun.

ACTIVITIES Swimming, canoeing, hiking, crafts, Bible study, games, campfires.

EVALUATIONS No
MEDICAL FACILITIES Nurse on duty.
VISITORS Not allowed
SPECIAL NEEDS FACILITIES Unspecified
DESCRIPTION Located on the north shore of Buffalo Pound Lake.

NEAREST CITY/TOWN Moose Jaw
AGE SPREAD 6 to 14 years
CAMPERS PER SESSION 40
STAFF PER SESSION 4 paid & 4 volunteer.
COUNSELLOR:CAMPER RATIO 1 to 5
BOYS OR GIRLS ☐ Boys only ☐ Girls only ☒ Co-ed
NOTES

CAMP CHRISTOPHER

SUMMER ADDRESS Box 20, Site 7, RR#1

Christopher Lake SASK
S0J 0N0 **SUMMER PHONE**

WINTER ADDRESS 7303 Dalgleish Drive

Regina SASK
S4X 2B8 **WINTER PHONE** 306-586-4026

CONTACT PERSON Donna Wilkinson
ACCREDITATION SCA
AFFILIATION Presbyterian Church
YEARS IN OPERATION 49
DATES OPEN July through August
FEES Varies from $85 - $150 per session; please enquire.
SCHOLARSHIPS Camperships may be available.
ACCOMODATION Cabins, hot water showers, main dining hall.
SPECIALTY Christian Development
OBJECTIVES To assist growth in personal understanding of God, personal committment to God as Lord, & a responsible attitude towards creation (other persons and nature).
ACTIVITIES Canoeing, Bible study, devotions, campfires, games, swimming, arts & crafts, music.

EVALUATIONS No
MEDICAL FACILITIES Infirmary with nurse on site.
VISITORS Allowed.
SPECIAL NEEDS FACILITIES Yes
DESCRIPTION Located 50 km north of Prince Albert.

NEAREST CITY/TOWN Prince Albert
AGE SPREAD 8 to 16 years
CAMPERS PER SESSION 50
STAFF PER SESSION 4 plus volunteers
COUNSELLOR:CAMPER RATIO Varies from session to session.
BOYS OR GIRLS ☐ Boys only ☐ Girls only ☒ Co-ed
NOTES Special needs refers to learning disabilities. The camp is also undergoing renovations for complete accessibility.

CAMP HARDING

SUMMER ADDRESS Box 1587

Maple Creek SASK
S0N 1N0 **SUMMER PHONE** 306-662-3695

WINTER ADDRESS As above

WINTER PHONE

CONTACT PERSON Mary Lee Villeneuve
ACCREDITATION SCA
AFFILIATION Anglican Church
YEARS IN OPERATION 32
DATES OPEN July through August
FEES $100 per session.
SCHOLARSHIPS Yes, please enquire.
ACCOMODATION Cabins, flush toilets, showers, main dining hall, craft cabin.
SPECIALTY Christian Development
OBJECTIVES To further Christian education for young people.

ACTIVITIES Canoeing, swimming, arts & crafts, riding, hiking, games & sports, paddle boats, mini golf, campfires, music, religious education.

EVALUATIONS No
MEDICAL FACILITIES Hospital 20 minutes away.
VISITORS Allowed
SPECIAL NEEDS FACILITIES Unspecified
DESCRIPTION Situated in beautiful Cypress Hills Provincial Park.

NEAREST CITY/TOWN Medicine Hat, Alberta
AGE SPREAD 6 to 14 years
CAMPERS PER SESSION Approximately 30
STAFF PER SESSION 4
COUNSELLOR:CAMPER RATIO 1 to 4
BOYS OR GIRLS ☐ Boys only ☐ Girls only ☒ Co-ed
NOTES

CAMP KADESH

SUMMER ADDRESS Box 598

Dalmeny SASK
S0K 1E0 **SUMMER PHONE** 306-254-4434

WINTER ADDRESS As above

WINTER PHONE

CONTACT PERSON Leroy Peters
ACCREDITATION SCA, CCI
AFFILIATION Evangelical
YEARS IN OPERATION 10
DATES OPEN July through August
FEES $125-$185 per one-week session.
SCHOLARSHIPS Financial aid is available.
ACCOMODATION Cabins, chalet with chapel & main dining hall.
SPECIALTY Christian Development
OBJECTIVES To encourage spiritual growth, social interaction & acceptance, & to provide a fun relaxing time at camp.

ACTIVITIES Swimming, canoeing, waterskiing, beach volleyball, windsurfing, basketball, floor hockey, drama, music, archery, handcrafts, hiking, nature study, trampolines, Bible studies, chapel, campfires.
EVALUATIONS No
MEDICAL FACILITIES First aid quarters.
VISITORS Not allowed
SPECIAL NEEDS FACILITIES Unspecified
DESCRIPTION The camp occupies 47 rolling acres on Christopher Lake, 48 km northwest of Prince Albert.

NEAREST CITY/TOWN Prince Albert
AGE SPREAD 8 to 18 years
CAMPERS PER SESSION 96
STAFF PER SESSION 40-50
COUNSELLOR:CAMPER RATIO 1 to 2
BOYS OR GIRLS ☐ Boys only ☐ Girls only ☒ Co-ed
NOTES

CAMP MCKAY

SUMMER ADDRESS Box 757

Broadview SASK
S0G 0K0 **SUMMER PHONE** 306-696-2565

WINTER ADDRESS c/o Brenda Bond
Box 741
Moosomin SASK
S0G 3N8 **WINTER PHONE** 306-435-4155

CONTACT PERSON Gordon Woods
ACCREDITATION SCA
AFFILIATION United Church
YEARS IN OPERATION 30
DATES OPEN July through mid-August
FEES $80 per 5-day session.
SCHOLARSHIPS Please enquire
ACCOMODATION Cabins, showers, washrooms, dining & recreation halls.
SPECIALTY Christian Development
OBJECTIVES To create & nurture awareness of God through the teachings of Christ. To share Christian leadership & experiences by living & growing together in a natural environment.
ACTIVITIES Christian education activities, crafts, recreation, canoeing, swimming, archery, nature activities, hiking, outdoor cooking, campfires, sports.

EVALUATIONS No
MEDICAL FACILITIES Small sick bay & first aid-trained staff.
VISITORS Not encouraged
SPECIAL NEEDS FACILITIES Unspecified
DESCRIPTION Located in the Qu'Appelle Valley on Round Lake.

NEAREST CITY/TOWN Esterhazy
AGE SPREAD 7 to 14 years
CAMPERS PER SESSION 40
STAFF PER SESSION Approximately 16
COUNSELLOR:CAMPER RATIO 1 to 5
BOYS OR GIRLS ☐ Boys only ☐ Girls only ☒ Co-ed
NOTES

CAMP OSHKIDEE

SUMMER ADDRESS Box 902

Saskatoon SASK
S7K 3M4 **SUMMER PHONE** 306-382-2264

WINTER ADDRESS 1221 Avenue J North

Saskatoon SASK
S7L 2L7 **WINTER PHONE** 306-978-1221

CONTACT PERSON H.J. Block
ACCREDITATION CCI
AFFILIATION Evangelical
YEARS IN OPERATION 23
DATES OPEN Late June through July
FEES 12 yrs+ $85/week; 8-11 yrs $55/week; 4-7 yrs $42/week.
SCHOLARSHIPS Please enquire.
ACCOMODATION Log cabins, main lodge, showers, toilets.
SPECIALTY Christian Development
OBJECTIVES To introduce campers to Jesus Christ & to teach a Bible-based lifestyle.

ACTIVITIES Swimming, sailing, windsurfing, hiking, waterskiing, archery, canoeing, horse-shoes, kayaking, paddle boating, volleyball, Bible study, campfires

EVALUATIONS No
MEDICAL FACILITIES First aid kit; hospital 60 km away.
VISITORS Not allowed
SPECIAL NEEDS FACILITIES Unspecified
DESCRIPTION The camp is located 350 km north of Saskatoon on the north shore of Jeanette Lake in the Meadow Lake Provincial Park. The buildings are all constructed of solid cedar logs.
NEAREST CITY/TOWN Saskatoon
AGE SPREAD All ages
CAMPERS PER SESSION 65-75
STAFF PER SESSION 14
COUNSELLOR:CAMPER RATIO N/A
BOYS OR GIRLS ☐ Boys only ☐ Girls only ☒ Co-ed
NOTES This is a family camp; parents camp with their children. Campers bring their own breakfast foods & are given facilities to prepare the meal at their leisure; morning time is for family togetherness.

CAMP TA-WA-SI

SUMMER ADDRESS			
	Fort Qu'Appelle		SASK
	S0G 1S0	**SUMMER PHONE**	
WINTER ADDRESS	2400 - 13th Avenue		
	Regina		SASK
	S4P 0V9	**WINTER PHONE**	306-757-9622

CONTACT PERSON Family YM-YWCA of Regina
ACCREDITATION SCA
AFFILIATION YM-YWCA
YEARS IN OPERATION 44
DATES OPEN July through mid-August
FEES $191 per 7-day session; $269-$369 per 10-day session.
SCHOLARSHIPS Sponsorships are available.
ACCOMODATION Cabins, dining hall.
SPECIALTY Traditional
OBJECTIVES To ensure fun, adventure, learning, & friendship for each camper in a safe, healthy outdoor environment.

ACTIVITIES Kayaking, canoeing, sailing, swimming, campfires, sing-songs, computers, archery, crafts, environmental activities.

EVALUATIONS No
MEDICAL FACILITIES Infirmary, first aid dispensary & full time health care worker.
VISITORS Allowed
SPECIAL NEEDS FACILITIES Unspecified
DESCRIPTION Located on the shores of Echo Lake in the Qu'Appelle Valley.

NEAREST CITY/TOWN Regina
AGE SPREAD 6 to 18 years
CAMPERS PER SESSION 140
STAFF PER SESSION 15
COUNSELLOR:CAMPER RATIO 1 to 5
BOYS OR GIRLS ☐ Boys only ☐ Girls only ☒ Co-ed
NOTES Fees are discounted if paid early; please enquire.

CAMP TAPAWINGO

SUMMER ADDRESS

SASK

SUMMER PHONE

WINTER ADDRESS 225 12th Street E

Prince Albert SASK
S6V 1B9 **WINTER PHONE** 306-765-4764

CONTACT PERSON Ed Cook
ACCREDITATION SCA
AFFILIATION United Church
YEARS IN OPERATION 46
DATES OPEN Late June through August
FEES Unspecified; please enquire.
SCHOLARSHIPS Available
ACCOMODATION Cabins, showers, main dining hall.
SPECIALTY Christian Development
OBJECTIVES To provide an opportunity for campers to know & grow in their relationship with God, each other, & God's world.

ACTIVITIES Swimming, camp-wide games, crafts, canoeing, nature trails, archery & sling shots, paddle boating, Bible study, vespers, campfires.

EVALUATIONS No
MEDICAL FACILITIES Nurse on staff; emergency doctor within 100 km.
VISITORS Not allowed
SPECIAL NEEDS FACILITIES Unspecified
DESCRIPTION Located on Candle Lake.

NEAREST CITY/TOWN Prince Albert
AGE SPREAD 6 to 16 years
CAMPERS PER SESSION Maximum 81
STAFF PER SESSION 7
COUNSELLOR:CAMPER RATIO 1 to 9
BOYS OR GIRLS ☐ Boys only ☐ Girls only ☒ Co-ed
NOTES

CAMP TRIDENT

SUMMER ADDRESS

Crystal Lake SASK

SUMMER PHONE

WINTER ADDRESS 1445 Shannon Road

Regina SASK
S4S 5L4 **WINTER PHONE** 306-584-8194

CONTACT PERSON Peter Charles
ACCREDITATION
AFFILIATION Canadian Parents for French (CPF)
YEARS IN OPERATION 10
DATES OPEN August
FEES $250 per 2-week session.
SCHOLARSHIPS Please enquire.
ACCOMODATION Dormitories, washrooms & showers, main dining hall.
SPECIALTY French Immersion
OBJECTIVES To promote the use of the French language, to help reinforce & strengthen skills, to develop the motivation to continue French studies & to have fun in French.
ACTIVITIES French conversation, arts & crafts, creative drama, choral-singing, folk dancing, music, physical education, hiking, nature study, canoeing, swimming.

EVALUATIONS Certificates are issued.
MEDICAL FACILITIES Nurse on duty.
VISITORS Not allowed
SPECIAL NEEDS FACILITIES Yes
DESCRIPTION Situated on a 10 acre site on the shores of Crystal Lake.

NEAREST CITY/TOWN Yorkton
AGE SPREAD 10 to 16 years
CAMPERS PER SESSION 75
STAFF PER SESSION 16
COUNSELLOR:CAMPER RATIO 1 to 12
BOYS OR GIRLS ☐ Boys only ☐ Girls only ☒ Co-ed
NOTES Parents must have current, paid-up CPF membership to send children to this camp. Special needs refers to wheelchair accessibility. Also able to accomodate some mild learning disabilities.

DALLAS VALLEY RANCH CAMP

SUMMER ADDRESS Box 83

Drake SASK
S0K 1H0 **SUMMER PHONE** 306-363-4766

WINTER ADDRESS As above

WINTER PHONE

CONTACT PERSON Laverne Jantz
ACCREDITATION SCA
AFFILIATION Canadian Sunday School Mission
YEARS IN OPERATION 10
DATES OPEN July through August
FEES $148 per session.
SCHOLARSHIPS Camperships are available.
ACCOMODATION Cabins, showers, dining hall.
SPECIALTY Christian Development
OBJECTIVES To encourage faith in God by providing an educational & recreational experience within a Christian context. Also to help campers grow in their self-worth & social skills.
ACTIVITIES Horsemanship, swimming, leather crafts, riflery, archery, canoeing, campfires, chapel, Bible study, outdoor living schools.

EVALUATIONS No
MEDICAL FACILITIES Unspecified; please enquire.
VISITORS Allowed
SPECIAL NEEDS FACILITIES Unspecified
DESCRIPTION Located 30 km northwest of Regina, near Lumsden.

NEAREST CITY/TOWN Regina
AGE SPREAD 9 to 17 years
CAMPERS PER SESSION 56
STAFF PER SESSION 12
COUNSELLOR:CAMPER RATIO 1 to 8
BOYS OR GIRLS ☐ Boys only ☐ Girls only ☒ Co-ed
NOTES

JUNIOR CHOIR CAMP

SUMMER ADDRESS Saskatchewan Choral Federation
1870 Lorne St.
Regina SASK
S4P 2L7 **SUMMER PHONE** 306-780-9230

WINTER ADDRESS As above

WINTER PHONE

CONTACT PERSON Valerie Brooks
ACCREDITATION
AFFILIATION Saskatchewan Choral Federation
YEARS IN OPERATION 4
DATES OPEN One week in July
FEES $225 per session; $175 for day campers.
SCHOLARSHIPS Yes, please enquire.
ACCOMODATION Cabins, central washrooms, dining hall, rehearsal in Abbey
SPECIALTY Music: Choral Singing
OBJECTIVES To introduce young people to the rich and rewarding experience of choral singing.

ACTIVITIES Swimming, hiking, painting T-shirts, dancing, concert, rehearsal 3 times a day, classes in reading music and music theory.

EVALUATIONS Yes
MEDICAL FACILITIES Nurse on site; 40 minutes to hospital.
VISITORS Invited to final concert.
SPECIAL NEEDS FACILITIES Unspecified, please enquire.
DESCRIPTION At St. Peters Abbey surrounded by woods and lakes.

NEAREST CITY/TOWN St Peters Abbey, Muenster
AGE SPREAD 8 to 12 years
CAMPERS PER SESSION 95
STAFF PER SESSION 21
COUNSELLOR:CAMPER RATIO 1 to 5
BOYS OR GIRLS ☐ Boys only ☐ Girls only ☒ Co-ed
NOTES

LUMSDEN BEACH CAMP

SUMMER ADDRESS 3548 Allen Avenue

Regina SASK
S4S 0Z9 **SUMMER PHONE** 306-586-9763

WINTER ADDRESS As Above

WINTER PHONE

CONTACT PERSON
ACCREDITATION SCA
AFFILIATION United Church
YEARS IN OPERATION 86
DATES OPEN July through August
FEES $70 - $150 per 6-day session; please enquire.
SCHOLARSHIPS Please enquire
ACCOMODATION Cabins, showers, dining & recreation halls.
SPECIALTY Christian Development
OBJECTIVES To create & nurture an awareness of God as revealed through Jesus Christ & to share Christian experiences by living & growing together in a natural environment.
ACTIVITIES Swimming, hiking, crafts, archery, campfires, canoeing, games, cookouts, Bible study, evening worship services.

EVALUATIONS No
MEDICAL FACILITIES First aid cabin with medical personnel in charge.
VISITORS Not allowed
SPECIAL NEEDS FACILITIES Unspecified
DESCRIPTION Situated on a 267-acre site on Last Mountain Lake.

NEAREST CITY/TOWN Regina
AGE SPREAD 6 to 16 years
CAMPERS PER SESSION 50
STAFF PER SESSION 4
COUNSELLOR:CAMPER RATIO 1 to 5
BOYS OR GIRLS ☐ Boys only ☐ Girls only ☒ Co-ed
NOTES

ST. JOHN BOSCO CAMP

SUMMER ADDRESS

SASK
SUMMER PHONE 306-426-2227

WINTER ADDRESS PO Box 1330

Prince Albert SASK
S6V 5S8 **WINTER PHONE** 306-764-9194

CONTACT PERSON
ACCREDITATION SCA, CCA
AFFILIATION Catholic Church
YEARS IN OPERATION 33
DATES OPEN July through August
FEES Unspecified; please enquire.
SCHOLARSHIPS Unspecified; please enquire.
ACCOMODATION Wooden-floored tents, showers, main dining hall, chapel.
SPECIALTY Christian Development
OBJECTIVES To offer a challenging Christian camping experience & a chance to learn personal skills & share in community living & group participation.
ACTIVITIES Archery, canoeing, sailing, ropes course, singing, campfires, educational drama, wilderness skills, overnight hikes, woodsmanship, nature lore, sports, swimming, orienteering.

EVALUATIONS No
MEDICAL FACILITIES Nurse or EMT on site.
VISITORS Allowed
SPECIAL NEEDS FACILITIES Unspecified
DESCRIPTION Situated in the Nipawin Provincial Park on two northern fresh water lakes, Zeden & Ispuchaw.

NEAREST CITY/TOWN Prince Albert
AGE SPREAD 9 to 17 years
CAMPERS PER SESSION 125
STAFF PER SESSION 30-40
COUNSELLOR:CAMPER RATIO 1 to 7
BOYS OR GIRLS ☐ Boys only ☐ Girls only ☒ Co-ed
NOTES Motto: People experiencing people in God's nature. Camp is co-ed, but campers in each program are grouped according to age & gender. Summer phone number is for emergency use only.

TEEN CHOIR CAMP

SUMMER ADDRESS	Saskatchewan Choral Federation 1870 Lorne St. Regina SASK S4P 2L7
SUMMER PHONE	306-780-9230
WINTER ADDRESS	As above
WINTER PHONE	
CONTACT PERSON	Valerie Brooks
ACCREDITATION	
AFFILIATION	Saskatchewan Choral Federation
YEARS IN OPERATION	4
DATES OPEN	One week in July.
FEES	$225 per session; $175 for day campers.
SCHOLARSHIPS	Yes, please enquire.
ACCOMODATION	Cabins, central washrooms, dining hall, rehearsal in Abbey
SPECIALTY	Music: Choral Singing
OBJECTIVES	To introduce teenagers to the rich and rewarding experience of choral singing.
ACTIVITIES	Swimming, hiking, painting T-shirts, dancing, concert, rehearsal 3 times a day, classes in reading music and music theory.
EVALUATIONS	Yes
MEDICAL FACILITIES	Nurse on site; 40 minutes to hospital.
VISITORS	Invited to final concert.
SPECIAL NEEDS FACILITIES	Unspecified, please enquire.
DESCRIPTION	At St. Peters Abbey surrounded by woods and lakes.
NEAREST CITY/TOWN	St Peters Abbey, Muenster
AGE SPREAD	12 to 16 years
CAMPERS PER SESSION	95
STAFF PER SESSION	21
COUNSELLOR:CAMPER RATIO	1 to 5
BOYS OR GIRLS	☐ Boys only ☐ Girls only ☒ Co-ed
NOTES	

TORCH TRAIL BIBLE CAMP

SUMMER ADDRESS Box 84

Choiceland SASK
S0J 0M0 **SUMMER PHONE** 306-428-2989

WINTER ADDRESS As above

WINTER PHONE

CONTACT PERSON Matthew Teigrob
ACCREDITATION SCA, CCI
AFFILIATION Canadian Sunday School Mission
YEARS IN OPERATION 44
DATES OPEN July through mid-August
FEES $106 - $159 per 4-6 day session.
SCHOLARSHIPS Please enquire
ACCOMODATION Cabins, showers, main dining hall.
SPECIALTY Christian Development
OBJECTIVES To provide an educational & recreational experience within a Christian context, helping campers grow in their sense of self-worth & social skills.
ACTIVITIES Sports, trampoline, archery, sling shots, horsemanship, pool, canoeing, crafts, mini-golf, hayrides, Bible study, chapel.

EVALUATIONS Certificates for some skills (swimming, horsemanship).
MEDICAL FACILITIES All necessary first aid supplies to treat minor injuries.
VISITORS Allowed
SPECIAL NEEDS FACILITIES Unspecified
DESCRIPTION Please call for details.

NEAREST CITY/TOWN Prince Albert
AGE SPREAD 6 years & up
CAMPERS PER SESSION 120
STAFF PER SESSION 25
COUNSELLOR:CAMPER RATIO 1 to 8
BOYS OR GIRLS ☐ Boys only ☐ Girls only ☒ Co-ed
NOTES Fees are discounted if paid early; please enquire.

Camping Associations

Canadian Camping Association
1806 Avenue Road, Suite 2
Toronto, Ontario
M5M 3Z1
(416) 781-4717

Alberta Camping Association
Percy Page Centre
11759 Groat Road
Edmonton, Alberta
T5M 3K6
(403) 453-8570

British Columbia Camping Association
c/o Thunderbird Outdoor Centre
880 Courtney Street
Victoria, British Columbia
V8W 1C4
(604) 386-7511

Manitoba Camping Association
194-A Sherbrook Street
Winnipeg, Manitoba
R3C 2B6
(204) 784-1134

New Brunswick Camping Association
Regent Station
4 - 403 Regent Street
Fredericton, New Brunswick
E3B 3X6
(506) 459-1929

Newfoundland and Labrador Camping Association
Box 760
Bishop's Falls, Newfoundland
A0H 1C0
(709) 258-5862

Camping Association of Nova Scotia
Box 3243, South
Halifax, Nova Scotia
B3J 3H5
(902) 865-3523

Ontario Camping Association
1806 Avenue Road, Suite 2
Toronto, Ontario
M5M 3Z1
(416) 781-0525

Association des Camps du Quebec
4545 Avenue Pierre de Coubertin
Case Postale 1000, Succursale M
Montreal, Quebec
H1V 3R2
(514) 252-3113

Saskatchewan Camping Association
c/o Saskatoon YMCA
22 - 22nd Street East
Saskatoon, Saskatchewan
S7K 0C7
(306) 652-7515

American Camping Association
Bradford Woods
500 SR 67N
Martinsville, Indiana
46152-7902 USA
(317) 342-8456

Alphabetical List of Camps

Centre/Plein Air l'Estacade, QUE
Centre/Plein Air/Forestiers, QUE
Centre/Plein Air/Saisonnier, QUE
Centre/Plein Air Lusson, ALTA
Centre/Plein Air Marie-Paule, QUE
Centre/Plein/Beauvallon, QUE
Centre/Plein Air L'Étincelle, QUE
Chawuthen, BC
Christie Lake Camp, ONT
Circle R Ranch, ONT
Circle Square Ranch, BC
Circle Square Ranch, NB
Cité Joie, QUE
Colonie Ste-Jeanne D'Arc, QUE
Columbia Bible Camp, BC
Courtenay Youth Music Centre, BC
Dallas Valley Ranch Camp, SASK
Dinosaur Country Camp, ALTA
Domaine de l'Amitié, QUE
Easter Seals Camp Shawnigan, BC
Easter Seals Camp Squamish, BC
Edgewood Camp, ONT
Educo Adventure School, BC
Emmanuel Bible Camp, PEI
Evans Lake Summer Camp, BC
Foothills, ALTA
Foothills Camp, ALTA
Fraser Lake Camp, ONT
Frontier Lodge, ALTA
Gavin Lake, BC
George Pringle Camp, BC
Glen Bernard Camp, ONT
Green Hill Lake Camp, NB
Habonim Dror Camp Miriam, BC
Hilbre Bible Camp, MAN
Hockey Opportunity Camp, ONT
Hollows Camp, ONT
Horse People, ONT
Huron Hockey School, ONT
Huronda, ONT
I.F.A.C.E.F. Camp Coeur Joie, QUE
Johannesen Int'l School/Arts, BC
John Island Camp, ONT
John McInnis Forestry Centre, BC
Joy Bible Camp, ONT
Junior Choir Camp, NS
Junior Choir Camp, SASK
Kandalore, ONT
Kawabi, ONT
Kawkawa Camp, BC
Keats Camp, BC
Keewaydin Camps, ONT
Kemur Camp, ONT
Kiev's K-Hi Ukrainian Camp, ALTA
Kilcoo Camp, ONT
Knox Adventure Camp, ONT
La Villa Notre-Dame/Fatima, QUE
Lake Nutimik Baptist Camp, MAN
Lakefield Camp International, ONT
Lakewood Camp, ONT
Latona Catholic Camp, BC
Lavrock, NFLD
Lion Max Simms Camp, NFLD
Livingston Lake Camp, NB
Long Bay Camp, ONT
Long Lake Jr Forest Warden, ALTA
Lumsden Beach Camp, SASK
Manitoba Pioneer Camp, ONT
Marygrove Camp, ONT
McGill Redmen Hockey Sch., QUE
Merrywood Camp, ONT
Missanabie Woods Academy, ONT
Moonlight Bay Camp, ALTA
Moorecroft Camp, BC
New Frenda Youth Camp, ONT
N. Vancouver Outdoor School, BC
Northway-Wendigo, ONT
Northwood Camp, ONT
Okanagan School of the Arts, BC
Olympia Sports Camp, ONT
Ontario Pioneer Camp, ONT
Outward Bound, BC
Outward Bound, ONT
Pac Mtn Gymnastics Camp, BC
Pine Lake Camp, ALTA
Pioneer Chehalis Camp, BC
Pioneer Pacific Camp, BC
Pioneer Ranch, ALTA
Project C.A.N.O.E., ONT
Pugwash, NS
Red Rock Bible Camp, MAN
Rideau Hill Camp, ONT
Royal Winnipeg Ballet, MAN
RKY Camp, ONT

Index of Camps by Specialty

The camps are indexed under the following headings: **Arts, Cultural Development, Disadvantaged Youth, Language Development, Leadership Development, Science, Special Needs, Spiritual Development, Sports, Travel,** and **Wilderness Training.** These listings are further broken down into more specific categories.

The camps listed in this index are those which have indicated a special focus or concentration in a particular area. Camps which did not indicate a specialty are not listed here; these camps are indicated throughout the book by the term "Traditional" in the Specialty category. Many camps which focus on traditional camp experiences may include a number of the activities or facilities listed here. For example, many traditional camps offer horseback riding, although it is not listed as a specialty of the camp. As well, many camps are able to accomodate campers with physical or mental disabilities, even if that is not the focus of the camp. This index should be a general guide; the camp listings themselves should be the primary source of information.